# JUILLIARD TO JAIL

*A Memoir*

# Juilliard to Jail

by

Leah Joki

JUILLIARD TO JAIL
Copyright © Leah Joki, 2013

All rights reserved. No part of this book may be reproduced in any form, except brief excerpts for the purpose of review, without the written permission of the publisher.

Made in Montana Press
www.leahjoki.com
Cover Art by Roland Rosenkranz and Ashley Sisson
Cover Photo by Terry Cyr

Publisher's Cataloging-in Publication Data
Joki, Leah
 Juilliard to Jail / Leah Joki -- Missoula, MT : Made in Montana Press
 p. ; cm.
 ISBN: 978-1478190936
 1. Non-Fiction. 2. Memoir.
 I. Title.

9 8 7 6 5 4 3 2 1

Stephen —

Thank you for your stellar representation and for giving me thee best line ever! One which I hope to use in my next book.

"I just felt like an old whore who wasn't going to get paid --- so I decided to give the guy a good ride for the sake of professionalism"
  Stephen McLeod 2008

Jerome Butler vs. Leah Joki

## AUTHOR'S NOTE

*Juilliard to Jail* is a memoir and subject to the imperfections of memory. I have been faithful to what I remember and diligent to confirm these memories with others to the best of my ability. Inmates, prison staff, contract artists, colleagues, friends and family members may remember shared experiences differently. Most names of actual people have been changed for those both living and dead, with the exception of the names of public figures, elected or appointed State officials and well-known individuals in the Arts in Corrections program and in the arts and entertainment field. I kept my own name to emphasize that this story could only be mine. I couldn't have made this shit up if I tried.

*…for Burl and the kids.*

# Table of Contents

PROLOGUE
| | |
|---|---|
| Chapter 1: DICK | page 5 |
| Chapter 2: BELONGING | page 13 |
| Chapter 3: JUVIE | page 17 |
| Chapter 4: DOUBLE LIFE | page 25 |
| Chapter 5: THINK AGAIN | page 37 |
| Chapter 6: HOUSE OF MARRIAGE | page 47 |
| Chapter 7: FACILITATIN' | page 57 |
| Chapter 8: BLYTHE | page 67 |
| Chapter 9: RANK AND FILE | page 79 |
| Chapter 10: BLACK IRISH | page 91 |
| Chapter 11: GOOD PLAN | page 99 |
| Chapter 12: GENIUS OR KNUCKLEHEAD? | page 113 |
| Chapter 13: ALMOST PERFECT | page 123 |
| Chapter 14: GO DIRECTLY TO JAIL, DON'T COLLECT $200, DON'T WRITE A PLAY | page 135 |
| Chapter 15: THE BIG HOUSE | page 139 |
| Chapter 16: ZUMLARRY | page 155 |
| Chapter 17: VISITING LWOP | page 161 |
| Chapter 18: SHAKESPEARE GOES TO PRISON | page 167 |
| Chapter 19: JEWISH IN JAIL | page 171 |
| Chapter 20: MOVIE STARS IN THE JOINT | page 177 |
| Chapter 21: THE "C" FILES | page 187 |
| Chapter 22: THE FORCE | page 197 |
| Chapter 23: THE GOOD DOCTOR | page 205 |
| Chapter 24: MANIPULATION | page 213 |
| Chapter 25: CRAP | page 221 |
| Chapter 26: ON TRIAL | page 231 |
| Chapter 27: RETURNED | page 239 |
| Chapter 28: THE RUNAWAY KALEIDOSCOPE | page 245 |
| Chapter 29: THANKS FOR STABBING MY SECRETARY | page 253 |
| Chapter 30: DOWN HILL | page 259 |
| Chapter 31: THE FINAL BRIDGE TO ART | page 267 |
| Chapter 32: TO LIVE OR DIE IN LA? | page 277 |

EPILOGUE

# Prologue

For almost 20 years I drove into prison parking lots grinning ear to ear. I had a huge love affair with prison. It was my big, muscular, hairy-chested 240 lb. lover, full of surprises. On the outside he was a mass of gray concrete adorned with razor wire, electric fences and gun towers. On the inside he was a complex being filled with dark secrets, dreams, aspirations and a wonderful sense of humor. He wasn't the kind of lover that you could take home to your parents. My family could never really comprehend my choice and I rarely spoke of him around them. But I couldn't wait to introduce my lover to my friends. I spent hundreds of hours convincing friends and colleagues to come and meet him just once. People were always shocked at the enormity of my lover and his intimidating physical presence. He definitely had a temper and would act out at the most unexpected of times. But no one knew him like I did. No one loved him the way I did. I belonged in prison.

I loved walking onto prison yards, scanning a sea of men dressed in blue denim whose eyes longed to connect with another human. I was *Woman Hear Me Roar* inside the joint. I didn't flinch when alarms went off, just paused to watch the guards jog to the scene with their keys, clubs, handcuffs and pepper spray. The only gear I'd been issued for protection was a silver whistle, but somehow that made me feel safe and secure enough to walk past those incidents unfazed.

Prison became my lifetime partner. It consumed me. And like a torrid romance that ends badly in deception and betrayal, my love for prison was finally squelched. Near the end I'd sit for hours on a metal folding chair on my deck, smoking cigarette after cigarette. I'd gaze at the razor wire surrounding my inner-city Los Angeles backyard, rocking myself back and forth, drinking too much and finally numbed, sleeping too much. My life was stuck on the extra rinse cycle. I can't remember how, but I eventually realized that God had better plans for me and for my family. I crawled out of the Maytag, confident that I didn't have to churn away endlessly in the dark with a life I no longer recognized. I left Los Angeles and went to the woods to live deliberately, to live in a place quiet enough to hear myself think.

Now that it's over, my biggest fear is that someone from prison will track me down and slit my throat. That fear was rekindled recently when two inmates in California contacted me through Facebook. One was in a maximum-security prison and the other in San Quentin. I was shocked, but not surprised. The age of smart phones has led to a new security challenge. Inmates have the ability to use the internet to easily communicate with the world and with each other. When I was contacted in 2012, my memories of prison were re-injected into my system like a hefty dose of Cortisone into a sore joint.

Perhaps it is the response from prison staff that I should fear the most. I cannot tell my story without revealing what I have seen and heard: The politically powerful California Department of Corrections and California Correctional Peace Officer's Association would rather the public not know what I know. But whatever the repercussions, I am compelled to tell my story. So…

# Dick

### 1997: California State Prison – Los Angeles County (Maximum Security Prison for Adult Men)

Of course, there was a lockdown. There was always a lockdown if a deadline was around the corner. I had taken the time to read numerous screenplays and was intent on at least giving notes to the guys before they were sent to their cells. It looked as if this lockdown could last a couple weeks. Staff had found a number of weapons stashed in the ground about twenty feet from the Program Office. That was definitely not a good thing. It implied that inmates were planning an assault on primary staff members. Why else would they stash makeshift weapons near the entrance that accommodated the Sergeant, Lieutenant, and Captain? Almost every custody officer on the Yard went through those offices at one time or another. How could they not? Not only were the higher ranked there, that's also where the conference room, staff bathroom, copy machine, refrigerator and microwave were. It's a pretty safe bet to say that every officer came through that entrance, considering the fridge and microwave were in the hood. The number of weapons also suggested a well-organized assault on staff. At a designated time, they could quickly dig them up and get busy. It was impossible to know if the assault was designed for a specific person or group or just whoever was going to be there at the time. Oodles of handmade knives had serious implications. I wondered how they made them and when they intended to use them. On 1st Watch? 2nd? 3rd? Usually the best time for such attacks is at a shift change. That's when it's the most chaotic. One shift is focused on getting out of there, and the other is still rushing in. They're either coming or going, but not thinking about getting attacked on the bookends of the day. That's why it's the perfect time. Chaos.

I knew the drill. A thousand inmates on Facility "D" were going to be locked down for a while, for as long as it took to investigate and to search every single cell on the Yard and then some. Soon, I was going to have the opportunity to do lots of paperwork in my office and to catch up on phone calls. *Gee,* I thought. *Maybe I can catch up on the dreaded quarterly report! Wouldn't that be snappy?* It was the document held so dear by MUGsie. But for the moment, I had to focus on the task at hand: sharing my notes with the inmates.

The screenwriting class on Facility "D" was a prolific bunch of guys. There were a number of them who worked very hard in pursuit of the coveted first and second place spot for the Annual Screenwriting competition. The two winning scripts would be read in the prison by a group of professional actors. I had finished reading all of their scripts and was going to do my damnedest to make sure they all got notes before they would have to hunker down for a while. Lockdowns brought a perk for the writing class: lots of time to write. A Sergeant once said "There are three things I love about the Department of Corrections: payday, lockdowns and deferred compensation." Yes, lockdowns were financially beneficial to custody officers. I never saw an officer unhappy about a lockdown: They got easy overtime money. The inmates got more writing time without remuneration. In every other regard however, lockdowns sucked, big time.

In any case, turning over my handwritten notes to the inmates was not an option. First of all, they require explanation and secondly, some would piss people off. As a director in the theater, it was my habit to take notes during rehearsals and I rarely censored my thoughts. Just because I wrote down "you absolutely suck in this part," didn't necessarily mean that I shared that thought with the actor. I also didn't turn over my notes to inmates. I used them not only to keep track of my comments, but to vent too. The venting part was for my eyes only. So inmate Bob did not need to be handed a piece of paper that stated, "This stinks. Take me out of this hell now. One more misogynist remark and I will handcuff and spank you myself."

So off I went, embarking on a Leah-gives-comments-quickly session before the lockdown. No time for questions, discussion or anything: Just the oral presentation of my precious notes. The usual suspects feverishly jotted down my advice. I have no clue what the temperature was, but it was hot. If there was air conditioning in the classroom, I didn't feel it. Sweat gathered on my thin upper lip. I was aware of the presence of one inmate, in particular. Surely I was in a silent movie. I know I was talking, but it felt like there was complete silence in the room. Time slowed to a stop. His skin was intensely black, his inner lip a bright cherry that looked as if he'd just eaten a chemical feast from a pixie stick. His eyes were sad. They bulged from the sockets like his stomach bulged over his pants, a perfect match.

"Who in the hell is this guy?" I thought. He'd joined the class about two weeks prior. Many of the long-term writers despised my policy of allowing new people into the class at any time. I remembered that he came into the classroom a few weeks before and said "I'm inturr... rested in uh... writin' somethin'...ya' know... like uh... I don' know whut, but yeah... somethin'. Cans I join the class?"

Exasperated as always I said "Sure." So come to class he did, a couple of times. But I never heard a peep from him. He was so quiet I often forgot he was there.

But... not that day. That day, he was still quiet but his presence was looming large, his manly presence. Big-ol'-quiet-cat-had-his-tongue-Guy was sitting in a desk directly facing me. He was the only guy in the first row, just a few feet in front of me. His eyes looked so sad. This big ol' sad Guy looked right through me, as his left hand rested motionless on a notebook on top of his desk. But in his right hand underneath the desk, he held his dick as he ejaculated onto the floor. *Lovely. Just flippin' lovely. It's on the floor for chrissakes. Jesus Christ. His spunk is on the fucking classroom floor.* My face was draining the blood into my throat. Or was it becoming flush? A sensation that came easily years later with menopause, but this flush was induced by fear, not hormones.

Although I was reading notes out loud, another dialogue was being rehearsed in my head. It was a moment of pure, female, multi-tasking genius. "What's a girl to do?" I pondered. *I don't want to be the last one in the room with big-ol'-sad-comin'-on-the-floor-dude. I always remind my teachers of the danger of being alone with an inmate. Violette* (one of my female teachers) *let an inmate she'd known for months into her classroom while a lockdown was ensuing. She wasn't alone with him more than a few minutes, when he pulled his dick out of his pants. That was a horrible situation. I don't wanna' be left alone with this dude. If I say nothing, maybe he'll just leave afterwards? That would be bad too. He'll think I'm a wuss and do something worse next time. Damn-it!*

As an Artist Facilitator I knew precisely what I was "SUPPOSED" to do. I was supposed to implement standard procedure for inmate sexual assault on staff. Here's what the CDC (California Department of Corrections) would have recommended:

#1. Push the button on the panic alarm, which was attached to my overly distressed black leather fanny pack and riding on my left hip. (This would alert staff.)

#2. When the officers burst into the room, point to Coming-on-the-floor Dude and say, "This inmate is threatening me with sexual behavior and exposing himself." (They would then escort him out of the room.)

#3. Cancel class. (They would immediately send the inmates back to their cells.)

#4. Write concise report on the incident. (This would then be turned over to the Program Sergeant or Lieutenant, then ultimately pass through the hands of an inmate Program clerk or two, which is akin to announcing something on the loud speaker.)

#5. Try not to feel too guilty in the days to come when Coming-on-the-floor Dude is found in the shower room beaten and bloody, his teeth gone, his cheek bashed in, ribs broken and is moved to the infirmary then Administrative Segregation ("the hole") for his own protection. (#5 is the unwritten, unspoken part of what really happens when an inmate threatens a staff member in a sexual way, especially a well-liked female staff member. Word gets passed around and the inmates take it upon themselves to teach the guy a lesson.)

I did not want the burden of being responsible for big-ol'-sad-coming-on-the-floor dude getting hurt. Twisted huh? A 250-lb most likely but not necessarily convicted murderer jerks off right in front of me and I'm concerned about his welfare more than my own. Actually it made sense. I was in control. I could protect myself. But Coming-on-the-floor Dude, the poor sad fuck, wouldn't be able to protect himself. He was going to be in a world of hurt if I touched that panic button, so I didn't.

I firmly set my notes down, looked him in the eye and with stern resolve said, "You, you need to leave. Right now."

"Now?" he replied with amazement.

"Now." I stated. The room was awkwardly silent. He gathered himself together ever so slyly, placing a notebook over his crotch and he exited the room. I looked down and took several deep breaths.

Then, from the back of the room I heard, "What was that all about?" It' was quiet, old Ted the Redhead speaking first. He usually didn't say much. He was more like a doting grandfather who sat in the back of the room and just listened. Actually a sweetheart of a guy, Ted had retained some red in the grey hair that was battling to take over. He was an inmate I always wondered what in the hell he did to end up in there, but he was never a troublemaker so I never checked his file to find out.

"It doesn't matter." I said. And I went back to my precious, life-changing notes. Minutes later an exasperated officer came in. Our time was beyond up. As the inmates gathered their stuff, I asked if anyone knew the gentleman I had sent out of the room. When someone said they knew his cellie, I made a request. "Please get the message to him, that he is never to step foot in my classroom again."

"Why?" somebody piped.

"It doesn't matter why. Just deliver the message."

I too gathered my things. Just as I was about to leave the room Johnnie Go-To came up to me. The same Johnnie Go-To that I once thought had threatened to kill me now had a big-ass smile on his face. "Mannnnnn Miss Joki. That was real sharp. Dude musta' been doin' some weird sexual shit or somethin'. But since you didn't say shit I'll just get the word to homeboy and watch yur back. See, if ya' said he was doin' some weird sexual shit, Man we'd hafta take homeboy out. But you didn't say shit. I'll keep an eye on him. Don't worry 'bout it. You'll never have to see him again. Real sharp Miss Joki. Real sharp."

He turned with his big-ass smile shaking his head. I think Johnnie Go-To had a whole new respect for me. I had upheld convict etiquette. Johnnie Go-To was an original gangster. "One of the first Crips" he claimed. (I thought that was Stanley "Tookie" Williams, but what do I know?) Johnnie Go-To wouldn't think twice about hurting somebody who exposed himself to me. That would be a no-brainer. Expose yourself to a lady? That is just downright unacceptable. For a brief moment, I detected a glimmer of pride in his smile. I had finally figured out how prison really works.

The drive home was unusually hard that day. One third of the seventy-five miles was locked in canyons where the wind blew so strong that it felt like you could be picked up and tossed off the road. It was stressful. At the end of the day, when you catch an inmate jerking off to the point of orgasm, wittily sent him packing so you don't have to worry about the guilt you would feel if you returned to work the next day to find out that his throat had been slit... at the end of that day, I wanted a little support. You know, a hug, a "you're amazing", something! There in my 1950's pink kitchen, leaning on the O'Keefe & Merritt oven I got... "You need to get out of that hell hole. And I need to go to bed." That's all Husband had for me.

I stood. Alone. Like a southern belle in a Tennessee Williams's play... *There's nothing lonelier than feeling alone, when you're with the one you love. And besides, l liked my hell-hole.*

# Belonging

### 1985: Los Angeles, California

I was supposed to be a movie star. I was the little Montana girl who went to The Juilliard School in New York City where my acting teacher deemed me "better than whipped cream." But the Hollywood dream was slipping away and I was working as a real estate appraiser in Los Angeles. Then came "the call." Before caller ID existed, I answered my phone wantonly. There was no screening out the 800, 866, 877 numbers in 1985. Nope. Back in the day, a person simply answered the phone.

"Hello?" That's all I used to say. "Leah...it's Tom Provenzano."

"Aaawww.... Tommmm." I murmured. I had a fondness for Tom Provenzano, a soft spot. "Leah, I came across something that is perfect for you. I got this thing from a group at UCLA. They're a non-profit organization looking for male and female actors to teach improvisational theater in a juvenile detention center. As soon as I read it I thought of you."

*Why? Why would Tom Provenzano think of me as someone "perfect" for working in prisons? I was supposed to be a movie star. I didn't want to be an actor in prison.*

Four years before this call, Tom and I were part of a group of actors that worked in the Fort Peck Summer Theater, located in the remote northeast corner of Montana. Now he was running a successful children's theater company.

As Tom read the details for this part-time job, I jotted down notes and wondered if he remembered that while in Fort Peck, on a dare, I took my clothes off, went naked into another actor's trailer and sang "I'm a Little Teapot, Short and Stout". *Was it because I was crazy enough to do that that he thought I would fit well in prison?*

Maybe Tom remembered the time when we were partying in Ken, the artistic director's trailer and Ken yelled out "What do we all have in common?"

I raised my hand gleefully and blurted, "We all *care*?"

The group fell silent. Apparently they didn't all *care*. I was so disappointed I broke into tears over their non-caring. Maybe Tom Provenzano thought I could be a person who cared about inmates. *Or maybe he just thought I should go to a place where I couldn't be a danger to others.*

By 1985 I had completed my education at The Juilliard School and had done a few plays and student films in New York. For the most part, however, I waited tables and bartended in Times Square back when Times Square really sucked. Like everybody else, I had relocated to southern California to break into film and TV. Although I was now fully committed to Los Angeles, I'd already grown weary of devoting my days to looking for the right outfit, being the perfect weight or having my hair and make-up just so for one line on a bad TV series or the opportunity to be in some obscure play that no one would see. I still had dreams of Hollywood fame but so far, I was definitely not a success and as I needed to eat and pay rent, I took a job as a real estate appraiser. I thanked Tom for the call and wondered how this might work out.

\* \* \*

I attended the audition for the prison gig in downtown Los Angeles at the Music Center, which houses the Dorothy Chandler Pavilion, the Ahmanson Theater, and the Mark Taper Forum. It was the biggest opera and theater venue this side of the Mississippi. The prison audition was held in one of their rehearsal rooms. I went to the stage entrance off the street and gave my name at the security desk, then proceeded down the wide hallways with perfectly clean linoleum floors. The rehearsal rooms were made for musicians and opera singers, so a symphony could be blasting away, and you wouldn't necessarily hear it as you walked by. They had large, heavy doors, and inside were acoustically spectacular. Some of the world's most famous classical musicians, opera singers and performers had rehearsed in these rooms, and I was there for something I knew nothing about.

The audition wasn't remotely akin to singing "Teapot" in the nude. It was long, dramatic and arduous. There were more than thirty actors there and we were asked to improvise scenes about teen pregnancy, peer pressure, drug addiction and domestic abuse for hours. At the end, I was selected along with a young black actor, John Freeland, Jr., to join a group of actors who taught improvisational theater at the Fred C. Nelles School, a nice name for a prison for hard-core juvenile delinquents.

I got the coveted white girl spot that day, which added to the odd sort of karmic trend I had going. For some unknown reason I did tend to end up being the white girl in predominantly black plays. When I graduated from Juilliard, my first professional offer was from an up and coming black director, Lee Richardson, to be in a production of *To Be Young, Gifted and Black* in New Jersey. I declined and opted to honor a commitment to direct a play at Juilliard instead. When I first arrived in Los Angeles in 1985, the first non-equity play I was cast in was *To Be Young, Gifted and Black*. The production fell through, but clearly the universe wanted me to be young, gifted and black. In 1986 I was one of the few white contestants to make it to the finals of the Ira Aldridge Competition at the Inner City Theater Center. This was an acting competition for actors in the inner city, I guess. Since I lived in the inner city of Los Angeles, I gave it a stab. And even though I wasn't black like the other ninety-five percent of the actors, I was young and gifted enough to make it to the final eight. I didn't win. I was a white, glow-in-the-dark fish in black water that night!

Who'd have thunk that by going to some obscure audition I would be stepping into the world of enormous bureaucracies, where the art world mixed with paramilitary organizations, where there was a chain of command and volumes of acronyms. How did I end up in this place? Why did I get the coveted white girl spot?

Apparently Susan Hill, the Artistic Director of this group from UCLA, knew. Little did I know that this attractive, redheaded woman with the pale, lightly freckled skin at the audition was a major power player in the prison arts scene. At first I thought she was some flunky, some throwback to the sixties who happened to have an artsy job. I couldn't figure out what cachet she had to score space at the Dorothy Chandler Pavilion. Susan Hill was a visual artist who managed this arts organization called Artsreach, which was housed in some offices at UCLA Extension. She wrote in an article many years later, "We found that in fact the most important attribute for our successful longevity was that each artist carried some memory of being the outcast kid, and that their connection to the work and to the students came from deep empathy, from a true allegiance to inclusion, to stubborn survival." Susan Hill not only knew that I *cared*, she knew that I was looking for a place to *belong*.

# Juvie

I was first sent to the Fred C. Nelles School, a juvenile prison for male felons, located on busy Whittier Boulevard in Whittier, CA. From the street, one would never have suspected it was a prison. It looked like a nice private school with brick buildings and manicured lawns connected by a maze of newly poured concrete sidewalks. Except for the rusty chain-link fence with razor wire on top, it wasn't the vision of containment I had for young rapists and murderers. There wasn't even a security checkpoint into the parking lot. When I entered the first building however, the prep school appearance quickly vanished. Past the double glass doors employees were in uniform and behind bullet-proof glass. I was required to furnish a picture ID and take everything out of my pockets. Car keys were left there until after the session. One only went in with a pencil and a notebook or paper. Once I passed through security, a guard escorted us to the classroom. I admit that I was scared shitless. I had no idea what to expect. It was like being a foreign student in a foreign land, I just wasn't quite sure into what land I was dropped. I wasn't feeling the whole I belong here thing. I was feeling the *I need to get the hell out of here in a hurry* thing.

I was standing in the classroom with three other actors. That was the Susan Hill team teaching approach: two men, two women and racially diverse. I remember the moment the "wards" came in. I'd never heard that term before. I thought they were called prisoners or convicts, but I was quickly admonished, and told that they aren't called that anymore. Adults are called inmates; in a juvenile facility they're called wards. This group of kids consisted of thirteen to eighteen year olds who were in for serious crimes like murder in the first degree, murder in the second degree, manslaughter, rape, kidnapping, aggravated assault and might also be carrying a few infractions for burglary, theft, and otherwise unseemly conduct. (aka pretty serious shit.)

If you look up "ward" in Webster's you get: n. 1. a guarding 2. the state of being under guard 3. (a) guardianship, as of a child or person not capable of handling his own affairs (b)the condition of being under the control of a guardian; wardship; (c) a child or incompetent person placed by law under the care of a guardian or court; (d) a person under another's protection or care. Apparently, being a juvenile felon does mean you're a ward of the state and that you are under someone's care. Because if you look up "inmate" in Webster's you get: 1. a person living with others in the same building; an occupant 2. a person lodged with others, and often confined, in an institution, asylum, etc. 3. an inhabitant.

So the young wards are being "cared for," and the adult inmates are being "lodged". Interesting. If you look up "convict" in Webster's you get: n. a person proved or found guilty of a crime, and sentenced by a law court. 2. a person serving a sentence of confinement, as in a penitentiary. Wow! When in the hell did it become offensive to note that this group of individuals were guilty of crimes, had been sentenced in a court of law and were serving a sentence of confinement? I wonder what politically correct bureaucrat found a term that determined if they were young they were under someone's guardianship and as adults they were simply being lodged. That's a head-spinner ain't it? It's hard to call a spade a spade anymore.

When the wards first entered the room the air supply suddenly seemed to diminish. I felt lightheaded. What in the hell happened to the air? It seemed like I had just moved up a couple thousand feet, probably just pure adrenaline kicking in. It was intimidating to be in the presence of about twenty teenagers who swaggered with a don't-fuck-with-me attitude, with baggy blue jeans barely on their butts, and their eyes just glaring at me, checking me out, making sure I got the message that they had something over on me. They may have been "confined", but their swagger told me who was in control and it was not *Miss Leah*. Everyday teenagers can be threatening. They don't understand their physical strength, they're awkward and they make goofy choices. Hell, their frontal lobe isn't developed yet. But this room full of teenagers was not well educated, had screwed up family lives, was probably sexually active and had all been high enough or brazen enough to commit some deadly crimes. These kids scared the crap out of me.

I was an oddity, a white woman amongst teenage males of mostly color. That too was a bit surprising. The number of young black men in juvenile facilities was staggering. I have a photograph of one of our theater groups at Nelles and out of twenty wards, three are white, three are Hispanic and fourteen are black. Most of the white boys in a facility like this usually were the kids who snapped and killed their parents or got so high they killed their brother. The white kids tended to kill their families and the blacks and Hispanics tended to kill each other. I couldn't drop the Juilliard card with a fourteen-year old gang-banger from east LA. He probably had never heard of the place, so why would he give a shit? All of my Juilliard training did not prepare me for the likes of a juvenile delinquent challenging me on my very right to exist.

If they spoke English, I recognized little of it. I didn't know that if you were a Blood you drop the "C's" out of your dialogue. For instance, I remember a kid doing a scene and he said he wanted an "ease grater". We kept asking what the hell he was talking about until someone informed us that as a Blood he isn't supposed to say his C's. He was asking for a "cheese grater". It took me a while to wrap my head around that. The speech thing was no joke. You had to pay serious attention. It wasn't just the gang-speak, it was the drugs, too. Some of these kids had done so much drinking and pot smoking as teenagers, with some PCP or angel dust or crack, they had lost many of their motor mechanisms. Their brain just could no longer make the connection quickly and their speech was most likely permanently altered from what it could have been had they grown up alcohol and drug free. I was stunned the damage done by these substances to growing children, and I'd swore I'd try to keep them out of the hands of kids I knew.

The gang insignia was also way over my head. We'd be doing some innocuous exercise with everyone standing in a circle and saying his name simultaneously with a movement. We aptly called it the "name game". There we would be in this big circle and without notice, the room suddenly divided into four corners; in one corner were the Hispanics, in another were the whites, in a third were the blacks who were Cripps and in the fourth were the blacks who were Bloods, in a matter of seconds without words being exchanged. Apparently there were some signs thrown around that said more than words could and BAM, the homeboys divided and stood their ground in their own little corners. *Weird shit!*

One of the unexpected perks of being a woman in this situation was that for at least two sessions I could do no wrong. That's right. Any woman working in a male facility gets at least two weeks hassle free. That even transferred to the Big House later on, the adult men's maximum, security prisons. Guys young and old are so intrigued with being in the presence of a female, and especially an attractive female, that they'll do practically anything: stand on their head, quack like a duck, or sing a ditty just to be in your presence. And sometimes for white women, sometimes they would throw in a third week. But that really wasn't a compliment. Au contraire. In a facility that had that many young men of color and so few white kids, the African American and Hispanic female teachers were viewed as either whores or mothers to them. The white females were just viewed as whores. The thought of relating to any woman as a friend, coworker, colleague or boss, simply wasn't in their repertoire.

There was also the whole "scent of a woman thing". When guys are locked up for while, even young guys like these, it's as if they just quit smoking and are beginning to regain a sense of smell they didn't know existed. Instead of smelling the distinct aromas of their mother's kitchen, or the odor of their shoes, or the fragrance of the flowers blooming, they smelled *me*. They smelled me and got off on it. And it wasn't just my perfume. They smelled my bloody womanhood. Geez. I swear, every time I worked while menstruating, they knew it. They would get as close as possible to me and I could feel them take these big deep breaths in a really bizarre way.

Another aspect of being a woman in a juvenile boy's facility is that I quickly learned how to handle the "touching, no touching thing". The touching, no touching thing was a test. It was a weird test and sometimes lasted for weeks. I'd be sitting next to a kid on the floor watching other people perform and as I was watching the scene on stage I got a sense that maybe the guy was touching my arm. It was so subtle I wasn't even sure. So I ignored it. Then the next time I was by him I got this sensation that maybe he touched my back but who knew? Before I knew it, I got that sensation on my ass and breasts and homeboy enjoyed a big 'ole laugh at my expense as I looked weak and easily manipulated. Like women often do, we think it's just in our heads, that they meant no harm, but it was a tactic to test us and we all had to learn quickly that if you thought for a second that some kid was lightly brushing up against you, your instincts were right. If I was going to keep control of the room, (a kind-of-important-thing-to-do- in prison) then that kid needed to be put in check in a hurry. A simple whisper of "Cut that shit out." would usually suffice.

The more cocky ones would respond, "What shit?"

I'd respond back "You know what shit I'm talking about."

But the second time I said it, it was loud enough that someone next to him heard it. That was part of the whole "don't diss 'em" in front of their homies etiquette. The first time, I whispered the "cut the shit" remark quietly to the one touchy guy, only. If he didn't stop, I had to make sure that the guy next to him heard it, so that the touchy guy would know that I was still cutting him some slack and not dissing him in front of the whole group. He needed to get the message loud and clear that I wasn't afraid to put his shit on the table for everyone to see but I'd let him out quietly if he would just cut the shit. I learned some smooth operations working with juvenile delinquents.

Our male counterparts caught shit from these kids from the moment they walked in the door. The wards were hardest on the male teachers. If you were white you really had to prove yourself, and if you were black or Hispanic you had better be down with the street speak or they didn't trust you. If you sounded too educated and were a minority, they assumed you jumped ship and went to the white man's side. They were brutal that way.

For the first year with Artsreach I didn't come out of the box swinging. I was very much a follower and an observer. For a time, I was the only white girl and I even wondered if I wanted to keep the coveted white girl spot. The theater company consisted of three dancers (two black and one Jewish) and five actors (two white, two Hispanic and one black). Christine Avila and Peter Schreiner were the leaders.

Christine was a beautiful Hispanic actress with a gorgeous singing voice and a relatively successful career. She was calm but forceful in the way that makes a good mother, she knew how to set boundaries early on. Peter was a white guy who, according to Susan Hill, "played the audition so tough and so angry that no one thought he was a candidate until he sang "Amazing Grace" so off key and so heartfelt that we had no choice but to bring him in." He was a slightly overweight guy, maybe 5'7", very Norwegian looking with a turned up nose and boyish face. He could get so worked up however, that I swear steam would come out of the top of his head. Although he was a bit of a bull in a china shop in the early years, he was irreplaceable. No one had a bigger heart, worked harder and cared more for these kids than Peter.

J. Ed Ariza was the hippest Hispanic dude I ever met, a real gem. His presence was cool, calm and collected. The guy was tall, thin, good looking, bilingual and his voice had a rich, low, to-die-for timbre. Hands down, J.Ed was the guy you wanted in the room with you. His fluent Spanish was a plus, and he was unflappable with no fear of making a fool of himself.

There were three dancers in the group. Lula Washington was older than most of us, a dark-skinned black woman with a very serious look on her face. Her dance company later became acclaimed in Los Angeles. Myrna Gawryn was Jewish, but viewed as the other white girl. She had a gorgeous head of long brown curly hair and had made some claim to fame choreographing THE *TEENAGE MUTANT NINJA TURTLES*. I've always remembered her bemoaning the fact that hip hop had taken over the industry and there was very little work left for classically trained dancers, jazz, modern, or even tap dancers. Most TV and film work was all hip-hop in the eighties.

Then there was Flo, a tall, lean, muscular drop-dead gorgeous black woman who was not only a dancer, but a singer too. She was a single mother of two boys from separate fathers and worked her ass off to keep it together in Hollywood. She had sung backup for Natalie Cole when Natalie was whacked out on drugs and for a moment she was rehearsing to sing backup for Madonna until it was rumored that Madonna got rid of the back-up singers she hired because they were too pretty.

Susan Hill got what she looked for in that theater company: a group of people who exhibited "teamwork, resiliency, imagination and grace under stress." Despite our many accomplishments, we were still mostly unemployed actors trying to save the lives, or shall I say, the artistic souls of misspent youth. Every actor can relate to that. Like a shrink that goes to work each day ultimately to fix his own problems, some actors crave to be accepted and nurtured and have the bad hand that life dealt them understood.

The enthusiasm that existed in the early years at Nelles was contagious. No matter how left wing, liberal, hippie-like, criminal sympathizing the program was, one could not deny the impact of professional artists in a correctional setting. And we had proof. California's Arts in Corrections (AIC) program touted its' success based on the Brewster Report, published in 1983 by the ever-so- liberal University of California at Santa Cruz. The study documented that inmate participants in the AIC program showed increased levels of cooperation, less racism, fewer incidents, and a reduced rate of recidivism. The Brewster Report gave us credibility.

Most of the wards never made it far enough in school to have any real experience in the arts. The arts are consistently misunderstood. They are a staple, not a dessert. With the arts one learns discipline, patience, work ethic, cooperation and tolerance. Our goal was never to find the next best actor behind bars, it was to provide a teenager with an artistic experience that would challenge him and deepen his sense of possibility. Looking into the eyes of a fourteen year old, no one wants to believe his soul is irretrievable. They were kids, for chrissakes. Kids with drug problems and scars from machine guns, kids without doting parents and with parents who beat the crap out of them, kids who were afraid of being raped in the dorms.

Maybe, just maybe, the bureaucrat who came up with the term "ward" was onto something. They were kids who needed to be taken care of, to be under the guardianship of something positive because almost every one of those kids, no matter how bad the crime, almost every one of them was coming out again as a adult. And one would hope that that adult learned something as a ward, even if it was just to get along in a room full of people of a different race, gang, gender or just a different crowd. Then, maybe they had a shot at something close to a so-called normal life.

# Double Life

I was so hooked-up at age twenty-nine: Real estate appraiser by day, prison actor at night. A typical day consisted of dressing in acceptable but comfortable bank attire and commuting in my company compact Chevrolet to the San Fernando Valley to work for Home Savings of America. I liked the job of understanding the market value of real estate. It was a "grown-up" life.

This was the appraisal drill: arrive, say hello, look at the house, tape the house inside and out to get the exact square footage, draw the map of its exact location, take notes and pictures, then say goodbye. I'd spend thirty minutes or so in the car researching comparable properties, take pictures and more notes. Then I was off to the next appointment where I repeated the process. My goal was to be a good little appraiser with all my work done neatly and concisely, so I could ask the boss to leave early to teach the misguided juvenile delinquents in prison. Fortunately, appraising residential properties in the San Fernando Valley wasn't difficult, even for a theater major. It's common sense, market driven and data based. Every now and then a mansion in Encino or a geodesic dome in the foothills of Calabasas could throw me for a loop, but usually it was easy. Since my work didn't have many mistakes, I was allowed to lead my double life in prison at night.

Maintaining this Jekyl and Hyde existence took great planning and commitment. I had to be in Whittier at the Fred C. Nelles School at 6:00pm, so I mastered the art of changing clothes while driving. Brushing hair, putting on make-up and drinking coffee behind the wheel was for amateurs. Crawling along the 210 Freeway at 15mph, I actually changed my bra and top and took off panty hose while driving, and without the guy next to me taking any notice. That was almost as rewarding as the theater sessions themselves. Actually getting there *on time* was a big accomplishment. Even in the mid-eighties traffic from 4:00-6:30pm in the major areas, was a challenge. I reveled in my double life and even came to enjoy teaching the misguided miscreants.

It wasn't long after I got started with Artsreach that an opportunity came along to direct an original play. Directing had, like acting, been one of my strong suits and passions. The play was going to be produced at a small theater in Venice that was run by whom else? Tom Provenzano. I wondered if he thought this would be "perfect" for me as well. The play was titled LOVE ABUSE. Go figure, it was about an abusive marriage, a fun subject. The playwright was a beautiful, blonde beach-bunny-of-a-housewife with a rich husband and a flock of small children. It took a few weeks into the rehearsal process to realize that the guy I cast as the husband wasn't working out. I convinced the playwright bunny that I knew the "perfect" person for the job. He just happened to live in New York City, happened to be black (the character in the play was white) and he just happened to be OBBF (original black boyfriend).

In addition to those brushes with getting cast in black plays, I had also developed a reputation for dating black guys. My Juilliard sweetheart, my original black boyfriend (OBBF), was the first in a string. After we split there was the former NBA black guy, the older black writer, and the somewhat older and famous black artist. That was my run of black love interests. Throughout my dating history I was linked with four black men and eight white men and I still had a reputation for dating black guys. If you date a few black men in a row, the white community says you have a thing for black guys. You date a lot of white guys and nobody says a goddamn thing. One also hears from the black community that "once you go black you never go back". Heard it heard it heard it. Don't know where it came from, why it was reiterated over and over, or why it became a mantra. I suspect it's connected to the notion that black men have bigger dicks. Just for the record, that's not necessarily true.

OBBF was a terrific actor and even though we had parted company about two years before, we were still on speaking terms. I needed someone with the utmost professional demeanor who could come in and pull this sucker off in ten days. Granted, the playwright was apprehensive about the image of a black man knocking around a white woman. But I convinced her of OBBF being able to pull off the colorblind thing and in the end it was a success. (I can say that with credibility because I won the Los Angeles Dramalogue Award for Best Director that year. I swear to God I won it, but can't find it. I searched my house high and low looking for the review and the award. I've even tried to Google it, but came up empty handed.)

There wasn't money to pay OBBF to do the play, so he stayed in my apartment as remuneration. When the play was over however, he didn't leave. He didn't rush back to New York because he didn't have anything to rush back *to*. Besides, Artsreach needed a few more actors. When I recommended OBBF to Susan Hill, I didn't tell her about our past relationship. So, it was without any "nudging" from me that he was brought into the theater company along with another black actress, Violette. She had a beautiful round face with short, short hair, happy eyes and a small dent in her forehead that some doctor swore he could fix. At first I thought she'd been scammed, but she was so alarmingly convincing in her presentation of skull-reshaping that I believed he could too. Violette was one of the hardest working, most passionate actors I've ever known.

It wasn't long before OBBF and I were back together. Just months before we were leading separate lives on opposite coasts and then we were in the sprawl of southern California working together in prison and cohabitating again. We were happy campers. We taught classes in juvie together, wrote grants and got one of them funded together, attended meetings at Artsreach together, created a multi-media performance piece together and as we sat in "our" apartment, we talked about prison together.

I continued to work as an appraiser and he took a job delivering Chinese food at night. My dream had now become his dream. I willingly left behind the dream to pursue an acting career in Hollywood and was content to focus solely on prison and OBBF jumped on the bandwagon with me. Before I knew it, not only did I have a double life, so did we.

Our double life worked so well that even Susan Hill didn't know that we were an item and we decided to leave it that way. One year had passed before Artsreach made the connection between the two of us, even though we had the same address. It was during that time that we perfected the How-to-Work-Together-as-a Couple-Without-Letting-Anyone-Know-You're-a-Couple-Approach. Our relationship was always under the radar during teaching sessions, meetings, or at a conference. Intimacy between us went undetected. These were our self-imposed guidelines for success.

1. **Never sit next to each other in a meeting.** If you do, that gives it away every time, especially if you agree on something, which we often did. The idea was to give the illusion that we were always independent of each other, so that the group didn't feel they were being ganged up on by a couple. People hate being ganged up on by a couple.

2. **Never answer questions about one's personal life.** Now, this actually became a motto for the entire group of prison actors. After a while we realized that it's really not advisable to tell a convicted murderer where you lived. You never know, they might come looking for you one day.

3. **Go by first names only.** With a name like "Joki" I figured it wouldn't be too hard to be located by any ward with half a brain, so I got OBBF and the rest of them to comply in juvie. First names only.

4. **Nothing but the utmost of professional behavior at all times.** This was the ultimate for us as a couple. No yukking it up in the corner, no holding hands and winking at each other, no recognition of a relationship at all. And that was not just in the classroom with the wards, it was in planning sessions, group meetings, and at conferences.

We embraced those tactics wholeheartedly. We relished our duplicity, oh masters of disguise and maestros of the double life, we!

I admired how Susan Hill delegated. As a visual artist running a theater company, she had the foresight to hire well-trained actors, provide us with the best training available in prison theater: the late Rebecca Rice from Center Stage in Washington, D.C. and John Bergman of the Geese Theater in London. Then she let us take the ball and run with it. We ran so hard sometimes it was like running into a brick wall. We knew we made mistakes in juvie, but she never admonished us for trying.

We always took time to plan the session beforehand and a brief amount of time to evaluate it afterward. Ninety percent of the time we would arrive at Nelles and write down this list:

Name Game
Warm-up
Bulk of the session
Cool down

It was an ingenious plan for twenty hardcore gang-bangers. They'd strut into the room and look at us with this what-in-the-hell-did-you-call-me-here-for-bitch attitude. Once we got them to contain the gang insignia, the "Name Game" became our reliable ice-breaker. At the beginning of each session the entire group of wards and instructors would stand in a circle and, one at a time, each person would step into the center saying his name as he simultaneously made a repetitive movement with a sound. For instance, I'd go to the center of the circle and in a loud, resonant voice say "LLLLLEEEEEEE...AAAAAHHHHHHHHH" and simultaneously do a couple of lame karate kicks.

Then the whole group would repeat "LLLLEEEEEEE... AAAAAHHHHHHH!" and also do some lame karate kicks. The idea was to create a sound and movement that you could attach to each person's name and their physical image. Ironically, for someone with a piss-poor memory I had a knack for remembering every guy's name and movement even if it was the first time I met them. That was quite the impressive parlor/prison trick I picked up. It bought me at least ten minutes of grace each session.

Once we got them to pry their lips open and say a few names, we would start onto the warm-up. A warm-up is a warm-up is a warm-up: get the blood flowing, the mind thinking. Same with the cool down at the end: chill out, take a few deep breaths and relax. Actually if we got them to be quiet for one goddamn minute, it was a miracle! Silence was hard to come by in juvie. First we struggled to have them mumble their names. Then we struggled to have them shut up and be quiet for a minute.

Planning the Name Game, warm-up and cool down was easy. Planning the onerous "bulk of the session" was not. Every week we racked our brains for what to do and how to come up with something that would open these guys up, something that would challenge them but let them feel comfortable. It would be thought provoking or get them to laugh at themselves. Something that would make them see the error of their ways, or fuck it, anything that would expand their godforsaken criminal minds and teach them to cut the shit, stay out of the gangs and go home and be good boys.

We were under strict orders from Artsreach and the California Arts Council: artists/actors were not therapists. The CDC had trained shrinks and counselors for that. We didn't do therapy sessions. We just looked for fun methods that may or may not have benefited the wards therapeutically. Of course the public wouldn't have been too keen on us simply providing them with a good time so it was okay if they could learn something that helped to remedy their bad behavior, it just couldn't be therapy. That was the conundrum of working as an artist in prison! We always had to answer the "Do-You-Guys-Do -Therapy?" question.

We were a strong-willed group of actors, dedicated to doing the best we could and we were risk-takers. Of course some of the things we did back then, we'd probably be sued or fired for today. But that was before political correctness became the norm and people were still allowed to make mistakes. Not that we made mistakes so much as we designed some "Interesting Escapades".

We sat around the table one evening after a session and someone blurted "What every juvenile delinquent needs more than anything in life is the opportunity to take responsibility for his actions and to learn to cooperate with others." Yes indeedy, wasn't that the truth? Well we, the privileged and educated ones in the facility, had just the answer that day: a computer, a human computer.

I'm not sure who came up with the computer thing but in retrospect, it must've been me as I can still vividly recollect two childhood friends from Butte, MT, my hometown, Terry Blanc and Terry Bing. They made their own computer once. They were the "Two Terries" and had even written a short book called "Terrineese", a dictionary of their own language. They spent weeks in seclusion working on their genius computer project. The only thing the rest of us little gumbahs knew was that we weren't supposed to know anything about it. We were to stay out of the Bings' backyard where it was being constructed, until we were notified to come over. When the invitation came I was so excited. They had built a computer next to the yellow detached garage out of a huge refrigerator box (obviously a wee bit unfair from the get-go since Mr. Bing worked for Westinghouse Appliances). The outside of the box was painted to look like a computer, which of course, I'd never seen before. It had that *My Favorite Martian* look about it. We walked up to the computer, filled out a piece of paper with a question on it, inserted it into a slot, and a few minutes later that puppy actually spit out an answer. It was quite impressive. Although the Two Terries were in the refrigerator box armed with a dictionary, maps, reference books, a calculator, etc., we, as friends, appreciated their ingeniousness. We gleefully asked the computer many questions and applauded the swiftness with which it provided answers. At least that's how I remember it. Nice girls celebrating other nice girls' creativity and resourcefulness. Since I had nothing but fond memories of that experience, I was completely open to the prison computer idea.

We didn't have a huge refrigerator box from Westinghouse in juvie, but we did have a roll of brown craft paper. Typically, we were always there to greet the guys as they came in. But this time, we didn't appear to be there, at first glance. Four of us were in a corner of the room and we literally barricaded ourselves in with craft paper. Imagine, grown adults standing in the corner behind a piece of craft paper taped wall to ceiling. In the center of the paper were two slots. One was labeled "Outgoing Instructions", the other "Evaluations". We stood behind the brown craft paper with envelopes containing instructions such as: 1) Pick a leader. 2) Do five minutes of stretching. 3) Break into groups of four and pick a theme. We didn't have reference books and maps or calculators, just pieces of paper with simple tasks, extremely simple tasks that we had done a million times before. Our thinking was that they would learn something by having to perform the tasks as a group without our direct, physical assistance. From this, they would learn cooperation, responsibility, sharing and leadership. It was endless what they could have learned. It was proactive for chrissakes. It was brilliant! So brilliant, we planned this session for weeks.

Other than obnoxious pillars in the middle of this empty room with the shiny, laden-with-more-wax-than-should-be-legal, prison-clean linoleum floor, there was one other bothersome feature; two mirrors. The mirrors *had* to be covered. A group of teenage gang-bangers cannot be trusted with a large mirror. Mirrors conveyed domination. If a ward could see his reflection in a mirror, so could others. If he projected his affiliation in the reflection, that could be seen by others as well. The closest person to the mirror had the largest reflection, therefore the most space taken up, therefore the most powerful. Within thirty seconds of an uncovered mirror sighting, a mirror in a room of gangbangers was an instant display of reflective graffiti on the wall. No spray paint was needed to illuminate his affiliation, just the holographic illusion. Once, in the amount of time it took to tie ones shoelaces, we looked up and saw Tom Tom lifting his white T-shirt exposing four black indentations forming a horizontal line on his stomach. They were the proud display of his surviving being shot with an AK47. Like a stripper dropping that first cover to let everyone know she has the goods underneath, Tom Tom exalted in his treasures too.

The problem wasn't only that someone would start signifying in front of the mirror it was that once one did it, they all had to do it. And once they all joined in, it was like throwing the Sunni, Shiites and the Kurds onto a live canvas just to see what happens. The Bloods started pushing out the Crips, the northern Latino gangs attempted to overcome the Southerns and the Skinheads tried to physically squelch them all together. Hands forming C's, B's and W's were backed up with eyes bulging with fury. That was their reality. Gang affiliation was everything. If a kid wasn't allied to some group, he was probably some poor punk who offed his father after he had the crap beaten out of him and his mom for fifteen years. Other than that, they were all affiliated and they made damn sure it was known with whom. They had even been in fistfights after a brief, reflective display of gang affiliation.

So, on computer day, we had the good sense to cover the damn things up. They entered the room silently as usual, escorted by a counselor, and for the most part, still on good behavior. Naturally we couldn't see shit. I remember hearing from behind the paper someone mumbling "Whassup?" "What the...?" "What the fuck is that shit?" The 10' x 12' sheet of paper in the corner had definitely gotten their attention. That was precisely what we wanted, so we shot out the first envelope and heard it fall onto the floor. It contained something like "Walk around the room twice" as their first instruction. But curiosity killed our cat. Within moments there were large black eyes peering into the instruction and evaluation slots. Then came their fingers. They were like customers in a pet store who can't resist sticking their fingers into the cages. They knew they weren't supposed to but they couldn't help themselves. Before we knew it, we were being bombarded with paper clips and rubber bands. I remember being vexed, thinking, *where in the hell did they get all the paper clips and rubber bands?* It sounds stupid, but imagine paper clips and rubber bands being shot at you from a foot or two away. And shot at you with the intent to hurt you. There we were, four adults screaming and jumping up and down like some kind of bugs being poked at in a glass jar with no way out. Pathetic really. The guard, I mean counselor, blew his whistle. The commotion stopped. We sadly ripped down the brown craft paper to expose our foolish selves: half-wits, state-mandated morons. The wards were taken back to the cottages and class was over. That was their punishment for misbehaving. Our heads hung low as we quietly threw all the brown craft paper into the trash.

When the counselor and the wards were gone however, we laughed at the thought of them gleefully shooting us with rubber bands from point blank range. It was very funny in a twisted way, so lame that it was downright hysterical. It was zany, but harmless.

Another time we thought it would be fun if the guys went from one station to another, like different parts of a nightclub, and in each spot they improvised a little something. That was a brilliant idea. We came armed with props and music, ready to put on a jazz club the likes of which they'd never seen. We divided them into groups. Some started at the bar, some where the singer was entertaining and the rest were just milling around our make believe nightclub. We actually got Flo, an amazing singer and beautiful to boot, to agree to stand on a table and sing jazz songs in a beaded, antique-looking gown. Her vocals were captivating, but unfortunately the wards were mostly interested in her crotch. There she was belting out some brassy jazz tune on top of a banquet table, and our adolescent-hormone-driven-wards were lying on the linoleum floor beneath her, trying to look up her dress. Silly us, we were horrified.

At the other "stations" of our improvised jazz club the wards gathered around the bar and asked for whimsical, exotic drinks. When they didn't get them they started to threaten the teacher/bartender. And throughout the imaginary lounge where people were milling about and socializing they improvised snorting lines of cocaine. The counselor that evening was horrified. What educational / artistic value did that have? None. But it was pretty funny and it wasn't therapy.

Figuring out what to do for the "bulk of each session" was easier to solve than the conundrum of what to do for "The Performance". At the Fred C. Nelles School, it was a given that we would culminate each year with a performance. That's what made the administrators happy, so that's what we did. Personally, I never liked them. They were an exercise in crowd control, a war between the liberal arts clan and the thugs. Just to keep gang signifying out of the show was a miracle. I didn't like parading them in front of staff and their peers so we could justify our existence. For some wards the notion of getting up on a stage with lights in front of an audience was the ultimate thrill, but for others it was something to dread. Like the mirrors, live performances could be used as a power play. The performances were a great place to strut your stuff or to humiliate someone else. They always made me nervous.

Normally however, things went off with only a few glitches, some gang signing here and there, some unscripted comments here and there, some pants-dropped-lower-than-they're-supposed-to-be here and there. But they were pretty successful. My dim view of the juvenile performances was implanted when a ward was caught coming to the performance with multiple layers of clothes on, which implied that he was planning to escape after the show. I remember how shocked and disappointed we were that he would use the performance as a venue to escape. We were so self-absorbed we complained that our precious little theater performance wasn't being taken seriously, we were being taken advantage of! "Wah wah wah" we went on.

We got a little reality check however, when we learned that this fourteen year old white kid, fresh with newly formed acne, a little dandruff and blue eyes filled with sadness, had been raped the day before and just wanted out. He just wanted to not be in that place anymore. My heart ached at the thought of it, even though we couldn't confirm if the rumor was true. But I do know this, we never saw him again and our almighty theater woes were silenced with the realization that we weren't exactly working in a Disney version of an *American High School Muiscal*. This was a prison for kids and bad things happen in bad places. And the trick to surviving there was to never forget that, to always be aware of the kind of place we were in, and still be able to laugh. Like my "double life" this too, was a balancing act.

# Think Again

In California there were a whole lot of prisons built in the late 80's and early 90's. On one hand Governor Pete Wilson disgusted me with his rate of growth in prisons and the lack of growth in schools, but on the other hand I was delighted with all the new prospects of work. Yep, there was a whole lot of prison work up for the taking. OBBF, Violette and I started a stint at CIM (California Institution for Men) in Chino that lasted for years. We worked on the minimum-security yard and it was there that I became quite enamored with what would become my preferred status of the incarcerated: adult men. In the juvenile prisons, the wards weren't required to come to a theater class, but they were heavily nudged. In the adult prisons, it was completely voluntary and that made a huge difference. I knew how to reach these guys in a way I lacked with the kids. Working at CIM was hands down the most gratifying teaching experience I had as a contract artist. The Artist Facilitator was a middle-aged white guy named Tom Skelly. Skelly was a visual artist who dabbled in music, video and multimedia. He had a gorgeous head of dark hair and even darker circles around his eyes. He was really quite striking, but looked like he was always exhausted. What we loved about Skelly is that he didn't meddle. He let us come in, do whatever we wanted and as long as there was a lot of enthusiasm from the guys, he kept on bringing us back year after year. CIM was just plain fun. OBBF, Violette and I became a well-oiled machine. The three of us knew how to work a room. Without words we instinctively knew when to help the other out and when to back off. I adored working with Violette and OBBF. And performances? They were a blast. No concerns about inmates trying to escape before or after the show, no worries about gang signifying or humiliating someone else. They were adults. They were way past that. And that just made it a pleasure.

During the same time frame I also taught at CIW (California Institution for Women) with beautiful, black Flo. We did some great work but, I gotta' tell you, working with incarcerated women was not my cup of tea. First of all, being a white girl in a women's prison had no benefit. I didn't get that same break from the women that I got from the men. Hell no! The women automatically assumed I grew up privileged and couldn't possibly know shit about their world. Then, on top of the attitude, they were women being women in the worst way; catty, mean-spirited and backbiting. Don't get me wrong, they weren't all like that but a lot of them were, and boy did it come out in a theater class.

Another thing that annoyed me about the female prisoners was their preoccupation with men. The majority of women who are locked up are there, stereotypically, because of some guy. Some guy they held drugs for, some guy that pimped them out, some guy that beat the crap out of them and they just kept taking it until they snapped and blew his brains out. I swear to God, there was always some guy in the background, which in a way was "ironically inspiring": At least they don't commit much violent crime on their own. They're just obsessively needy.

The whole sexual thing in the women's prison is also peculiar. In men's prisons there were certainly some blatantly gay queens roaming around, but they didn't have these very public displays of affection. In the female joint? Girlfriend, it was going on. These chicks were all over each other, holding hands, making out, patting each others' tooshes and ninety percent of them didn't consider themselves gay. All sorts of straight women go to prison and hook up with another woman. A woman's need to be loved and nurtured is that intense. The dikes were a bit intimidating, I must admit. I wasn't used to being undressed by another woman's eyes. That was a weird new thing. I realized that for a lesbian who had unsuccessfully hit up on heterosexual women in the past, prison had its' perks: Most of the straight girls were going to cross over, especially if they had a significant amount of time to do. It was a wee bit of dike heaven.

We sat in a circle on a dirty hardwood floor. There were ten women in class. Flo was on the opposite side and I was completely fixated on the woman to her right. She had that dark, dark African skin and was slight but very muscular. She had striking features but manly in a way. I couldn't place her but was confident I had known her from somewhere. At the end of class I asked if we knew each other somehow, asked why she seemed so familiar. It turned out "she" had been in a class of mine two years ago at CIM. That's right. CIM, the California Institution for Men. She was a male inmate who was released, got the surgery and then, got locked up again. I mean, talk about a test in social graces that wasn't ever mentioned in *Miss Manners*. My inclination was to let my jaw drop, my eyes bulge and shout "What? You've got to be kidding!" Instead, I squelched that urge and said a good Jerry Seinfeld "Wow!" Understated and yet, amazed!

In addition to CIM and CIW, we also worked at CRC (California Rehabilitation Center). CRC was the only prison that housed both men and women, although not together. The women were up on the hill in the Hotel California, the place that had been confiscated from Al Capone in a tax fraud case. It was gorgeous and overlooked a tiny man-made lake, had lush landscaping all around and beautiful tile work within. At the bottom of the hill however, there was razor wire fencing separating the makeshift bungalows that housed the male inmates from the once-famous resort. CRC was a minimum-security prison that mainly housed "N" numbers. That's someone who had been convicted of a narcotics charge. Basically, male and female drug-related offenders were there. They were a squirrelly bunch to work with. Need I say, *spacey*?

CRC had a distinguished attribute: "flaggers". Flaggers were women on the top of the hill, and men at the bottom of the hill, who would send each other messages through a series of coded, broad movements. The urban, prison myth at CRC was that a whole lot of, otherwise verboten, communication went from one side to the other through the flaggers. (Who said cheerleading skills didn't come in handy in the joint?)

CIM, CIW and CRC had all been around for a long time, like San Quentin, Folsom and Soledad. Although Soledad was kind of in the middle of nowhere, the others were either in, or close to, a major urban area. But when all the new prisons were being built every economically disadvantaged small town in the middle of nowhere was dying to have a prison in their back yard. Prisons were popping up in the Central Valley and in the southern deserts near Mexico and Arizona like warts on a toad and became eyesores on the natural California landscape. But *hoorah*, there was even more prison work to be had! There was so much work, Susan Hill had to add a position for a company manager to the roster and I was the logical person to herd those cats into one barn.

With more work for the theater group, more actors were needed to cover the sessions. Suddenly when we attended meetings they included a handsome but volatile white guy with a great head of hair, a tall redhead, a dramatic black actress-trained-in-England, and the laugh-out-loud-funny Irma Escamilla. With all these new people coming into the fold it also meant more training and Susan Hill believed in a great deal of training for artists working in the prisons. For me there was something very gratifying about getting paid to take an acting class from awesome new teachers.

When we began working with John Bergman of the Geese Theatre and the late Rebecca Rice from Living Stage in Washington, D.C. it started to kick in that my life was pretty darn sweet.

I had the cool corporate job at the bank appraising homes, which not only provided a decent, stable income but health benefits, paid vacation days and a company car. I also had my very cool prison gig working in the adult men's prisons and I had my cool Original Black Boyfriend, too. I had it all.

The really, really big, big serious fun started with a little play called *THINK AGAIN, JACKSON!* John Bergman, Geese Theatre guy, was training us. He was a hippie-Englishman who looked Jewish and acted like an abrasive New Yorker who spoke with a heavy British accent liberally laced with profanity. He was awesome. No one had more energy than this guy, no one was louder than this guy and no one could cut to the chase like this guy. From the beginning he warned that we "would go in a white-bleeding-heart-liberal and come out a fascist pig". I just couldn't conceive of me becoming some sort of fat, Nazi-like dictator in the classroom and didn't feel that was a potential problem for me. But there was one "Bergmanian" piece of advice that stuck with me: "Never forget ladies! Never forget you're the one they're thinking of when they jerk off at night!"

We spent several days coming up with a large collection of characters through improvised monologues. Bergman put them on a list on our always-handy-brown-craft-paper and then linked them together in scenes. Before we knew it, we had the beginning of a nifty little play. Several of us worked on scripting that play, which ultimately became *THINK AGAIN, JACKSON!* It was a morality tale about an inmate who was released into the real world, and while on parole he made one mistake after another and ultimately ended up back in prison. *THINK AGAIN, JACKSON!* was designed for two male and two female actors. OBBF, J. Ed, Sheila Scott-Wilkinson and I were the selected four. Our little theatrical gem did so well in southern California prisons that we took it on tour all over the state. It was one of my favorites because the prison audiences loved it and they were always so vocal about it, like performing at the Apollo. If you weren't good, you heard about it in a New York minute. The inmates didn't have horns to blow or fruit to hurl, but they weren't afraid to yell at us.

We called the play our "show in a bag". We could perform it anywhere with just a couple bags of props, a boom box and cassette tapes. We performed it in a boxing ring in the gymnasium of the prison in Susanville, CA. That was a dandy. There must have been about three hundred inmates in the audience. I remember my voice being sore afterwards because we had to project so loudly in order to be heard. OBBF played Jackson, the parolee, throughout the entire play whereas J.Ed, Sheila and I played all the other characters. In one scene I played Jackson's young daughter and was sitting on his lap when we heard a deep voice from the back of the gym yell "Yo, man, we don't do it like that."

It suddenly fell silent and then in no time you could hear the rumblings of discontent. A wave of anger was rolling towards us like thunder in the distance. Evidently they thought we were implying that there was an inappropriate relationship between the father and daughter, which of course there was not. It was okay that Jackson stole things, slept with hookers, bailed on his wife and kids, did drugs, etc. But even the inkling that he might behave inappropriately with his daughter was flat out unacceptable. OBBF knew immediately what their beef was and took action. He pushed me off his knee rather aggressively. At first I was pissed, but then I quickly understood what he was doing. He was asserting himself as the alpha male in front of them by manhandling me, an adult female. That's okay in the joint, that type of minor aggression towards women. He leaned up against the boxing ropes that separated and kept us elevated from the inmates. He looked at them as if to scold an errant child. "Hey brother!" He yelled. "This is my daughter, man. I's don't do it like that." Then he glared at them with one of those, do-I-have-to-hit-you-upside-the-head-looks and lifted his brow with a do-you-get-my-drift look, then rolled his eyes with a can-we-get-back-to-business look. He pulled me back onto his lap and the grumbling ceased. Then, a smattering of applause began. He had set them straight and we could go on. I loved working with OBBF in prison.

We performed *THINK AGAIN, JACKSON!* in San Quentin, Folsom, RJD (Richard J. Donovan) in San Diego, and DVI (Duel Vocational Institute) in Tracey. Playing in the SHU's (Secured Housing Unit) at Soledad was the most bizarre because there were two of them next to each other. The first SHU contained notorious inmates such as Sirhan Sirhan, who assassinated Robert F. Kennedy, and Juan Corona, a serial killer of migrant workers. For the first time we were going to perform for "famous" criminals. As much as we knew that it was meaningless, it still gave us the butterflies, accompanied with the knowledge that we'd have the perfect anecdote for David Letterman and his "Brush with Fame" segment.

Prior to entering the SHU we heard a rumor that no other women, other than female custody officers in uniform with stab-proof vests, had entered these units in seven years. That certainly caught us girls' attention. Nothing like feeling added sexual pressure to the existing anxiousness of playing the Big House. This SHU was at Soledad, the Soledad of Soledad brothers, the Soledad of George Jackson and his letters. The reputation of Soledad with its horrific riots still lingered in the late 80's. Walking into it was like entering Oz (the original movie *Wizard of Oz*, not the HBO series). We entered a hallway in what looked like a big public school and moved through an oversized door that entered into a separate, small holding area, which then connected through another door to the SHU itself. Holding areas are a big component of prisons and are critical to security. There is never more than one door open at a time between areas and the door into the SHU would never just open into a hallway. Without the holding area, inmates could overpower staff and push their way out of the SHU and into another less-secure area and attempt an escape.

The actual SHU itself was a three-tiered unit. There were cells on each level with stairs in the center. Hollywood loves this look and uses it all the time. According to the movies you'd think that everybody in prison is in a Secured Housing Unit, not just the PC (protective custody) dudes but the main line maximum, medium, even minimum, security guys. Hollywood is messed up that way and always goes for the most intimidating physical location and that would be a SHU, especially an old one like this in Soledad. As we entered the place, all eyes were upon us and we quickly realized that we were the only ones without stab-proof vests. I wanted one badly. Fashion be damned, I felt naked without one. We were escorted through the unit to the outdoor area where we would perform. The outdoor area was a concrete pad about the size of one half of a basketball court. It was enclosed by the walls of the SHU, with the small windows of the inmate's cells looking down on it. On one side were the cells of the famous convicts and on the other were the cells of big-time gang members, shot-callers. You know, the ones that run the show from within. The concrete pad surrounded by brick, windows, iron and razor wire was the only "outside" these SHU inmates saw. Some had been there for decades. They saw one small patch of sky a couple times a week. No flowers, no trees, no horizon with sunsets.

Gun coverage was also required to perform in the courtyard of the SHU. Juilliard hadn't really prepared me for live rounds. I don't remember discussing how distracting and perplexing it might be to have an officer about three feet behind you strolling along with a loaded gun. That never came up in acting classes. I wasn't concerned that some incident would flare up in the audience and warning shots would be fired, I was worried that I would skittishly bump into the officer, his gun would accidentally discharge and I'd be shot in the back. *I don't want to fall down and hit my nicely veneered teeth on the concrete with Sirhan Sirhan observing from his cell above. I don't want the inmates fighting over who is going to pick me up, not because they care, but just so they can cop a feel. I don't want to die doing a one-act play in prison. It would upset my family who doesn't understand why I do this anyway. I don't want to be killed during a performance.*

Even with all that gobbledygook in my head, it was hands down the most thrilling performing experience I'd ever had. It wasn't necessarily the "danger" that made it thrilling. It was confirmation that in a very stressful and intense environment, I was unflappable and capable of handling a situation into which few women would ever put themselves. I was proud of that and perhaps it was on this day, noted by the twinkle in my eye, that I began to fall in love with my 240lb. hairy-chested lover, prison.

## House of Marriage

There was my 240lb. hairy-chested lover and then there was OBBF. Every time I taught or performed in prison I came home more and more in love with OBBF. He always treated me so well in prison. I was his queen there. OBBF listened to me intently when we worked together. We completed each other's sentences in prison. We were a single unit working towards a common goal, the "artistic duo" that inmates never suspected was a "couple". We worked so well together, lived so well together, laughed so much together that it was inevitable that we would be together for the rest of our lives.

There was never a proposal, never a bended knee accompanied with an "I want to spend the rest of my life with you". There was just a lot of partying on the weekends. Sometimes our debauchery led to late night discussions about getting older, about wanting a monogamous marriage and children. Then, one day we made plans; wedding plans.

It wasn't the smoothest road to travel being a white chick from Montana and marrying a black man. But despite a couple of minor what-if-you-have-children-it-would-not-be-fair-to-the-children-they-will-not-be-accepted arguments, the race thing was just an itty, bitty blip of insignificance. Our friends and colleagues now were of many different races and beliefs.

Not only did I love OBBF, he was my best friend and soulmate. The wedding and reception was going to be upstairs in the Dorothy Chandler Pavilion. We couldn't use the room where the ceremony was to be held for rehearsal the day before, but Artsreach was allowed to use rehearsal space there. Since I was the company manager who now booked those rooms I called up my regular gal and requested a rehearsal room for a Friday evening. I didn't mention that it was for my *wedding* rehearsal and I didn't get permission from Susan Hill. Both of our families and the wedding party were instructed to say that they were there for "the prison theater thing". Somehow they all bumbled their way in, not looking one bit like actors who worked in prison, especially my 4'11", eighty-seven year old grandmother.

In the same room where John Bergman and Rebecca Rice taught us the nuances of working with the incarcerated and we rehearsed *THINK AGAIN, JACKSON!*, I was now rehearsing to be a real wife. I loved how prison was woven into my personal life. OBBF and prison were like braids of sour dough twisted around each other and baked into one hot loaf.

The wedding was scheduled the next day for 8:00pm. At 5:00pm I arrived as planned at a hair salon in Beverly Hills. When I first opened the door I thought it seemed a bit dark. A handsome Italian man was sweeping the floor. He definitely wasn't the janitor. He looked a little like Julie Andrews in *Victor! Victoria!* I told him I was there to see Luanne and he replied, "She no work here anymore."

"How can that be? I just saw her last week."

"I'm sorry Madame, but Luanna no longer working here."

"What do you mean?" My voice was starting to quiver and get louder. "She just did a trial run on my hair last Friday and promised that she would be here at 5 o'clock today. I'm getting married in less than three hours. Can't you check the schedule or something? Can't you call her?"

"Holy shit" he answered. "One minute Madame. Maybe I help you." Victor Victoria went to a calendar and looked in dismay. Then he picked up the phone and rambled on angrily in Italian. After several "Luanna? Luanna?" and a few "Mama Mia's" he turned to me and said " No Luanna. Luanna fired. No more Luanna. So sorry."

"No big deal" I thought. "I'm just getting married in two and a half hours on the other side of town. No big deal." Trying to convince myself that it was no big deal apparently wasn't working because I found myself sobbing on his newly swept tile floor. Poor Victor Victoria wasn't quite sure what to do. But I must have cried hard because he eventually offered his assistance. He made it clear however, that he was a cutter and didn't do the kind of work that Luanne did.

"I don't need a haircut, I need a hair*do*." I bawled.

One hour later I emerged with a gorgeous, ballerina-like chignon.

I returned to the hotel and put on my veil. "Oh crap!" The crown tipped over my eyes. Victor Victoria's chignon was *not* working. I either had to dump the crown and veil or come up with a new do. The wedding was an hour away. I didn't know what to do so I opened the little refrigerator in my room at the historic Biltmore Hotel and poured myself a gin and tonic. Then, I poured myself another and called OBBF.

"Leah" he reassured me. "It'll be fine. I'll send your sister over."

That was perfect. My oldest sister could fix *anything*. She studied Home Economics, by golly! So at 7:45pm when the guests were already arriving, I stepped into the shower and washed my hair. OBBF and I had talked about how we were going to think of the wedding as one, big prison improv. So that's what I did. I pretended I was in prison, and rolled with it.

By 8:30pm my sister had figured a way to do my hair and we jumped in a cab to the Music Center. I was running across the street carrying a wedding dress and curlers as I passed a homeless guy looking for a handout. *Sorry, no hands!* Inside, our guests had been assured by the best man it was a minor glitch and not to worry. Our guests didn't worry, they walked down the hall to the bar and started drinking.

The ceremony started an hour late. The lyrics of the first song began "I don't know what's going on." The crowd burst into laughter, delightful laughter. *What a great prison improv!*

Before the actual vows we took a moment to convey our personal thoughts. He began. "When I first saw you, you were a bird on a grey sky." This was a reference to seeing me in a movement class at Juilliard, where the floors were steel-like grey. He didn't write his words down and we never videotaped the ceremony so after that who knows what in the hell he said. I recited a poem that used to come on TV at 11:30pm just before the station was going off the air. I always stayed up too late as a teenager and for years this poem marked the end of my day. I stood there in my 80's low-cut wedding gown with Elizabethan sleeves and a beaded crown with veil attached and apologized to my mother for staying up so late all the time. I took OBBF's hand and recited:

*There's a comforting thought*
*At the end of the day*
*When I'm weary, lonely or sad*
*I'm glad that I live*
*That I battle and strive*
*For the place I know I must fill.*
*I am thankful for sorrow*
*And will meet with a grin*
*What fortune may send, good or ill.*
*I may not have wealth*
*I may not be great*
*But I know I shall always be true.*
*For I have in my life*
*That courage you gave*
*When once I touched shoulders with you.*

Okay. It wasn't a *great* poem, it was from my childhood for chrissakes, but there wasn't a dry eye in the house. It was the happiest day of my life, little glitches and all. We both felt so loved and supported. It was grand. It was the beginning of a partnership that was filled with love and respect and loads of laughs. OBBF became Husband.

After the wedding we kept our work schedule, me as an appraiser, new husband with odd jobs and together in prison. Working in real estate was a wake-up call. It was like studying for a role, like I was an actress infiltrating in someone else's life, except it was actually *mine*.

My branch office was located in Encino where people were buying up 800 sq. ft. boxes for $65,000, updating the 6' x 12 ' kitchen and tiny bathroom, throwing down some hardwood floors, a coat of paint, some strategically placed flowers and Voila; selling them a year or two later for $110,000. It was wild. The more I worked in real estate, the more I wanted to buy some of it. People were raking in the dough in the eighties real estate boom. Husband and I didn't have a dime in savings, but my sister and her husband presented us with an opportunity to buy an attached condominium in Fullerton. The market was really hopping in Orange County. People were making fortunes. They offered to put the required 10% down, if we would live there for two or more years and make the payments. When the time was right, we'd sell that sucker and all laugh ourselves to the bank. Ha Ha Ha! It was going to be grand and it made perfect sense. The dollar signs flashing in our eyes weren't symbolic of our collective greed, but an indicator of the future. We were finally going to do what everybody else supposedly did; make money without working for it. Finally, oh finally, we had arrived.

The first setback came, however, when the builder was almost a year late in completion. They were from the east coast and I believe this was their first foray into the southern California market. The high quality of construction was one of the things that attracted us to this development. It wasn't your typical wham-bam-thank-you-mam' stucco box with aluminum windows. It was quality shit, it was "Maison de Fleur"; my house of flowers! Even though we were impressed with the builder's high standards, as time went on our mantra became "quality schmality". We needed a turn-around. We weren't exactly looking to live there forever, just long enough to cash a check.

On top of the delay in completion, I began to have some serious misgivings about moving forward and closing on the property. Although the market still appeared to be hot, it made me nervous. But Husband remained steadfast in his determination to close this deal. He insisted on going through, and we did. We were like a 400 lb. man getting stuck in the water slide, when eventually enough people pile up behind him and the pressure shoots him out into the water, ready or not. That was us. We sat in an escrow office for the first time. In addition to having my sister and brother-in-law on the title, the lender wanted yet more assurance that Husband and I would not default on this loan, so my younger brother had to co-sign as well. There was nothing more motivating to not screw up than having two siblings and an in-law co-signing our first home loan.

After the deal was closed we still had to figure *how* to make the whole thing work. Living in Orange County and working in the San Fernando Valley would have been insane, so I transferred to a branch of Home Savings in Fullerton. I thought my life would be the same, only twenty-three miles farther south as the crow flies.

Husband on the other hand, had a much more dramatic solution for his conundrum: He took a job in Kansas City at the University of Missouri teaching theater and doing a play for the Missouri Repertory Theater. Off the newlyweds went. I went to Orange County to live alone in "our" first home, and he went to Kansas City.

I was living in a three bedroom, two and a half bath condo with vaulted ceilings. It was so beautiful I took my shoes off so I wouldn't ruin the white carpet or scratch the wood floors. It had a master suite with a glass shower and a big tub from where I could see the stars. Actually, I could only imagine seeing them due to the streetlights and pollution that formed an orange glow overhead.

There was, however, one problem with my lovely new home: me. I couldn't find me anywhere. I looked in the double sinks of the master suite, in the guest room and in the sparkling clean garage. I even looked outside in the twelve foot wide, yet-to-be landscaped yard. But no such luck. I was nowhere in that house to be found. I thought maybe I got lost in Orange County along the way somewhere, but I realized that there was no sense looking for me there. I hated Orange County. I hated the suburbs and their gated communities. I hated the woman at the video store who would gaze at Husband as if he were going to steal a video from her white store. And, most of all, I hated being married and being alone.

It wasn't long before I quit my job at Home Savings of America and went to work for my sister and her husband who had their own appraisal business. In pursuit of the almighty dollar, I now lived alone in an area I hated and gave up my easy-going job at the bank to work in the over-the-top stressed-out world of independent appraising. It was funny. (Not funny Ha Ha, but funny strange.) I'd lost my independence as an independent appraiser. The sister that had co-signed my home loan was now my boss. I worked for her and her husband and I lived in *their* investment. My younger brother who had also put his John Hancock on my home loan was now my co-worker. He too, had invested in me.

I certainly didn't feel free to flick JELL-O from a spoon against the beige walls of my "Maison de Fleur". This wasn't a JELL-O flicking house, this was an investment. I needed to stay invested so I ate donuts. Lots of donuts! I was surrounded by such invested, familial love I ate bagels and cream cheese, too. Lots of bagels and cream cheese! I loved my sister and brother and brother-in-law, but I pined for my 240lb. hairy-chested lover. It was in his presence where I craved to be. With him, behind bars, is where my daydreams took me.

I gave up my company car, lunch time workouts at the gym and twenty minute drives to properties so I could drive to East LA, Alhambra, Pasadena, Mission Viejo, Torrance, Huntington Beach, Chino, Manhattan Beach, Diamond Bar, Laguna Nigel, driving north, south, east and west. *Funny... strange.* I had no sense of direction and got off the wrong exit frequently. I couldn't always find good comparables because I didn't have the bottomless bank of knowledge about every market in every neighborhood that my sister, brother, and brother-in-law had. I longed for the simplicity of the card board boxes in the Valley. I wanted to tape the house, take pictures of the comps, go to the gym, eat lunch, whip out the appraisal and leave early to go to prison, where I could quack like a duck or pretend to be a retarded girl lost at a bus stop and memorize everybody's name in the circle. But, no. I had to suck it up for long, grueling days in which you cannot hate your boss because you love your boss because she is your sister, and you cannot get annoyed with your coworker because he is your one, and only, brother. I had to pony up for the drive to Aliso Viejo to look at another Spanish style tract wondering if it was under the flight path of an airport. I had to figure out why a property was $30,000 over market value, and if there were any interesting financing terms like lenders providing undisclosed incentives and who knows what else. While I was figuring all this shit out, I gained twenty pounds.

I may have been fat, but I was focused goddammit. Steadfast in my search for the almighty dollar, I took on a roommate. She was younger, less stable emotionally and had dated my brother. She couldn't get my brother so she settled for me in a condo where she couldn't leave a mess of any kind because that would threaten my investment. It wasn't sheer domestic bliss. We drank a lot of beer.

In the mid-west however, Husband was thriving. He was in a play at the Missouri Repertory Theater, playing a black convict who fell in love with his white writing teacher. I traveled to see him and beamed with pride as he clutched the faux prison bars with remorse, yearning to be with his lover. This particular performance of Husband's was some of the best work I'd ever seen him do. He made me proud.

His costar, Louise, embodied the essence of a woman wound so tightly, that her falling in love with a black convict was inconceivable. She was a talented actress with dark hair, blue eyes and lovely skin. Louise wasn't very nice in-person though. She had spent all this time working with my husband, and yet had no interest in meeting me: the prison lady.

Although I missed him, we were banking on the notion that Kansas City might just be the ticket. Maybe I could be married to a tenured theater professor soon? Maybe I could leave my common-wall condo and move into a quaint brick house near the university?

*This could be very cool.* I really liked Kansas City. I envisioned myself downtown going to art shows, sitting in trendy restaurants eating mid-west beef, and walking along streets kicking the coral autumn leaves into the air. We'd have lunch on campus together and out of the brown, wicker picnic basket that Peter Schreiner gave us as a wedding present, I'd produce tuna and cucumber, lightly salted, wrapped in pita bread. Hiding beneath the red and white, checkered napkins would be homemade chocolate chip cookies.

Surely there had to be a prison nearby. I imagined there was at least one in Kansas, and another in Missouri. Eureka! Each time I visited Kansas City I went to a lot of open houses.

# Facilitatin'

It was a shame. Husband lost the job at the University of Missouri. He was embarrassed, and I was disappointed I didn't get to be married to a tenured professor and live in a brick house. He asked me to videotape him as he walked down the halls of the theater department for the last time and cleared out his office. "Yep... they fired me!" he complained on tape. I remember scolding him from behind the camera for knocking over our wedding picture on his desk. He was so engrossed bemoaning his termination that he hadn't even noticed. Even though it wasn't the best of days, there was a silver lining in his cloud. He was offered a job at the Dallas Theater Center. That was a plus, a plus in the wrong state, but a plus nonetheless.

I returned to our condo in Orange County and Husband was off to Dallas. I cried a lot. I didn't like working as an independent appraiser, didn't like living with a roommate and was tired of donuts, bagels and beer. I wanted something more. I wanted more prison in my life.

It wasn't possible to make a living as a contract artist teaching classes in the evenings in prison, but it was possible to do so as an

Artist Facilitator. The IAF (Institutional Artist Facilitator) was the person at the prison who hired the contract artists. That was the person who called up Susan Hill at Artsreach and said, "I'm thinking about offering some theater classes on the minimum yard. What 'ya got?" It was a sweet gig for an artist. Every time Governor Pete Wilson built another prison, they were looking for another Artist Facilitator. I was determined to get that job. The notion of spending the rest of my life in a peach-colored, stucco condo was unfathomable. The stressing about how-to-determine-the-impact-of-arterial-traffic-to-a-property's-value-when-you-can't-find-a-good-comp days needed to be over.

As I pretended to be perplexed about the value of a bonus room vs. a garage, I was thinking about what else I might need for my state application as an Artist Facilitator. When I said I needed to retake pictures of comps in Yorba Linda, I went home instead, and called Susan Hill and other Artist Facilitators for advice. I put the application in the mail and waited, for months.

The call. "You're rated a three." Being rated a three was very exciting. Isn't number three a medal position? So what if I wasn't number one or two, I was happy, bronze number three. If I was third on the list to becoming an Artist Facilitator, I thought, then I should have a job soon because Pete Wilson can't build them fast enough. It wasn't long after that I was asked to interview for the position at CVSP (Chuckawalla Valley State Prison), a new prison in Blythe, CA. I interviewed and was offered the position a few days later.

I immediately called Dallas. "I got it! I got the job in Blythe! I was rated number three and I got it!" I screamed. My dream had come true. I was going to run my own fine arts program in a medium-security men's prison out in the middle of nowhere. I had made the big commitment to my 240 lb. hairy-chested lover. It would be grand. It didn't phase me that the job was three and a half hours away on the Arizona border in one of the most miserable desert towns I'd ever encountered. It didn't phase me that I was living in Orange County, Husband was in Dallas, and I was taking a job and another apartment in Blythe. My sister surely thought I'd lost my mind and was rightfully concerned about her investment. But, none of it phased me.

I blathered on and on to Husband in Dallas about this turn of events for so long I hadn't noticed that he was no longer on the other end of the phone. I heard a soft voice in the background. "Your husband is so proud of you." She said.

"What?" I asked.

"He is so proud of you. He talks about you all the time.

"What?" I stammered. "Who is this?"

"We're making ceramics at the Senior Center."

"Excuse me, who is this?"

"I'm sorry." She paused. "I'm Candy. We're in the play together."

"Oh...okay. Hi."

How sweet. His theater buddy Candy was talking to me as if she knew all about me, as if he had expressed love and concern for me and was proud of my prison pursuit. He must have handed her the phone while he tended to the kiln or something. Yep, it was one sweet day. I'd just got my dream job and Husband and his theater buddy were making me large, peach-colored ceramic bowls.

I was off to big, bad, sandstorm ridden, 115 degree Blythe. It all worked out. I would rent a small studio in the crappy desert town, drive there on Tuesday mornings and work 'til 9:00pm, then stay there three nights and drive back to Orange County after work on Friday nights. I would work the 8, 12, 12, 8 scenario. And when Husband returned from Dallas, I would spend three-day weekends with him. It was a grand plan. I figured I could write two or three plays while there and have two or three children, courtesy of the state of California. My inspiration to work and procreate was strong.

(Being rated a three wasn't a compliment. I had naively thought that I was third on the list to be an Artist Facilitator. Instead, I was in the third category of artists ranked for that position, the third of four levels. Ultimately, I was at the back of the pack, a bottom feeder. I was lucky to have gotten the job. The director of Arts in

Corrections shook his head with dismay at a meeting and said, "We're having to look at category 4's right now. It's very disheartening. A category 4 artist really isn't qualified for this position, but what can we do?" I'll tell you what I did. I never mentioned again that I was rated a three. Zipped that little piece of info right up.)

Yep! I was gonna' do me some facilitatin'! All the years that I taught theater workshops in the prisons, I was known as a contract artist. But I wasn't contracting anymore, I was facilitating. According to Websters:

**fa cil i tate** 1. to make easy or less difficult.
2. to free from difficulty.
**fa cil i ta tion** 1. a facilitating.
2. in psychology, increased ease of performance of any action, resulting from the lessening of nerve resistance by the continued successive application of the necessary stimulus: opposed to *inhibition*.

Sure glad I had looked that up. I had no idea that in addition to facilitating arts in the prison, I was going to make them easier, less difficult and increase the ease of any actions they performed by lessening their nerve resistance by applying continued, successive stimulus. Wow! Maybe instead of calling us Artist Facilitators, we should have been known as Artist Stimulators. That might have helped, actually, and was more accurate. Whenever asked the question "What is an Artist Facilitator?" I stumbled over my words and rolled my eyes because, by golly, it just wasn't a one-sentence answer. But had I been an Artist Stimulator, the response "I stimulate arts in a prison", may have been sufficient. It just never really worked to say, "I facilitate arts in a prison." Believe me I tried it, and people just looked at me weirdly.

Even though I had worked for different Artist Facilitators over the years, as a contract artist I never really understood the entire scope of what they did. All I knew was that they could be very difficult to get on the phone and I didn't know why. I wanted to find out however, since I was now one of the few holding that coveted position. What made it so coveted? There were only about twenty of us in the state of California. For every state prison in California, there was only one Artist Facilitator. We were a teeny, select group of individuals with union representation. The majority of us tended to be visual artists of variable mediums, but there was an occasional musician, writer or performing artist. I was the first actor to become an Artist Facilitator.

In order to learn just how one facilitated, I was sent by the Director of the Arts in Corrections program to different prisons nearby to see how the others did it. The first director of the program I'd worked with had been Bill Cleveland, a wild and gregarious sort of guy. Bill was tall and had a luscious salt and peppered mustache and was the only person I knew who could continue a conversation while juggling. Bill Cleveland was a hoot. He was legendary for his leadership of the Arts in Corrections program, but he had moved on to other things and now, Jim Carlson was his successor. Jim wasn't as flashy as Bill, but he was just what the program needed at the time when more and more prisons were being built: a politician. Jim had that Scandinavian look: he was tall with broad shoulders, a square jaw and looked good in a Nordic sweater. He had been the Artist Facilitator at San Quentin for many years, before he opted to give being an administrator in Sacramento a whirl. Even though he was a visual artist, he had once pulled off a high-profile production of Beckett's *Waiting For Godot* in San Quentin. He was no schlep. I was always struck by how grounded Jim was. Unlike most artists who bend toward a more bohemian lifestyle, he was straight-up (and strangely) middle-class. His wife was an adorable nurse and his kids were smart and athletic. They were such a neat, normal family that you wouldn't have suspected that Jim was quite the dynamo in prison.

First I went to visit Tom Skelly at the California Institution for Men (CIM). Since I had worked for Skelly for a few years, I didn't think there was much for me to learn there. I was dead wrong. Skelly was the quintessential, prolific prison rogue. For Skelly it was all about the inmates, and he gave them as many opportunities as conceivable. His program was complex and multi-faceted with strong programs in several areas: painting, pottery, video and theater. Skelly also had a very long leash at work, so he was able to come and go as he pleased and develop strong connections in the community. Nobody brought more to the community through his arts program than Skelly. And I figured out why.

He was the guy who taught me the art of spending state money, specifically funds allocated for the Department of Corrections. This secret form of fiscal art was developed long ago and perfected by a select few: state employees. And now I was one of them. An Artist Facilitator, who shall remain unknown here, once referred to spending government money as "sucking the tit of the great state of California". Nummy! Nummy! I was going to love being nourished by the third largest state in the union, the mother of all mothers. What a *rack*-et! I thought I'd died and gone to heaven. I had a job with a budget, medical and dental insurance, sick time, holidays off and paid vacation. Oh, Lordie, I was happy!

Not only did Skelly teach me the yummy art of spending my government allotment of cash, but he also tipped me off on how to spend other peoples' state money. How cool was that? With new prisons popping up all over the central valley (a.k.a. the prison Middle Kingdom) and near the southern deserts, came new Artist Facilitators. Many of the newbies struggled with spending all of their money. The paperwork was onerous and the restrictions were mind-boggling. When a new Facilitator couldn't spend his money, it was usually put up for grabs to the old-timers rather than returned to the general fund. Skelly had been the benefactor of others "inability to spend problem" a few times. That skill augmented his budget and allowed him to do things that with his own limited funds would have been impossible. I couldn't wait to spend my money and other peoples' too. Yep, that visit to Skelly encouraged me to get off the traditional calendar, off the school calendar and onto the calendar of the fiscal year. Sugarplum fairies danced in my head as I reveled in the thought of spending money at the beginning of each new fiscal year. I left Skelly jazzed, jazzed about paperwork without nary a thought of whether I ever would be able to be weaned from the luscious breast milk of my new mommy; the engorged state of California.

After Skelly, I paid a visit to Kim Kaufman at the California Institution for Women (CIW). Kim was a medium-built white girl with bedroom eyes and a hefty cackle. She could be heard laughing a mile away. While Skelly was easy going as he roamed around the prison, Kim was militaristic and circumspect. Her leash at CIW was only two feet long. The woman could barely leave the main trailer she worked in. Unlike the other Facilitators she had no flexibility with her hours. Unlike Skelly who came and went as he pleased, her every move needed to be accounted for and that's how she ran her program, too. Kim taught me the art of accountability, also known as covering-your-ass-with-a-trail-of-paperwork. The ass covering with paperwork was implemented in many forms which included sign-up sheets for classes attended by inmates, ducats (passes sent to inmates so they would be released to come to class through whatever gates it took to do so.), fliers to advertise classes, quarterly reports and the Big Kahuna: the IAP (Institutional Arts Plan), an annual program proposal.

The most important component however, was the almighty memo. Memos make or break you in prison. Memos were the key to keeping one's job whenever it looked like there'd been a fuck-up. Memos kept officers from shutting down classes when they thought you hadn't made arrangements to use another teachers' room. Memos allowed you to carry a skull of a dog into the prison for drawing classes and not have it confiscated. Memos made officers put out their cigarettes and pat down sixty inmates attending a one-act play. Memos were our lifeblood.

Kim also respected the mandate to adhere to a strict chain

of command. She didn't balk at the prisons' paramilitary chain of command, she embraced it, she was cognizant of its' power. Kim taught me never to go out of order, over the head of or around the something of anything: Respect the chain of command. The Institutional Artist Facilitators (IAF's) were at the bottom, then the Community Resource Managers (CRM's - they were our supervisors at the prison) then the Program Sergeant, the Program Lieutenant, the Program Captain, the Custody Captain, the Associate Warden, the Chief Deputy Warden and the biggest cheese of all, the Warden. That was the list. That was the order in which we asked for anything and everything, every time needing all of their signatures.

"Remember Leah," she said with a stern look "that annoying officer that you'd like to chew out could one day be your Lieutenant or Program Captain. Then they'd have real power over your life. Then, you might have a hard time begging them to help you out. Just because they're at the bottom of the totem pole today doesn't mean they will be in five years. We're the only ones who aren't going anywhere."

I also left Kim Kaufman jazzed—jazzed about memos!

My third and final training visit was at the California Rehabilitation Center (CRC), the land of "N" (narcotics) numbers. The Artist Facilitator there was a middle-aged black man named Ernest. Ernest had a mid-life mid-section and a calm demeanor that made me feel like I was from another planet but amusing for him to watch. Since there were both men and women at CRC, it was as if he ran two separate programs and consequently, he had perfected the art of delegation. Most of the time Ernest looked like he had nothing to do, but his program was hopping! The flurry of activity was largely due to grant money in the form of the Artist in Residence (AIR) programs funded by the California Arts Council (CAC). The Artist in Residence grant program basically funded an artist to work part time at an institution, (not necessarily prison; but schools, community centers, hospitals, etc.) for up to eleven months in a fiscal year. It paid about $1300/month plus a small supply budget. It wasn't a career, but for most artists it was a stability factor. They could work two days a week and have their rent and some groceries covered. It was a great program and it wasn't just utilized by down-and-out artists, it attracted some of the best talent in the state. For the prisons, it was a huge coup. We could have up to two Artists in Residence at a time and that was awesome.

Ernest had the dream grant in his back pocket. Her name was Aileen White. Aileen was doing a residency in creative writing on the women's side of the joint. She was in her late thirties, a single mother with long blond hair, very attractive and yet she talked like a truck driver. The defining factor about Aileen was that she used to be an inmate at that prison. She stumbled into a writing class, excelled in it, paroled and now was the teacher. She was the only Artist in Residence who had done time. She was trotted out to the public as "The Success Case of Arts in Corrections". She was what every Arts in Corrections Facilitator longed for; someone who discovered they had talent in prison, got out and became a huge success. Aileen wasn't really a huge success, but she was functional. She was writing, she was attending lots of conferences and her daughter was a well-known daytime actress on *General Hospital*, certainly that all counted for something. I left CRC jazzed—jazzed about grant funding!

Looked like facilitatin' was gonna' be fun. I just needed to make sure I knew all my acronyms. I was an IAF (Institution Artist Facilitator) for AIC (Arts in Correction), a CDC (California Department of Corrections) program supervised by a CRM (Community Resource Manager) at CVSP (Chuckawalla Valley State Prison). I hoped one day to have an AIR (Artist in Residence) funded through CAC (California Arts Council) and not the NEA (National Endowment for the Arts). Although I wasn't a CO (Correctional Officer), I would definitely get to know the CCPOA (California Correctional Peace Officers' Association). I embraced my correctional acronyms. They were my new literary Buddies.

Skelly, Kim and Dillihay were all helpful in my training, but no one prison was the same. Each Artist Facilitator had a unique situation. Each Facilitator worked in a different discipline, the physical space they worked in differed from one prison to another, as did the expectations of the Community Resource Managers, our supervisors. No individual Facilitator could tell another how to run his program because no two prisons were alike. Whether a prison was for medium or maximum-security inmates also dictated how and when you did things. The environment in which the prison was located differed from prison to prison. We were in the middle of an urban metropolis or in the middle of nowhere. We were in one hundred-eighteen degree heat or schlepping through two feet of snow. All the training in the world could not have prepared me for what would become my unique situation.

# Blythe

Chuckawalla Valley State Prison (CVSP) was located a few miles west of Blythe, California, which is near the Arizona border. It was a dreadful little desert town in the middle of nowhere. It's only redeeming quality was the nearby Colorado River, where everyone with a boat went zooming along with a cooler full of beer and a skier in tow. I grew up around cowboys but I'd never really been around such a redneck crowd before. The odd thing was that they weren't all white, more of a multi-cultural redneck crowd. The summers were horrific with temperatures up to one hundred sixteen degrees. For kicks, God threw in sand storms. Lovely!

Like most new employees from out of town, I accepted Blythe as best I could. CVSP looked like every other new prison being built at that time; four mini prisons (Alpha, Beta, Charlie, Delta) of two-story concrete buildings surrounded by an electric, razor-wire fence and guard towers. But there were things about CVSP that made it wacky. For starters, as I got off the interstate exit and drove toward the prison entrance, there were beautiful rows of palm trees. It doesn't sound out of the ordinary, except those tall, mature palm trees weren't exactly indigenous to that area. They were brought in for a hefty price. Now I completely understand pumping up Beverly Hills or Palm Springs with numerous species of palm trees where people have the time and money to make a desert look like an oasis, but why did they need palm trees along the road coming into a medium security prison? What bureaucrat in Sacramento thought that was a necessity? I mean, who do you think paid for those palm trees? The taxpayers naturally. It was rumored that the stupid trees cost about two million dollars. That's right. Million. Not a few thousand, but million. Now, don't get me wrong, I was still grateful to the California taxpayers that I felt better as I soaked up the stunning beauty of rows of palm trees hovering over my Toyota pickup. I just didn't understand the need for importing them when there were perfectly good plants around that were indigenous to the area.

Like cactus. What would have been wrong with rows of prickly cactus along the prison entrance? Was the image of needles poking out of a thick, rubbery stalk too harsh as you entered a place of incarceration? A place where possibly people were tortured or did intravenous drugs? Was that too disturbing for some bureaucrat in Sacramento? Maybe some local yahoo convinced the CDC that rows of majestic palm trees swaying in the wind would ease the sting of having a prison in his backyard. Who knows how, or by whom, that decision was made, but it was an extremely odd and expensive one.

The second grand scheme they hatched was to build CVSP without air conditioning in Blythe, CA with summer temperatures in the one hundred and teens! Some dolt must have thought that they could save taxpayers money by leaving out the air conditioning. It was probably the same bean counter that decided on palm trees then realized there weren't enough funds for AC. Anyway I didn't notice at first, because the Administration Building was so cool, so welcoming, as I came in from the blistering heat. I didn't suspect that beyond the primary areas for staff that there was no air conditioning for the inmates in their cells. I mean, they were convicted felons being housed there, not college students. That argument was rather flimsy however, since inmates dropped like flies of heat stroke and were airlifted to San Bernardino or Riverside county. How much money do you think that saved the taxpayers? Apparently the townspeople tried to warn them, but the CDC architects knew better. If it hadn't been so unbelievably stupid, they would have done it again when they built Ironwood State Prison down the road a few years later. As far as I know, CVSP had the unique label of being the only new prison built in a desert without air conditioning.

The final whoops? What was with that name, Chuckawalla? According to Webster's it's a large, edible lizard living in northern Mexico and the southwestern United States. But wait, that lizard is a "chuck-walla". Not a "chuck-a-walla." Jesus! They stupidly misspelled the name of the place right outta' the gate! Lordie! No wonder the inmates referred to it as "Chuckies Place".

As a new employee to the prison, if you weren't a native to Blythe chances were you didn't uproot your family to move there. Very few of us laid stakes there. The town was full of employees like myself, just passing through waiting to get promoted to a better place. Like many others, I rented a studio apartment at the popular Oasis. Some oasis. It was a motel turned into studio apartments when the prison boom hit town. There were numerous strings of one story rooms scattered around a narrow paved road that wound its' way through patches of grass and trees. My studio was located in the back, where it always seemed too dark. I always thought of it as a great place to hide from Arnold Schwarzeneggers *Terminator*. He'd never find me there. The Oasis hosted many CVSP employees but I rarely saw any of them.

My room had a double bed and that lovely wood paneling that everyone was so fond of in the 60's. About four feet from the end of the bed was a small TV on a cardboard box next to a plaid couch. Just behind the wall to my right was a tiny square table with aluminum legs, a small stove and a microwave and the bathroom.

I always felt like some sad woman in a bad horror movie. At 10 o'clock at night I'd return with a Drumstick ice cream cone that apparently I could not live without for one entire year, and I would slip back into my own little Oasis. It seemed like no one was ever there but the parking lot was always full. Surely people were hiding in their own wood-paneled oasis and smoking pot or doing lines of cocaine on their own aluminum-legged tables. Surely some prison guard was fucking another prison guard, who was someone else's wife, on his plaid couch. Surely seedy and sordid behavior lurked behind the thin Oasis walls. I was convinced it was there, so I locked my door, ate my Drumstick (preferably with caramel) and laid on the bed hoping that sleep would overtake me as soon as possible. If I could get to sleep then I could forget about the plaid couch that no one was fucking me on and the bizarre environment of the Oasis, and could rest up for where I really wanted to be: prison.

It was at the Oasis however, that my Intruder phobia started to kick in. I wasn't a stranger to intruders, I'd encountered them before. The Oasis reminded me of the first night I moved into an apartment on the upper eastside of Manhattan with a Juilliard opera student. After weeks of searching, opera girl and I found a one bedroom in the upper nineties that we could share. It had a small living room, teeny kitchen and bathroom off to the side and a black iron, spiral staircase that went down to the bedroom. She was going to stay in the bedroom and I was going to set up camp in the living room. We had just gotten keys to the apartment late that afternoon and had no furniture yet, just our suitcases of personal belongings. She slept with her short, white, longhaired boyfriend in the downstairs bedroom while I rolled out my sleeping bag in the middle of the living room floor. The room was probably only eight feet wide, because at 5'5" I covered most of the width.

I was snoring away when the light from the bathroom woke me up. I could hear somebody moving around in there and assumed that it was opera girls' boyfriend. I laid my head back down on my pillow and waited for boyfriend to emerge and turn off the light so I could get back to sleep. When he stepped into the hallway I couldn't see his face because the light from the bathroom lit him from behind. I didn't need to see his face to realize that whomever emerged from the bathroom was definitely NOT boyfriend. Intruder was way tall, had a big 'fro and in his left hand he held a flashlight and in his right hand, a gun.

*Welcome to New York*. I laid my head down and pretended to be asleep. I didn't know if Intruder was stupid, slow or painfully meticulous in his criminal behavior, but he sure did take his sweet time going through what little we had. He went downstairs in the bedroom and took forever to come back up. He had the audacity to put his stolen treasures into my suitcase. The guy literally stepped over me as he packed up our stuff and the last thing to go was the alarm clock that was next to my head. It had to be close in order to see the time because I was practically blind. As his large black hand unplugged the clock from the outlet I prayed *Dear God Almighty please, please, please do not let him see the gold chain on my neck!* Wearing gold chains was all the rage in the 80's. Unfortunately so was stealing them. Thieves grabbed the chains off women's necks, then shoved them into a subway car. I don't know what I would have done if he had grabbed my neck. I thought I might have screamed my head off, but then there was still that bothersome gun to deal with. I didn't want to die in the down sleeping bag I brought from Montana. I didn't want to die on the hardwood floor of my first apartment in New York and I certainly didn't want to die with opera girl, whom I hardly knew, and her longhaired boyfriend. So I just prayed.

Intruder left out the back door with everything I had of value: cash, jewelry, clothes, identification, and my alarm clock. My heart pounded, my thin lips were parched and the imaginative Intruder that lurked in my dreams at night had become a reality.

I thought about my big, black Intruder many nights at the Oasis, usually right about the time David Letterman was introducing his first guest. I wanted to sleep, but the wind landed an empty soda can onto my porch. *Uh oh. It's him*. Was he a high-on-drugs intruder or just plain evil? Was he white, black, Hispanic or Other? Would I be stupid and plead for mercy or would I take the lamp on the nightstand and try to bash his head in? Letterman just didn't seem as funny with the notion Intruder being out there.

Uninvited images in my head, not late night TV, controlled my late night thoughts. Spending three nights a week, alone at the Oasis was the hardest part of my dreamy job.

I walked into the Administration Building, down the hall to the Wardens' area to see my boss. In that one area was the Warden's office, the Chief Deputy Warden's office, the Community Resource Manager's office, the Public Information Officer's office, a conference room, and numerous secretaries manning the fort. That's where all the movers and shakers in prison were. Even though we Artist Facilitators were considered to be the lowest on the CDC totem pole, even though we made less than a new CO with overtime, we were welcomed in the king's castle: the Warden's Office. Arts in Corrections danced a political tango with the CDC. Wardens were appointed by the Governor and sent to their respective prisons to work while they waited to be confirmed by the legislators. For years State Senator Henry Mello sat on the confirmation committee and what was jiggedy about the good Senator was that he was a staunch advocate for the Arts in Corrections program. Despite the fact that we were just a spit in the bucket in the big scheme of it all, Senator Mello grilled every Warden about his knowledge and support of the Arts in Corrections program. Every wanna'-be Warden had to be a fan of the program, at least while awaiting confirmation. Once a Warden was confirmed, all bets were off.

My first Warden at CVSP was Theo White, a soft-spoken, handsome middle-aged black man. And I think it is safe to say that he was genuinely supportive of my program. I liked Theo White, but he was nothing like prison wardens in the movies. He was far from being a mean, middle-aged white man with a penchant for sadism, that lurked down the dark, dank hallways of a cold, musty prison with stone walls. *Au contraire.* Mr. White was an intelligent, well-spoken bureaucrat who worked in a carpeted office with a large wooden desk and upholstered chairs. He looked like a successful stockbroker.

Inmates told wild tales about Wardens. It was as if he was the President and had some grand scheme that would lead to their personal demise. Like he woke up in the morning and deliberated on how he could create more misery for those sorry-ass convicted felons. They believed the Warden plotted and schemed on how he could waste millions of taxpayer dollars and continue to keep the black man down while he was at it. What most inmates didn't get is that the Warden was just a flippin' bureaucrat. That's all. They were administrators, paper-pushers and political animals. They usually became far removed from the daily grind out on the yard and spent most of their time going from meeting to meeting to meeting. The Wardens' hands were tied with red tape like everyone else's. Most of them just wanted peace at their institution. No escapes or riots. No staff being assaulted or drug trafficking. No one escaping and killing an innocent family down the road. Plain old peace and quiet. Of course, that was impossible in a prison. But it was still their main objective.

The Arts in Corrections building at CVSP was located at the end of the Facility "B" (Bravo) yard. I had to walk the entire length of the yard to get there. It probably doesn't sound like much, but the reality was that those long walks across a yard were daunting. I'd done them many times, all over the state. But it was usually with Husband, or Peter and Violette. Now I was doing them on my own. It was probably the closest I ever got to walking a runway, because I was always aware that I had to be *on*, physically, mentally and emotionally. I never knew what was gonna' come up. Inmates would mumble all sorts of things. Most of it was gobbledygook about my breasts and how they'd like to get with me. Occasionally a faint voice from afar would cry "Miss Joki Miss Joki" and some guy who took a workshop from me in Folsom was filling me in about the trials and tribulations of his current life at CVSP five hundred miles to the south. Then there were those questions from afar; "You a counselor?" "Are you the Coach?" "Are you the phone lady?" "Hey

Lady, wha' chu do here?"

The Arts in Corrections program at CVSP had it's own little concrete building. Large, metal double doors opened into a 20' x 20' space. To the left there was a row of windows that looked into a classroom and to the right a staff office with a bathroom and two large storage rooms. It was actually a great space, but an empty space with two inches of desert grit covering everything. I didn't have keys or a phone. That was part of my job now: figuring out how to get things I needed. It was like being on an episode of "The Apprentice", except there wasn't The Donald greeting you and wishing you "good luck" on your new task. For this task, I was on my own and there was no set time frame. I was in the "get" mode for the next three months: get keys, get phone, get office furniture, get word processor and typewriters. (That's right. Word processor. We didn't have computers in prison in 1990. Not out on the yards anyway.) For a long time I just "got" a lot.

The budget was twofold: One budget was for contracting teachers (about $20,000 annually) and a second budget was for purchasing equipment and supplies (about $6,000 annually). Spending the larger portion of the budget to contract teachers was a snap. All we had to do was call Artsreach at UCLA and start making requests. The beauty of Artsreach at that time (although some would say to their detriment) was that if you didn't have an artist or program in mind they were happy to recommend one. It was dreamy spending. I could pick up my phone (once I had one) and start booking my calendar with all sorts of artistic programs. It was very cool.

I was enthralled that I could pick my employees, decide what projects to do each year, teach whatever and whenever I wanted and had access to a fruitful supply budget to make my dream projects come true. Oh yes. That annoying supply budget! That's why Artist Facilitator's could never be found. We were arduously getting quotes. I'd have a list of fifty items: different colors of oil paints, ten different sizes of brushes of variable quality, four sizes of canvas, etc. For each and every item, the state required three quotes. It probably doesn't sound like much but not every vendor carried the exact same catalogue of stuff. Dick Blick, the beloved vendor of the Hobbycraft program (no relation to Arts in Corrections) didn't necessarily have the same shit as Art Supply Warehouse. It was tricky stuff. Skelly was a genius at that crap and he still had dark circles under his eyes.

Yep, it was an exciting time. I didn't realize it at the time, but a large part of what was fueling that excitement was the sheer fact that building prisons in the state of California was the largest growth industry since the defense industry went down the toilet. When I entered as a state employee in September 1990 it had just begun to hit its' stride. The Department of Corrections and the California Correctional Peace Officers' Association (CCPOA; a.k.a. prison guards' union) was becoming this gigantic steamrolling engine that was beginning to determine the political future of the state of California. Despite the size of the CCPOA, much smaller than the AMA (American Medical Association) or the Trial Lawyer's Union, they were becoming the biggest contributor to political campaigns in the state. They wanted more prisons built, more jobs, more benefits, more pay, more, more, more, more and more. And they always seemed to be justified. Just like Kevin Costner in *Field of Dreams* said "If you build it, they will come". They sure did build them and they surely did come. Within a year of opening, every prison was typically at 190% capacity, literally overflowing with convicted felons.

People were pretty darn happy about prisons back then. I think the public was appalled at the number of them being built, but by golly Governor Pete Wilson was gonna' get the crime under control once and for all. Having bonds passed in the elections was a snap. Hell, California had become so laden with crime that fear alone got the voter to check that box. We didn't need schools, hell no. We needed more prisons. We didn't need to control the flow of immigration. We needed to take those thugs off the streets and put them away.

Rural communities with few economic opportunities for its' citizens, suddenly had good middle class jobs with great benefits available to those with a high school diploma. The dropout who previously was pumping gas at the local station could now become a respectable middle-class citizen. All he needed was a GED. Then of course, there was overtime for the CO's. How sweet was that? The niftiest thing of all was that if you were scheduled to work Monday through Friday, you could call in sick on Friday, get paid for it and then pick up a friends' shift on Saturday and get paid time and a half or double time since it was your day off. Officers up and down the state of California figured that one out in a heart beat and believe me they took full advantage of it. Officers all over the state were buddying up with each other: One feigned illness while his buddy covered his shift at a higher rate of pay, and then vice versa. Any knucklehead could pull down $40,000 - $50,000 in 1990 and that was living in Blythe, Avenal or Susanville. This was hot stuff in small towns like that.

Artist Facilitators were paid a salary and didn't have access to over-time pay, but we had something equally desirable that involved time, instead of remuneration. We had the coveted CTO (Compensated Time-Off). If I worked two extra days one week I could take them off some time later. The beauty of that was with a little effort I could make sure I had some good long vacations. *Sweet!*

Even warehouse workers and secretaries didn't do poorly. The Department offered good honest jobs. And if you had a college degree, the sky was the limit. Good officers quickly promoted to Sergeant, Sergeants to Lieutenant, Lieutenants to Captain, teachers to supervisor or administrator, every time a new prison was built. Yessirree. It was like the Roarin' 20's back then. You could climb that corporate ladder with a few years' experience and half a brain. It was shamelessly exciting!

But wait! What about those sandstorms? Wow! Having grown up in the mountains with four seasons, it was beyond me why anyone would choose to live there for any length of time other than job-required. Nothing cleared the yard faster than a sandstorm. If you were on the yard when it hit, it was hard to see it coming. Each yard was a self-contained 360 degree circle of buildings. The wind would hit hard and fast and within ten seconds the sand would come blasting across. If I couldn't get inside a building, I at least tried to get up against a wall, shut my eyes and ride it out. It whipped my legs like my Irish grandmother did with a wet dishtowel.

God forbid I had to ride it out in the open with nothing to even lean against. That was the worst. It was hard to keep my eyes closed, be pushed by the wind, not fall and figure out when to open them to see. Sandstorms were the craziest thing I've experienced. It was like God throwing dirt in my eyes. Staff and inmates alike, could be momentarily paralyzed with a sandstorm five feet high. The boys at San Quentin looking at the ocean or those soaking up the gentle rays in San Diego had no idea how good they had it. One had to come to Chuckie's House to fully appreciate how brutal the desert could be.

# Rank and File

Working in prison was like living in a foreign country: In order to succeed it was critical to understand the culture, language, customs, attire, resources, work ethic and the peculiar chain of command amongst inmates. At CVSP a cast of characters appeared at my doorstep. Most of my time was spent cleaning out the two inches of accumulated dust and getting things. The inmates tended to wander into the building wondering what was going on there. Many offered assistance in cleaning and moving equipment around.

There was a black guy I'll call Stanley, who was a thief. Stanley took pride however, in not being some junkie that broke into a house and stole shit, leaving behind a chaotic mess and a sense of violation. He was more professional than that. He observed a place for days, waiting for the family to leave before making his move. Stanley had some self-respect and didn't go into a home and dump the contents of drawers all over the place. He didn't arrive unannounced in the middle of the night, scaring the crap out of the occupants, nor did he ever pack a gun. At least he had the good manners to burglarize your home while you were on vacation and to leave it looking untouched. Junkies who made a mess were way beneath Stanley. Although a convicted felon, Stanley considered himself above street thugs, junkies and gang-bangers.

Wyatt, however, couldn't stand guys like Stanley. I mean, going into someone's home? How rude! He comprehended that burglarizing homes not only caused emotional trauma, but it also compelled the homeowner to contact their insurance company which also caused them to take another hit paying the deductible and/or an increased monthly premium. In his opinion, that lame-stuff was for small-time thieves. Wyatt was a handsome guy. He might have been in his 60's. He certainly had the long grey ponytail to prove it. But he also had those Willie Nelson blue eyes and a V-shaped build with pecs a woman could be intimidated by. Wyatt was a bank robber. According to him, the only one that took a hit when he robbed a bank was the bank itself, not the customers. He figured that the "white man" could absorb that cost with no problem since the "white man" had been screwing people over for years. Even though he was white as well, Wyatt considered himself a victim of the "white mans' repression". His shtick was to walk up to the teller and hand her a note as he coyly revealed the gun under his jacket. He boasted of never once having it loaded. It was an empty scare factor. There was no way that he was ever gonna' hurt someone during a robbery, but scare the shit out of you? That he would do. Apparently he'd had some success with this system, but obviously, being in prison, his win/loss record was somewhat tarnished.

Next came Carlo. He was about 5'3", Hispanic, and 120 lbs. soaking wet. Good Lord, he was cute, but in a devilish way. His black eyes twinkled as they undressed me. Carlo was the self-proclaimed king of thieves. He didn't rob you in your home, leaving you to wonder how he got in and crying over the brooch that had been in the family for three generations. He also didn't scare the crap out of you at lunchtime in the bank thinking that if you looked up, a bullet would shatter your skull and fling your brains onto the ATM machine. No sirree! Carlo deplored those class-less criminals who victimized innocent bystanders. Carlo claimed to be the brains and brawn behind sophisticated, well-planned jewelry heists. According to Carlo, he was so confident in his ability to pull these off that, not once, did he even bring a weapon along with him. He figured that if he was stupid enough to get caught then he deserved to go to prison. He claimed to be tremendously successful for a number of years and then Poof!

Carlo, Wyatt and Stanley were all thieves of a sort but none of them knew each other. Why would they? They were each of a different racial background and in prison the races don't mix. Whites stick with whites, blacks with black, Hispanic with Hispanic and if you're "Other"? You get to pick.

The pecking order of criminals was something I hadn't considered before. One kind of thief was better than the other but no one could be worse than the child molester. To be a child molester was to be the ultimate bottom-feeder. Child molesters who were on the mainline, living amongst the general population, not segregated from inmates with other types of crimes, had to operate below the radar, convincing others that they were there for something else. Otherwise they were isolated with other child molesters and snitches on a "Special Needs'" or "Protective Custody" yard where they didn't have to worry about getting shanked on the way to the chow hall.

To be a murderer, however, had some cachet. There are some surly folks out there who probably deserved to be taken out and on top of that, one must admit, it takes some balls to take another man's life. And balls are definitely well respected in prison. The murderers appeared to get a pass as righteous individuals, unless they were total whack jobs, in which case both inmates and staff kept their distance.

As for rapists, they too were a confusing crowd. They weren't automatically lumped in with the child molesters. A rapist could possibly be there for something any man might do; misread the acquiescence of the female participant. Unless the rapist was a nutcase, he usually did okay on the mainline. Female staff like myself however, always had to keep an eye out for inmates who wanted to work for us. Guys with an "R"(Rape) in their jacket (file) weren't good candidates with which to work alone.

There were also "fish" in prison. "Fish" is a term for a newcomer. The poor fish sometimes didn't know what had hit them. Guys who had done some hard time could spot a fish in a New York second. They'd hit them up for all sorts of things; cigarettes for protection, ice cream for protection, extra socks for protection. It appeared everyone wanted to protect the fish. And I imagine the fish had a hard time deciphering what was bogus protection from real protection. Everyone tried to get the fish's attention: The gangbangers who wanted to use him for something illicit, the junkie who always needed help procuring goods, or the born-again Christian who thought he could guide the fish to the straight-and-narrow path of Godliness.

Fish, however, were not to be confused with those who had "gone fishing". Those who had "gone fishing" were definitely in the Administrative Segregation Unit (AdSeg). It was an isolation unit that attempted to discipline the errant men. If an inmate was sent to AdSeg it was most likely for getting into a fight, attacking a staff person, getting caught with drugs, stuff like that. At CVSP they unofficially referred to being sent to AdSeg as "gone fishing". The officers in AdSeg liked to play a little game with the inmates there. The CO's would drop a few cigarettes on the concrete floor several feet from the guys' individual cells. When inmates were locked up in an individual cell with no contact with others, cigarettes were pretty hard to come by. The officers stood back and watched the inmates *fish* for the cigarettes. I'd heard of guys snagging cigarettes with floss and a paperclip, with sheets, with shoelaces attached to a gum wrapper. Leave it to men, they always find some form of competition.

In addition to the complex prison hierarchy, there were uniforms. Everybody had a uniform. Licensed Vocational Nurses were called Medical Technician Assistants (MTA). They wore brown slacks with a beige zip-up shirt/jacket. The officers had their green pants with yellow piping, fully pressed khaki shirts and green caps. When they promoted to Sergeant or Lieutenant they got to add woven badges with stripes to their shirts. The more stripes you had the more money you made. They also had a hard hat like the military wear for dress. That was cool. But officers had really arrived when they got to leave the uniform at home and put on a suit and tie. Then they were either Program Captains or administrators of some sort and had really hit the jackpot.

Prison was all about uniforms. I took the cantankerous John Bergman's advice and wore a self-imposed uniform in prison; black or beige Dockers and about seven different T-shirts. I rarely strayed from that. I considered it a sign of respect on my part to not wear clothing in the workplace that would be distracting for the inmates. I mean let's face it, it wasn't easy for guys who had been locked up for years to be around a female who wasn't in a custody uniform with pepper spray, handcuffs and a baton attached to her. It was just little Leah in her Dockers and T-shirt with a panic alarm on my side that looked like a garage door opener. It's not like I was some bombshell, but the very few times I walked onto the yard wearing a dress or a suit because of some scheduled meeting, the inmates didn't know what to do with themselves. Suddenly guys who had worked for me for months were stumbling all over themselves.

As for the inmates, their uniform had been around for years: dark blue denim pants, blue chambray shirts with white T-shirts underneath. They had grey sweat pants, shorts and tennis shoes for working out but wearing those to class was considered a sign of disrespect. They were required to wear their jeans and blue shirts to class or on their job assignment. To leave the yard for a visit or concert they needed to be in dress blues (shirts buttoned all the way up) with their brown boots.

Prison was the only place I knew where not only did the people who lived and worked there had uniforms, but so did the visitors. It was like belonging to an exclusive dinner club, except the attire wasn't black tie. Visitors could be family members visiting an inmate, religious volunteers, teachers working for me, or guests coming to see a performance. They all had to adhere to strict rules. Visitors could not wear denim of any kind, anywhere. Denim was for inmates only. Theoretically, if there was an incident on the yard, an alarm went off and everyone had to hit the ground, it was imperative that the visitor's legs stood out from the inmates, since that was what the tower officer would attempt to hit first with a rifle. After the warning shots failed, of course. Visitors could also not wear double layers of clothing, nothing blue, nothing sleeveless, shoes had to have closed toes, and women with dresses had to wear nylons. You also didn't wear metal snaps and zippers because you'd never make it through the metal detector. The most embarrassing visitor moment of all was when my best friend Jean, a woman I'd known since college, came to see a performance and had to give up her under-wire bra to the gate officer in order to make it through the metal detector. Thank God Jean had small breasts and clearly, she was a very good friend.

And God forbid women wore perfume! That was just plain unfair. You could feel the inmates edging closer so they could smell it. When guys had been locked up for years, the female presence was a powerful thing, you know, the "scent of a woman" thing.

Another essential component in prison is the canteen, the CDC version of a mom-and-pop store for inmates. Inmates were only allowed to go there a couple times a month. They were issued a ducat for the canteen line and if they weren't there when their number came up, then too bad, they had to wait until next time. Canteen is critical in the joint. John Q. Public thinks that inmates are given everything in prison. Actually, they're not. Inmates are required to purchase their own toiletries. So if an inmate gave a damn about hygiene, he needed to get to canteen. They could buy soap, deodorant, toothpaste, shampoo and conditioner and they paid a pretty price for it; what we would pay at a gas station with an attached convenience store. Expensive! Of course, selected vendors had a contract with the state to provide canteen materials and once they got the contract, could charge whatever they damn well pleased.

The other sundries that could be found at the canteen were food items. Food items were very valuable in the joint. When the same crap was served day in and day out, (especially the complimentary daily lunch of two slices of bread, one slice of bologna vacuum-sealed, a packet of mustard, and one apple that was about as crisp as a banana), having food to eat in the cell was a dandy thing. Not only was it dandy, it was critical. If the joint was locked down that meant there was cell-service only: Meals were delivered to the cells and they weren't hot like the ones served in the chow hall. Getting through a lockdown usually required some substantial additions to the food chest. The most popular items were Cup O' Noodles and canned tuna or shrimp. They could take that stuff and with the help of a makeshift heating coil, cook up a veritable feast. Add some crackers to that and it was called a "spread". Ice cream was also a coveted item. Since they didn't have their own refrigerators, there was no other option than to eat the whole pint as soon as they got it! Lordie... to watch grown men savor an entire pint of Lucerne's strawberry ice cream was a sight to behold.

That's what I loved about prison. It was a different country with different rules and customs. And being the Butte, Montana girl that I was, I was totally amused and fascinated.

One of the most entertaining aspects of my job was annual In-Service Training (IST). Artist Facilitators were required to have forty hours of IST each year. I was enchanted with IST. Everyone else in the prison thought it was a huge pain-in-the-ass but to me it was my connection to what other staff felt about their place of employment. The itinerary of IST included classes on Emergency Procedures (what to do if an inmate escapes), TB and Hepatitis B and C (how to protect yourself from contracting contagious diseases that were rampant in the joint), Completing Time Cards (how to document your inmate workers' whereabouts) and of course the most popular, most necessary training class in the country - Sexual Harassment (what to do if someone harasses you in the work environment, what your rights are, how to file a complaint or how to dodge the bullet of one).

I was fascinated by the swagger of this one Lieutenant, in particular. He taught a class in Emergency Procedures. I had no idea how emergencies, like an inmate escape, were handled. He spoke of the inner-workings of the "War Room"; the conference room in the Warden's area where key staff would meet and figure out how to capture the escaped convict. This swaggering Lieutenant gave an example of a good shoot. " Say you and me..." as he motioned to a male officer in the class. "Say you and me are in the car. We're drivin', scopin' things out in our designated area and then we get the tip. Somebody thinks they saw an inmate in McDonalds. Well, McDonalds is in our area. So what are we gonna' do?"

"Check it out. " the officer stated matter of factly.

"Thas right, bro'. Weeee " as he pointed his finger back and forth from himself to the officer, "weeeee gonna' check it out! Now we got loaded rifles in the vehicle, do we take them with us inside Ronald's House?"

"Yes sir."

"Damn straight we do. We're going into Mickey Dee's with guns loaded. Now, if I see the guy running down the street before I get to McDonald's, can I shoot him in the back?"

"Yes, sir." The officer responded.

"That's right." The Lieutenant sat on the desk in front of the class and crossed his arms. " But let's say it wasn't that easy and we got to go inside. Now, say we walk into McDonald's, at first look, we're not seeing anything. Then this chubby white kid behind the counter, all nervous and shit, with zits and his Mickey Dee cap off to the side, say he whispers that the inmate is in the men's room. Okay. Good. I go into the men's room. You back me up. I walk in. I don't see shit at first. Then I look down on the floor behind the stall and I see prison blues around his ankles and his state boots. And right then and there I shoot. Was that a good shoot?"

The class weighed in with mostly "Nooooos."

"Goooood. You're thinkin'. Why not?"

"You would need good intelligence that the guy is armed," the officer replied.

"If chubby tells me he thinks he has a gun, is that good intelligence?"

"Yes sir."

"Then, I can shoot him with his pants down?" grinned the Lieutenant.

Once again the class weighed in, "Noooooooo."

"What the hell? Damn straight that's a good shoot. I probably only hit him in the leg but even if I killed him that was a good shoot. He's a convicted felon who just escaped. He ain't got no rights. I don't need to warn him. I ain't giving him his Miranda rights. If chubby thought he was packing, I do not need to ask. I'm gonna' shoot first and ask later. Doesn't matter if chubby was right or not." He jumped off the desk, looked at the clock behind him. "All right. You got forty minutes for lunch. Be back here in forty minutes. Not forty-one." Then he swaggered off into Admin. Land.

As painstakingly boring as it could be at times, it was full of relevant information. Prison was full of a cowboy attitude. Many instructors felt they were some sort of sanctioned vigilante who was gonna' teach you how to tame the inmates or not get seduced by them. Others were like insurance salesman jauntily walking you through the numbers, and occasionally we'd get a shrink who would put us to sleep talking about rather fascinating subjects like psychotropic drugs and how they affected the inmates, henceforth how they affected our jobs. IST was interesting stuff, as long as it wasn't taught by the walking dead.

The challenge at CVSP was finding local artists who were qualified to work with our program. According to California Arts Council guidelines, artists had to have three years of "professional" experience in their field. "Professional" was a squirrelly term, sometimes up for interpretation, but it still wasn't easy finding many professional artists lurking around the dusty streets of Blythe. There were a few, but not many. I had a grandmother who was an excellent watercolor artist working for me. Seeing her dote on these big inmates was quite endearing. I also had a knockout fifty-year old woman who used to play piano in the Vegas casinos, teaching beginning keyboard. She wasn't a bad teacher, but she did wear white linen pants without underwear to work one day. That wasn't good. We had to finally part ways because she couldn't figure out how to keep the guys from hitting on her. (She just couldn't connect the "attire" dots together.) That was unfortunate because she was a local artist I fought hard to get. I'd begged Susan Hill of Artsreach to give the voluptuous piano lady a try, but in the end I was wrong and Susan was right. I also had a very funny African-American comedian from nearby Palm Desert. That was a hoot.

After those locals, I brought in my so-called big guns. I hired the Bobby Matos Band. That was a coup, since they were quite known back then. I also hired a prolific playwright that was a former Juilliard student, Shem Bitterman. I didn't know Shem but was familiar with his work in New York and LA and it was an honor to have him. He is one of the brightest guys I've ever known. I also brought in a long-time contract artist at Soledad Prison, the British actor/director Nigel Sanders-Self, to direct a couple of plays, and hired Husband. Yeppers! I convinced Artsreach and Sacramento that I needed to hire my spouse to work with me doing an improvisational theater class that would spawn a book of original monologues.

Husband was starting out a new life as well. He finished up at the Dallas Theater Center and while he looked for acting work he took whatever he could find. He even worked a night shift at a Texaco Station in Orange County. Bless his heart, half the time he didn't know if it was night or day. Having him work for me was well-intentioned nepotism. I mean, if finding local artists was a struggle what was wrong with using the one that slept in my bed? Technically that bed was in Orange County, but we did have an address in Blythe and he was definitely qualified.

## JOKI

\* \* \*

We were standing in the kitchen of our Orange County condo. "Honey, there's something in the oven."

He opened it several times, puzzled. "What are you talking about?"

"There's a bun in the oven. " I reiterated.

"Ohhhhhh. " He opened the oven door again. There was a blueberry muffin, to be precise, in our oven. "Ohhhhhh, " he said. "Thanks. I'm sorry. I don't really want a muffin right now. But thanks anyway."

"Jesus, don't you get it? A bun in the oven? There's a bun in the oven." And then I patted my stomach. He looked at me awkwardly, opened the oven door again and took out the blueberry muffin.

"What the hell is this?" he asked, as he pulled a small white dipstick with a blue-ish top out of the muffin. "I don't get it."

"Geez... some people know how to spoil a good laugh. There is a bun in the oven, dear. I'm pregnant!"

"Ahhhh...." his eyes lit up, and he hugged me, he hugged me hard.

Who knew that our plan to have two kids on the state would be implemented so quickly? We'd only had unprotected sex once. I thought at the age of thirty-four, all bets might be off. Who knew what kind of shape my reproductive department was in? I could have filled my condo with women I knew in their late thirties and early forties struggling to get pregnant. They checked their temperatures, called their husbands home and afterwards kept their knees folded to their chest for thirty minutes to keep the precious semen from spilling out uselessly. The world of many thirty-somethings was full of miscarriage, tubal pregnancy, and fertility drugs being shot in the ass. We had been the lucky ones. We barely had to try.

Despite our jubilation at the news, telling my boss and the Warden I was pregnant just three months into my job was embarrassing. It was definitely not the way I wanted to start my career as a state employee.

# Black Irish

The timbre of his voice was familiar. He was a guys' guy, all guy. He was a guy like the kind-of-guy-I-grew-up-with-in-Butte kind-of-guy! A beer drinkin', fun lovin', loud, prankster with a heart of gold, from Irish descent guy, named McMurtry. Those dancing blue Irish eyes with pale, freckled skin and brown wiry hair were set upon a lean frame. His energy was frenetic to say the least. He was loud, boisterous and opinionated. The lines on his face revealed years of hard living, yet he was only in his late twenties.

He was also missing one leg; amputated as the result of a motorcycle accident. He had a prosthesis that—in Blythe during the summer when it could get up to one hundred fifteen degrees— would fall off. The sweat would accumulate at the edge of his thigh where the suction grip took hold and before he knew it ... Squish Squish Blam! His prosthesis would fall off. Prison was no beauty pageant and McMurtry didn't really give a fuck anyway. Everyone knew he was short one limb, but in honor of his Irish ancestors, he also made sure that they knew he could still kick their ass if need be, with or without a leg.

I once saw him jump a guy on the yard as he left our building. They were talking as they walked along, they stopped, faced each other, exchanged words and suddenly McMurtry tossed his crutches to the ground and leaped onto the guy's back. It was like a hornet shoving its stinger into unsuspecting flesh, refusing to abandon its mission. His victim started turning in circles trying to shake this one hundred-fifty pound human pest off of him. McMurtry was beating him with two fists, as his complete left leg wrapped around him like a snake. The right stump was just along for the ride, flailing in the wind. McMurtry would have done anything to win. Poked his eyes out. Whatever.

His C-file was the first I had ever read. All the years that I had taught theater classes in the joint, I'd never actually seen a C-file before. They were usually brown, or that military green and always legal, not letter size. They were impressive and contained everything known about an inmate. A C-file housed a complete profile about the person and never divulged opinions, merely facts. Looking at the facts that were chosen to go into a C-file made it challenging for any reader to not form an opinion. It was similar to reading a fictional character's breakdown in a movie script: Sam Somebody is a 43 year old, white male with homicidal tendencies. No apparent relationships with women, no known children. Estranged from family. A frequent drug user, admits to using pot, cocaine, meth. Desires to be an electrician. 9th grade education. Missing right front tooth. How do you not form an opinion about a guy like that? Isn't that a perfect character for John Malkovich to portray?

I sympathized with McMurtry when I read his C-file. Simple things like casual drug use, disorderly conduct, broken family, they all sounded so bad on that legal paper with numbered lines to the side and blue ink stamps all over the pages. Hell my family was broken, I'd encountered drugs a few times in the past and I'd been asked to leave a bar or two. I just didn't have it recorded and stamped "RECEIVED". C-files were funny things. I read the whole story of a person, but didn't necessarily get the whole picture.

McMurtry's case was a tale of mishaps, as I remember it. He wasn't exactly the "golden child" growing up. He drank too much, was rowdy and flirted with the juvenile system many times; petty theft, driving under the influence, disorderly conduct; the usual, bad boy stuff.

In honor of McMurtry's birthday, a friend agreed to host a keg. They came, they saw beer and they drank. A lady friend gave him a cool little gift, a key chain with a Swiss Army Knife attached. At about 3:00am however, the friend grew weary of his drunken guests, and unlike most of them, he was gainfully employed and had to get up and go to work in the morning. He started pushing McMurtry around. Not only had his leg been amputated, but he also had residual pain in his chest and shoulder. McMurtry warned the guy to stop... to "please" stop because that shit hurt more than the friend could possibly know. When the asshole didn't stop, McMurtry upped the ante. "You touch me one more time and I'll stick you." One more time came fast and furious and McMurtry pulled out his brand, spanking new key chain with the knife accoutrement, flipped it open with the bar code still attached and thrust it into the asshole's side.

Girls, especially twenty-something drunk girls, tend to overreact at the slightest bit of blood at three in the morning. The chicks called the police and McMurtry explained to them that he was to blame for the one inch cut on the right side of his friends' abdomen. I believe he was sentenced to three or four years for that in a medium security prison.

I felt like I could relate to McMurtry. I understood his black humor and admired his ability to focus on the absurdity of the more painful aspects of life. It was an Irish thing. McMurtry once told a story about riding on the back of a motorcycle on the beach with a friend. They wanted to impress some chicks in string bikinis so they drove in front of them and attempted to do a wheelie for the girls. Instead they got thrown off the bike. McMurtry's prosthetic leg ended up facing the wrong direction. Unbeknownst to him, he was being watched by the bikini girls. He reached down and turned his leg 180 degrees so that his toes were facing front again. Bikini girls screamed in horror and took off running. So much for making a good impression!

I hired McMurtry as an inmate clerk. He was one of many in the future, with whom I had to straddle a line between their enthusiasm and commitment to the job, and their inability to tolerate fools and slackers. I think McMurtry encouraged some inmates to join the classes and threatened others if they walked in the door. And God forbid if any of them looked at him sideways.

McMurtry was joined in AIC with inmate Watts. He not only got along with McMurtry, (a requirement for sanity's sake) but he was a former theater student, as well. Watts was a pleasure to look at, a smaller, better looking version of Magic Johnson in his heyday. He was in his early 20's, maybe 6'3", lean athletic body, beautiful smile, and hair that was meticulously groomed with a wooden brush and set to condition under a do-rag. He looked and acted more like he belonged on a basketball court than in the theater, yet he was a pretty good actor. It was guys like him that gave credibility to the maxim: Prison is full of good black men.

So what was homeboy doing in prison? While attending Cal Arts, a prestigious theater school in Valencia, he also had a gig slapping sandwiches together at a Subway. I imagined he was spreading mayo on wheat and putting folded slices of turkey next to triangles of provolone cheese when it dawned on him that he knew the combination to the safe. He probably added lettuce, tomato, green peppers and pickles with a little vinegar and oil as he wrapped the foot-long sandwich in green and white paper, when it occurred to him that he could pull off robbing Subway.

Actors can be stupid. I don't recall exactly how it was bungled. If they found his fingerprints on the safe because he forgot to put on the plastic gloves, like he did every other day, or if someone spotted him leaving Subway at three o'clock in the morning. Whatever the scenario, one day Watts was taking acting classes on the plush green campus of Cal Arts from some of the best teachers in the country, and now he was taking them in prison from me.

We were *The Art Squad*: One black, one Irish and one white. During the day we were busy AIC bees typing up orders and ducats (passes to get inmates to class from their cell), sweeping and mopping the classroom, and brainstorming about all the fun things we could do in prison. We could do plays. I'd direct and they'd star in them. They could write plays and I'd direct them. Hell why stop there? We could encourage inmates from every prison in the great state of California to write a one-act play and submit it to a competition, which would be judged by professionals in the business. Good golly, prison was fun.

*Indian Wants the Bronx* by Israel Horovitz was my first theater production in the joint. Watts and McMurtry played two street thugs and a Hispanic inmate played the East Indian guy they harass. I asked a cronie from Juilliard, Joe McGrath—who ran his own design company in Tucson, AZ—to design the production. Joe was one of my favorite people in the Juilliard class of 1982. Like McMurtry he was of Irish descent, a guy-guy but with flawless Juilliard speech. He put together a whole package for me: portable stage, lighting, and props that included a knife made from rubber.

About a week before the performance McMurtry and Watts came to me with dire concerns. The reality had finally hit that they were actually going to perform this in front of an inmate audience (*Duh?*) and that they wouldn't know every inmate who attended the multiple performances. They were concerned. There were some serious idiots in prison. Just because the races mixed in Arts in Corrections didn't mean that it was that way on the yard. Out there, everything divided by race. Blacks ate and shared cells with blacks. Whites ate and bunked with whites, Hispanics with Hispanics. Like Watts and McMurtry, guys of different races could befriend each other in Arts in Corrections, but they didn't sit at the same table in the chow hall. It finally dawned on them that some of the other inmates could be offended by the image of a white guy and a black guy chumming it up on stage. McMurtry finally blurted out "Miss Joki I don't want to get my ass whooped for doing a play!"

It was a legitimate concern. I knew racist idiots existed, and sometimes they went after guys who, in their eyes, crossed the line. But the work that Watts and McMurtry did was so impressive that I was confident that the inmates would be blown away. No way could one watch the play and not be impressed with the amount of work it took to be on stage for a full ninety minutes, non-stop. I gave them the 'ole "believe-in-the-power-of-theater" speech, the "theater-transcends-reality" ploy and the "you've-worked-too-hard-to-throw-it- away, you're-better-than-them" lecture. And then, I prayed.

It went off without a glitch. They were stars on the yard for a week, McMurtry's leg didn't fall off once during the play and none of my actors got their ass kicked. That's what I called: success. Actually, in retrospect, there were two little teensy, eensy moments that I didn't anticipate.

Opening night of the play I proudly paraded Warden Theo White and Lucia, my boss, to the front row. The play started but I had forgotten to prepare him for the "fight" at the end. For a brief moment he wasn't sure if the fight was part of the play, whether or not it was under control and unsure about his own safety. My bad. The poor Warden's black skin looked white for a moment. In the end however, Mr. White was his classy self. Never broke in front of the inmates, congratulated everyone on the fine work and winked as he whispered, "Next time forewarn me." *Just... a small glitch.*

The other mishap connected to the Bronx play transpired after one of the performances. We were taking the show down; putting props away, taking down lights, unplugging recording systems, etc., when it came to my attention that the rubber knife used on stage was missing. The knife had been approved on a list of props all the way up through the Custody Captain and Warden White himself, with my assurance that if it wasn't being used on stage, it was under lock and key. One would think that a knife made of rubber would be no big deal, but not here. You couldn't physically hurt anyone with it but anything that looks like a knife from a distance could be perceived as a real knife and was fair game for battle amongst inmates or for guards in the tower standing with loaded guns. It was not a good thing to even wave a rubber knife in jest in that place. I gathered the guys together and explained if we didn't find the knife, I would have to go to the cops and there would be no more shows. This would be our last performance. *Hell if I screw this up about the only play I'll get approved to do in prison will be a reading of children's nursery rhymes.* They understood that not only would we be shut down, the whole yard would probably be locked down until the custody staff found the knife.

People in prison know how to keep people in prison in check. The place works because they want it to. The majority of inmates just want to do their time and be left alone. Once they hit thirty, gang banging holds little attraction except for the seriously hard core. Most of the time bringing in custody staff was a necessity, but not all times. In training to be a Facilitator we were advised that if you had a missing item or tool always check with the group first and assume that nine out of ten times it was an oversight.

The group concurred that there were one or two suspicious jerks in the crowd. They probably meant no harm, but were stupid enough not to realize how much trouble they could cause the program. My friend Joe and I kept looking in the building while Watts and McMurtry hit the yard. Thirty minutes later Watts walked in with a smile and stated "Miss Joki here's the knife."

"Where was it?"

"I promised I wouldn't say. I need to keep that promise. He was just being stupid."

"You got it." I said. "Let's lock it up and get out of here. Great show."

I mentioned the rubber knife story to someone in the office at Artsreach. I wanted to make sure there were no negative repercussions for Joe who made the thing at my request and I also thought it was a good tale of how to handle a potentially volatile situation. Not long after we closed Indian Wants the Bronx, I attended a training session on the UCLA campus led by John Bergman. The usual suspects were there; contract artists, Artist Facilitators and Artsreach staff. Husband and I were staying in a crappy hotel for the weekend. We sat in big, cushy chairs. I was very fond of training sessions, especially those led by John Bergman.

Bergman started out at signature breakneck speed. "What are your most important concerns in prison right now?"

I raised my hand. "I believe censorship is an important issue."

John was standing in front of everyone. You'd have thought by his reaction that I just said "Your mother is a whore and I'm going to cut your balls off with this machete in my hand."

Good Lord, the man's face was starting to get red with anger. It was like watching a plastic cup fill with cherry Kool-aid. "You, my dear, are a dangerous, fucking idiot. If you were working for me I'd have you fired. I've never heard of such stupidity."

I didn't have a clue what he was talking about. I sensed confusion and embarrassment in the group. I could only surmise that someone from Artsreach had told him the rubber knife story and he was morbidly pissed off. Personally, I didn't relish getting flogged in public when I was eight and a half months pregnant and just about ready to pop.

Before I knew it, John had stormed out. Like most of us, he was utterly predictable. What does an over-the-top, underpaid, stressed out genius do after ripping a friend/colleague's head off in front of others? Smoke a cigarette.

I went in search of an explanation. I found him trying to light up under a lilac tree. As I moved towards him, my mouth attempted to form the word "What?"

"Get out of my way." He boldly stated. His hand touched my left shoulder and pushed me aside. (Ask any eight and a half month pregnant woman if it's okay to intrude into her space? It's not.) I hopped in a cab shortly after and went back to our stinky hotel room. No matter how much I admired him, no matter how much he taught me, no matter how much I may have screwed up what he did wasn't okay. I have never laid eyes on John Bergman again.

# Good Plan

It's a funny thing making plans. It all sounds like such a good idea, at the time. My plan was off to an excellent start. I was working for the state, pregnant with child sooner-than-I-ever-anticipated on the state, spending money for the state, saving artistic souls for the state and writing plays for the state. My state was in a good state.

What was alarming about this world I intentionally concocted for myself, were the unknown, long-term ramifications. In California there were hundreds of thousands of lawyers, doctors, pizza delivery guys, thousands of prison guards and plumbers; and gazillions of actors and screenwriters. But there were only about twenty of us, and as an Artist Facilitator I felt isolated.

The inmates understood better than staff what the program was about, but I couldn't talk with them in a normal manner. I couldn't chat with them about my weekend. I couldn't tell them Husband was my husband. I couldn't divulge where I grew up, where I lived and what restaurants or bars I frequented. Water cooler talk with inmates was dangerous territory. I was trained to talk shop, and only shop.

Artist Facilitators also didn't hang out with other prison staff. We pretty much kept to ourselves. Only our supervisors, the Community Resource Managers, really understood what we did.

Some guards were even annoyed with us. They resented our easy access to Wardens, the trouble we could make if we had to and the attention the program got in the press. Our job looked cushy from their point of view because most of us came and went as we pleased. None of them knew the long hours we poured into training arts' teachers to work safely in an unsafe environment, ordering art supplies with three bids, the hours spent on the phone with a contract artist in distress, or the weeks spent writing and revising grants. We were an enigma.

Many of the Correctional Officers were high school graduates with three weeks of training. It wasn't exactly brain surgery babysitting the bad boys. The more educated, motivated faction of the bunch tended to have college or masters degrees. They were the supervisors of Education, the Associate Wardens or the Medical Dept. To half of them I was some artsy-fartsy buffoon with a degree from some fancy place who would either work for a song or volunteer to work for free.

One Captain in particular would smile and wink as he passed me on the yard. "Give it up, Joki. Put on the green." He knew I was well educated and that in Arts in Corrections I could only go so far. It wasn't a career with upward mobility and great retirement. Salary-wise we topped out in four to five years and the retirement benefits sucked. The Captain with the flashy smile knew he made three times the amount I made, worked half as hard and would one day retire and by legislated largesse, receive 90% of his regular salary. It was a no-brainer for him. Why I wouldn't go to the academy for three weeks, work a few years as an officer and promote my way into administration was beyond him, and he did have a point. Artists are stupid that way. Most of us like to ignore life's realities and think retirement is something for old people, which we will never be.

I was also in the midst of creating a family. That too was a plan that, like prison, I willingly signed up for. Little did I know that it wouldn't take long for my life to become consumed with prison and children and nothing else. Husband was becoming my only anchor, my only connection to the outside world. As for my own family, they largely remained baffled by what I did. This was definitely no *Leave It to Beaver* lifestyle.

Some guards abhorred that I was allowed to work the mainline while pregnant. They scowled as they begrudgingly opened the gate. If a CO was pregnant, she would have been sent to the mailroom or up to the admin building to do something. She wouldn't have been allowed out on the yard where she could get hurt in an incident. A pregnant woman was a huge liability, a danger to the other officers or a target for some sicko. But they didn't have any choice other than allowing me to continue status quo. I couldn't facilitate an inmate program from a desk where I never saw inmates. CVSP and the administration in Sacramento closed their eyes, held their breath and hoped that nothing would go dreadfully wrong.

As the only pregnant Facilitator at the time I felt even more isolated. It was hard enough being one of the few females to teach unconventional classes in prison, but it was even weirder teaching them while pregnant. It freaked the inmates out. They weren't used to seeing pregnant women inside and the bigger I got, the more protective I was over my belly. I wanted no one near me.

Since I was intent on staying strong and flexible in preparation for childbirth, I implemented a yoga/stretching class into my plan. Twice a week for one hour I would teach a session of grueling stretches to a committed following of six convicted male felons. One day however, some Hispanic guy wanted to give it a whirl. About fifteen minutes into the class sitting on the concrete floor with his legs straddled in front of him, I noticed the guy had a huge boner. I quickly asked him to leave. No big deal, I thought.

Weeks later I received a complaint he'd filed. In it, Boner Guy accused me of sexually harassing him. I wore a full-body leotard that was black with 1980's splattered colors everywhere and an oversized T-shirt over that. Evidently my colored splatters made a pattern that, like a corkscrew, wound its way right up to my vagina and that disturbed him. Like I said: I wore a big T-shirt over my leotard and I was eight months pregnant! *Please.* I had to file a response to his complaint. In the end Boner Guy was no longer able to attend my class. This was a good example of the gratuitous complaints that inmates could and would file. They cost the state a fortune.

Morning sickness was never an issue, but fatigue was. In the first and third trimester it was almost unbearable. When they locked the inmates down for count prior to chowtime, I would pull out my four inch Folger Adams key, lock the main entrance to my building from the inside, stroll to my office and lock myself in. I would try to work on paperwork until my eyes felt so heavy I feared my forehead would come crashing down onto the word processor and I'd be found out. So I lock myself in my private state restroom, laid on the cold, prison tile floor curled up in a fetal position and took a nap. Drool from my mouth invariably formed a little pool on the floor.

August had just begun but it felt like the first day of school. The anticipation of my new journey kept me awake most the night. I was just so darned excited it didn't matter that I was exhausted. It was my last day of work for a few months. My daughter was due to be born in one week. I was going to take a whole week off to get ready for the birth and to contemplate this new phase of my life, parenthood. The anticipation made me giddy. Husband drove with me to work that day. I didn't feel great, kind of nauseated actually, but it was my last day and all I had to do was go through a few things with Husband who would be taking over for me for the next few weeks.

Back in the spring Husband had applied for and received an Artist-in-Residence grant with the California Arts Council to run a video program at Chuckawalla. Although nepotism was frowned upon by the state, it was possible for couples to work together so long as one spouse didn't supervise the other. The only hitch then was that I could not act as his supervisor, but Lucia, the Community Resource Manager, was happy to do so. Fortunately the precedent for allowing this had already been set by another couple in the north, where the Facilitator's husband taught drawing as an Artist-in-Residence. A residency grant could bring an additional 15K to a program so we didn't want to pass on that. His grant was scheduled to begin in October.

In addition to that I also got the prison, Artsreach at UCLA and Sacramento to agree to let Husband take over for me for a few weeks. There really wasn't anyone else available and once again I would not be supervising him.

I wasn't planning on returning to work right away. Two weeks after my daughter was to be born I was planning to accompany Husband to the Massachusetts' Institution of Technology (MIT) in Cambridge, where he was going to teach theater. No kidding. Apparently the powers at MIT realized that it was turning out more worker drones than leaders, so they decided it would be good for the math/science geeks to acquire some creative skills. In came Husband. How? The guy heading up the new theater department at MIT just so happened to be the writer/director of the play about the convict who falls in love with the English teacher that Husband did in Kansas City. Alan Brody loved Husband's work. He begged him to join him in this new adventure. *Suuuurrrrre*, we were going to have a baby any day and Cambridge was on the East coast and *suuuuurrrrre* I was going to continue to work in the prison in California. And what about his new video grant at the prison in October? It was brilliant how we dovetailed CVSP and MIT together.

Here was the plan. I give birth. For two weeks he steps in as the Facilitator, then turns my job over to Joe McGrath, my designer buddy, and the two of us head to Cambridge with newborn child. For two months the baby and I would just hang and then I would return to California to work. At which point, Husband would start a weekly commute. Every Sunday he would fly to Boston, on Monday and Tuesday he would teach at MIT, on Wednesday he would fly to California, on Thursday he would watch the baby, and on Friday and Saturday he would teach at the prison. Then repeat the process. Most people thought we were insane. I thought we were adventurous. I mean why let a baby stop you from taking a once in a lifetime opportunity?

There was more to the plan, however. For his Artist-in-Residence grant he was going to do video dialogues with inmates from CVSP and students from MIT. He would pair a geek with an inmate and each week they would dialogue via video camera. That too, was a first. In retrospect, it's astounding that we ever got permission for that.

Keeping the program going in my absence was a big priority. No one could take a two-week vacation and not have the piranhas nosing around your space. An empty, unused room in a prison is like shit to flies. People are all over it in a hurry. Teachers in education get to thinking if a room isn't being used, they will arbitrarily designate it to education and quickly fill it with English as a Second Language (ESL) students. The Hobbycraft Manager would hear about nobody being in a room during the day and would think how easy it would be to distribute the inmates' orders of hobby supplies from there. The Warehouse officer certainly needed a place to hand out mail and packages to the inmates. He was like Santa all year long, except he didn't really have a spot of his own to hand out the goodies: packages of home-baked cookies and school photos of their children smiling extra big for daddy in prison, packages of canned shrimp and Top Ramen with bundles of paper, envelopes and stamps, packages of CD's and cigarettes and a new TV that their mother scrubbed floors in order to buy it.

An empty Arts in Corrections room would have been mighty handy for handing out those bundles of joy. Not to mention the Yard Officer who often needed a place to strip down inmates for one reason or another. I can't tell you how many times I'd be in my office working on ordering supplies or negotiating a contract with an artist and an officer would walk into the main area of my building and have a group of guys strip down and do the Kiester squat... you know... they squat down naked and cough to make sure no interesting things like drugs or weapons come out of their butt. You'd be amazed at what has come out of peoples' ass. Officers frequently acted as if it was perfectly fine to have a bunch of guys strip down without asking my permission. Some officers, not all, but some, thought that if they had a uniform on and you didn't, they could do whatever they wanted, when and where ever they wanted.

Oddly enough, I worried more about staff stealing my shit than inmates. Over the years, I've had CD players, guitars, typewriters, chairs, tables and office supplies stolen. You name it. Anything that wasn't locked in a cage or bolted to the floor was fair game for officers to use for their own purpose. I guess they figured state property was community property and as long as they didn't take the shit home, it could be used for their state purposes. I made damn sure that while I was on maternity leave somebody was minding the store.

The day flowed so easily that it wasn't until about 4:00pm when I normally took a break for food, that it sunk in that I was having labor contractions. No big deal. I would just stop for a moment, take a deep breath or twenty, then move on. We sat in the cafeteria, Husband and I. I don't remember anyone else being there, except for the inmate workers and their supervisor. The inmates made me the biggest burger and plate of fries imaginable. If the inmates liked you they always loaded you up with extra fries. What the hell did they care? They weren't there to make a profit. It was the state's money and if loading favorite staff members up with extra fries or a drink could score some points, why not? In any case I was determined to enjoy my prison cheeseburger, mountain of fries and a coke. Although, I think I was enjoying it a bit too much. Husband sort of watched in horror as ketchup oozed out of my mouth and onto my huge belly. He didn't have that neurotic delight in eating forbidden foods. He would actually forget to eat sometimes, a concept that was incomprehensible to me. He sat in terror as I flipped from exuberance over my cheeseburger and fries, to holding the edge of the table firmly and breathing deeply into a contraction, then back to cheeseburger delight. He was just plain horrified that I could eat like that, at a time like this.

When asked about my choice of having such a big dinner, I reminded him that it could be 24 hours before the baby comes and once I get to the hospital they weren't going to let me have food. Apparently no one wants to clean up a bowel movement from a woman in labor. I had learned this little tidbit of info in my avid search to find the determining factors that make having a natural childbirth possible. In fact it was just one week before we were sitting in the cafeteria that I decided to leave my Beverly Hills doctor and look for a new one.

Throughout my entire pregnancy I had been seeing Dr. Beverly Hills with the intent of having my child at Cedars-Sinai. He had been my ObGyn for years. But after Bergman went off on me that day at UCLA, I had a monumental realization. I had seen Bergman venomously criticize people numerous times before. I just never thought he would do it to me. I wrongly assumed I was above that. After that situation, I began to think about Dr. Beverly Hills. He had a picture of a Hollywood starlet on the wall thanking him for the C-section he'd given her. I also remembered how he lightly chuckled when I told him I didn't want an episiotomy. He said he'd give it a try, but felt that most women needed them. I realized the likelihood of having a C-section or an episiotomy was pretty darn high with him. So thanks to John Bergman I decided to drop my ObGyn one week before my baby was due.

After a ton of phone calls I stumbled into the perfect doctor; Dr. Michael Rosenthal, who ran The Family Birthing Center in Upland. He was also an ObGyn at the hospital across the street. The biggest distinction between the two places was that the birthing center offered the possibility of water births and didn't hook you up to an electronic fetal monitor. It was the perfect situation. I was too skittish to have a homebirth with a midwife. I feared that I'd be the one where some emergency happens and be airlifted outta' there feeling like a fool. But I was smart enough to know that 95% of the women I knew who had given birth in the last several years had either a C-section, drugs or an episiotomy. At the age of thirty-five in southern California I knew a lot of friends who'd had kids. It didn't make sense that an entire generation of women got to a place where they couldn't do naturally what they'd been doing for thousands of years?

The biggest factor I came to understand was that a woman paid a hefty price to be hooked to an electronic fetal monitor. In order to monitor the baby's heart rate that way, it requires that you lay down. I watched a bunch of birth movies, even a few at Cedars-Sinai, and in each film the woman in labor always wanted to get up. She was always trying to sit up, then, being restrained by the monitor, she would collapse back onto the pillows. It is my understanding that when you're in labor your body stops working with you and the baby's heart rate easily becomes inconsistent.

Shortly after meeting Dr. Rosenthal, I knew I was in the right place. He wasn't some hippie-drop-out-touting-nature-this-nature-that. He was the first doctor I'd met that had a genuine concern for the women's experience in the birth process. Believe me, every woman I knew relayed tales of horror and highly recommended as many drugs as possible. None of them ever said, "I had a great birth." What also sold me on the handsome doctor was his candor about his own disbelief that women could give birth without an episiotomy and without tearing. He said that when he first started trying it, women ended up with horrible tears, until he learned that they couldn't be lying flat on their backs. They needed to be standing or squatting like the way women used to do it. (A guy wouldn't try to pass a watermelon out of his ass lying down. He'd be squatting and grunting, letting gravity do its part.) Rosenthal was *my* guy.

Talk about calling it close to the bone. I just met the doc the day before and here I was in labor, in prison. After that terrifically greasy food, Husband suggested that we ought to head home soon.

But I was feeling dandy and ready to finish the evening. Blythe is 100 miles from Palm Springs, where we'd recently moved. (Raising my daughter alone in the Oasis motel wasn't an option, nor was the really far-away Orange County condo which we were lucky to sell.) Palm Springs was another 80 miles from the birthing center. No bother, we went back on the yard. I was merrily writing some last minute memos, clueless to the fact that I was going through my nesting phase right there. The contractions didn't take long to become more and more intense. It freaked the inmates out to see me at one moment tap tap tapping away on the word processor and the next minute standing, clasping the back of a chair, exhaling moans of a deep-seated pain.

"Miss Joki, don't you think you ought to leave?"

"Leah, let me get you out of here." chimed in Husband. We closed up the office, the AIC Building, and made our way to the gate. On the other side of the yard I saw Watts and McMurtry waving and singing the theme song from the TV show, *Gilligan's Island*. "Ohhhhh...the ship set sail from the shore one day to an un-chartered desert isle... blah blah blah ...with Gilligan, the Skipper too, a millionaire and his wife, a movie star, the Professor and Marianne... here on Gilligan's Isle." They had been teasing me whenever I wore these white bib overalls to work. I think my resemblance to the Skipper was disturbing to them. But, to be serenaded with that song as I was headed to give birth, was pretty fuckin' funny!

Not long after we got on the road, the contractions became mighty powerful. Poor Husband, there wasn't much he could do for me as I braced my feet against the glove box and screamed in pain. He drove as fast as possible. When we reached our house in Palm Springs, the plan was for me to alert the Family Birthing Center that the contractions were coming closer, and for Husband to pack a bag. They always tell you to have a bag packed but we thought we had another week. I was having severe back labor. Every contraction felt like a sledgehammer railing against my spine. With years of voice classes, I was one loud woman in labor.

I laid sprawled out on the living room floor as Husband stepped over me trying to put the bag together. He was in desperate search of honey and a teaspoon, something he remembered as being essential to the natural birthing process. Our kitchen was long and had more cabinets than we could ever dream to fill, and in his search of honey and a teaspoon, every one of those cabinets was open. In an hour's time, he had managed to tear our whole house apart looking for that crap.

Our neighbor from across the street knocked gently on the door. Linda was thin with pale skin and short brown hair, cute in a schoolgirl way. She knew I was about to deliver and heard me moaning from across the street. She noticed every light in the house on and thought she'd check to see if we needed anything. It takes an experienced mother to quickly assess the situation and take over. I was a helpless lump of screaming clay that needed attention and couldn't get it from Husband who was overwhelmed with putting a bag together and getting the car seat into the car. It was an odd thing, but he really did just drop off the planet for a while. He roamed from room to room, stepping over me, or around me, in search of... things. Linda detected chaos and offered to take us to the hospital. She felt I needed to get to the hospital in Palm Springs right away, but I was adamant I was going to the birthing center in Upland. As Husband struggled with the car seat in our vehicle, Linda wisely offered to drive us in her van. She popped that car seat in like a pro, grabbed the bag, locked the house up, and threw the two of us in the back of her van where I could lay down and Husband could be there to comfort me. We got off to a good start, until Linda realized she didn't have enough gas to get to Upland.

While Linda was inside the Shell Oil station paying for the gas, a mother of a contraction came upon me and I screamed my head off. A group of young men knocked on the tinted windows in the back of the van. "Mam', are you all right in there?" They pressed their noses onto the glass as if I had been abducted and was being tortured. Linda shooed them away as she returned to the car. As they walked off I remember them muttering "Oh sorry... wow!"

Linda couldn't drive me to Upland fast enough. I was in so much pain that every time I saw the speedometer at 55mph I wanted to put my hands around her thin neck and choke the living daylights out of her. Nothing under 80mph was acceptable at the moment.

Arriving at the birthing center was like being dropped off at a convent. It looked like a lovely, quaint home from the outside. Linda looked on in disbelief. I think she thought I was a goofball for coming there. I'm sure she questioned the necessity of driving 80 miles to get to a small convent in the LA suburbs. A woman opened the door and explained that a midwife would be there soon. I was disappointed that Dr. Rosenthall was not on duty and would only be called in an emergency. Since we were the only ones there, I had full roaming privileges. I could go anywhere in my birthday suit, and I did. The Family Birthing Center consisted of four birthing rooms, one room with a large tub for water birth, a kitchen, receptionist area and a classroom. It wasn't huge, but very inviting. The birthing room had a queen-sized bed that was low to the floor. It had a desk and nightstands, and was dimly lit. There was a bathroom off to the left. There was no hint of hospital. No steel gadgets, no beds that go up and down with buttons, no monitors, just a nurse and a midwife.

I wasn't exactly the poster child for natural childbirth. Linda opted to stay, since it was late and we had no way back. They let her rest in another room. I didn't see or hear a peep from her until the next morning, when she commented that my screaming would probably frighten most women away from having natural childbirth.

The problem was that I had extreme back labor. My daughter's head was hitting against a nerve, and every time I had a contraction it felt like that sledgehammer was hitting me in the back again. I would have taken whatever drug they had and handed them the knife to cut me open just to make the pain stop. But they didn't have any drugs, and they didn't have any knives either. Those were across the street at the hospital. One didn't take a gurney ride to the hospital until all her options were exhausted. So I went from the hot tub to standing on all fours, to sitting in the shower, to pressing against a wall, to roaming the halls of the center in search of pain relief. About every ten minutes or so, wherever I was, the midwife would check the baby's heart rate with a Doppler stethoscope to my stomach. Sometimes she literally got on her hands and knees to do so. I was pretty much beside myself, when the midwife made an offer. They would try one act of motion and I would give them twenty minutes to see if it made a difference. If not, they would take me across the street for an epidural. Great! Whatever! I didn't know if I could make it twenty minutes, but yeah let's get on with it, I thought. I wanted drugs and I wanted them right then and there. So bring on the act of motion. They had me lay on my left side on one side of the bed. The midwife reached under my shoulders and the nurse went under my legs. On one, two, three... they lifted me up and flipped me over to my right side on the other side of the bed. It was nothing short of freaky. I was then told to lie quietly on my side for about twenty minutes and at that time if the pain didn't subside they would take me across the street for an epidural.

The pain never returned. That sudden movement was enough to make my daughter's head turn just enough so that it was no longer pressing against the nerve. After that it was smooth sailing. It was amazing. I gave birth to my daughter standing up. Unlike a conventional hospital where once the baby's head comes out, they usually give you an episiotomy and pull the rest of the baby out. Here, they just let nature do it's thing and gave my body time to adjust for the widest part of the baby, the shoulders, to come out. My beautiful daughter's head came out, her black eyes looking right up at me and she stayed there looking at me for about ten minutes. To have just her head out and looking right at me, while the rest of her body was still inside me was a trip.

The other freaky thing was that after I pushed the rest of her body out, I laid down and they placed her on my stomach. They didn't immediately cut the umbilical cord, so she wasn't breathing yet. She was still getting her oxygen through the cord. It was wild.

In about ten minutes she started breathing on her own, and when they cut the cord she didn't even flinch.

I had two stitches, a nap, and went home six hours later. My instincts were right. Women have had babies for eons and, for the most part, we are fine.

# Genius or Knucklehead?

We arrived in Cambridge late and exhausted. It was nine o'clock in the evening and we desperately needed to eat. Alan and his wife offered to take three week old Girl-Child while we grabbed dinner nearby. I remember returning from the quick meal horrified as I walked into the Brody's apartment. There was Alan sitting on the sofa with his full head of grey hair holding my Girl-Child and smoking like a chimney. I could barely see her through the cloud that engulfed the two of them. 'Oh my, I'll take that' I thought as I whisked her from his grasp. They were from the generation that didn't think twice about smoking around children, and smoke they did.

The Brodys seemed to be enjoying their New England adventure on the MIT campus. They had a spacious apartment and were in that energetic phase of life when the children were grown, they themselves were healthy, still working hard, yet having lots of fun. Husband and I lived in a small studio nearby. It had a small kitchen, a bathroom and we came equipped with a blow-up mattress and a bassinet.

It wasn't long before our mattress started giving us problems; a small leak that we simply could not find. Every night we would fill it up with air from my hairdryer and by three o'clock in the morning we'd be on the concrete floor with the thinnest carpet that was ever made. We joked and laughed at our situation like it was such a kick-in-the-pants that I was thirty-five years old and sleeping on a concrete floor just weeks after giving birth. *Wasn't that a laugh?*

Husband worked hard to figure out ways to get the geeks to lighten up and think outside the box. Hell, we were living in a box and flourishing. Most days he spent at the school either teaching or planning how he was going to go back and forth from there, to CVSP on a weekly basis. Basically the money from the grant was going towards weekly airfare, but at least he got to take this one-time opportunity at MIT and still be home on a regular basis.

It didn't take long for the three of us to be out and about and get the "Bi-racial Triangle Stare" (BTS). We'd be walking along and as we approached someone coming the opposite direction, they would look at my white face, move their eyes in a straight line over to Husband's black face then south to a point between the two of us where Girl-Child was. We got the BTS a lot. Total strangers were very interested in what our bi-racial baby looked like. If they couldn't get a glimpse of her with the BTS, they'd crank their neck around as we passed by. I'd never felt like such an object of curiosity before.

Back at CVSP, Joe was holding things down as best he could. We spoke every day he worked and every day we talked about guitar strings and the impossible task of accounting for them. The E-string, in particular, was a pain in the ass. Because it's fine and breaks frequently, inmates were always asking to replace them. Our job however, was to make sure that the E-string was being used to play the guitar and not being put on the end of a pen with a makeshift motor to create a tattoo. It was common knowledge that was the typical mode of prison tattooing.

Joe was collecting stories from inmates that we thought could be put together in some sort of community project and he was struck by how much effort they put into committing crime. He wondered why, if they were going to work so hard, they didn't focus their time and energy on something positive. He was humored by some of the stupid things they did like stealing pallets from an industrial lot and reselling them for fifteen dollars to do drugs. The number of inmates incarcerated for drug-related crimes and the lack of treatment was particularly shocking and as a builder, he was horrified by the amount of money it took to build in prisons. One couldn't drive to Home Depot to buy a door lock. A simple purchase like that required onerous paperwork and was never cheap. While gathering their stories, Joe learned that my presence at CVSP was a positive one. He concluded that I had a "bulletproof personality" in the joint. I was flattered by his report, because I took great pride in what I did there.

My return from Cambridge came none too soon for Joe. He was tired of commuting from Tucson, tired of staying at the Flying J Motel and anxious to get back to a normal life and schedule with his lovely wife. It was November 7, 1991. As I walked towards my boss' office the room was buzzing with disbelief. The secretaries' eyebrows furrowed and the Public Information Officer held his shaved head in his hands mumbling, "I can't believe it." Magic Johnson had just announced he was HIV positive and leaving the NBA. *Magic Johnson?*

Heterosexuals in this country seemed to think that the only people who were HIV positive were gay, drug users, hemophiliacs or living in Africa. It was uncommon for a straight guy to be HIV positive back then. Adult heterosexuals pooh-poohed the necessity of condoms in the 80's. They were for teenagers who needed quickie birth control. Adult women had the pill, the IUD and the diaphragm. What did we need condoms for? No one slept around that much. Magic's announcement however, was one bizarre wake-up call.

Husband embraced his insane weekly commute with fervor. They liked him at MIT. The inmates enjoyed the video program and surely Girl-Child relished having her daddy all to herself one day a week. It was taxing, but he persevered. The video exchanges between the MIT geeks and the CVSP inmates became comical.

The students would ask dopey questions about prison life and crime and the inmates would dole out fatherly advice to over-achievers. Privately, we coined it the "Genius or Knucklehead?" project. We thought maybe if the inmates didn't wear their prison blues that a viewer might not know who was at a prestigious institution of higher learning and who was at an institution of incarceration and rehabilitation.

The real question was: Were we geniuses? Or were we knuckleheads? It was hard to tell. Sometimes his weekly bicoastal commute seemed like a half-baked idea. I was smart but was eating stupidly. I was just soooo hungry. The holidays came fast upon us and soon after I was not only famished, but bitchy. Turned out I was pregnant with child number two. I had planned to have two children on the state. I just didn't think I'd have them so soon. *Genius or knucklehead?*

Inmate concerts were a blast, and this year for the first time I was putting one on for Christmas. As long as concerts were handled properly, they were a win-win situation. The inmates usually had a great time whether they were playing in one or just attending. It was a great way to score points with staff. Hell, I'm no dummy. Good music just makes people happier. And what does one want most in prison? To be happier, a lot happier. What's wrong with the notion that for one flippin' minute an inmate can forget where he is, where he buried the body, where he left the money, where his wife was, where, where, where? There's also nothing wrong with staff taking an eight-hour shift and breaking it up with a little entertainment. They appreciated being able to kick back and not have to think about where the drugs are, where the weapons are, where's their report, where's their key-ring, their paycheck and goddamnit, where's their lunch?

Arts in Corrections was a win-win deal. For a little bit of money, we calmed everybody's ass down. And the calmer it was in prison, the better it was for everybody; including the general public's wallet. It was cheap to keep a place calm with a little music, a little mural painting, some storytelling... way cheap. What was a real drain on the pocketbook (the taxes that keep prisons operating) is when the place wasn't calm. Instead of buying a guitar, taxpayers paid for hundreds of hours of overtime while custody staff turned the place upside down looking for something that didn't keep the place calm. Putting together a little entertainment to calm the masses down was a good thing, so long as it was "handled properly."

When putting on an inmate concert I assumed that I was going to get screwed by some idiot that would ultimately make me look the fool. I always kept that notion firmly planted in my "noggin." I knew that if I gave a rogue con a microphone, I had a serious problem, especially with rappers. I'd seen inmate concerts, not sanctioned by Arts in Corrections, where inmates got up and started spouting off some shit about killing cops and giving it to some Ho' up the ass, and the staff sat and clapped like they were singing *Mary had a Little Lamb*. None of them wanted to admit that they didn't have a friggin' clue what "shit" these guys were saying, so they just played along, bopping their heads to the beat and applauding. All while the inmates laughed their ass off, knowing that they had just pulled one over on staff. If that would have happened in an AIC concert, the Artist Facilitator would have looked like a fool and there would have been repercussions. The inmates assumed that we didn't know shit about shit and were just as stupid as the okie guard with the pimply face shuckin' and jivin' to rap. We did not want to be in that group.

I not only feared the wayward rappers, but was also concerned that Billy Bob might go off track with a country band or some Metallica Wanna-Be would grasp the mike and wail "Fuuuuuuck youuuuuuu. Fuuuuuuuuck Youuuuuuu." So, before accepting a song into a concert I always checked the lyrics. Improvisation was for instrumental jazz bands only. We always did at least two runthroughs and at the final one, I'd threaten them with ever being involved with the program again, if they changed one word of their performance. It was a nifty system.

This particular winter however, I begged a group of inmates to do a Christmas show. The reason I had to beg was that usually inmates wanted to do the music that interested them, and holiday music didn't fill that bill. In addition, Christmas was usually ignored in prison. Even though it was a hard time for inmates, I thought they'd enjoy having it recognized.

I had an energetic inmate clerk, Mr. H., who claimed to be the lead guitar player for a popular band in the 80's. His C-file stated that he was a professional musician who was convicted of receiving stolen property, but it didn't state his band affiliation. I also had a very rare prison commodity, a trumpet player. Everyone in the joint thinks he can play a sax, but a trumpet? Only a real player would dare to pick one up. Lenny was a soft-spoken black man in his late 50's. The combination of these two was phenomenal. They could play anything. In addition to their primary instruments they could also play keyboards, base and percussion. Since Mr. H worked forty hours a week for me, he had plenty of time to plan and rehearse the show. He was a dream come true inmate, a consummate professional who cared about music above and beyond any prison bullshit. It was hard to find guys in prison to cross the racial line. Usually it was the black band, the white band, and the Hispanic band. But Mr. H played it all; rock, country, blues, jazz, R&B and Christmas music.

Mr. H. and Lenny concocted a smoking jazz version of *Silent Night* and a few other holiday standards. About half way into the rehearsal process, a group of black queens on the yard approached me about doing *Jingle Bell Rock*. I was happy to comply, so happy to comply that I not only helped with the choreography, I brought in costumes for them.

Getting permission to bring any kind of costume into prison was no small feat. A memo had to be submitted requesting permission to bring "the following items" in. I had to explain how important it was for me to bring in four red fake-fur tree skirts, four Santa hats, and four pair of big ornament earrings. I stated on what day

I was bringing them in, where they would be kept until the performance, how I would account for them afterwards and at what time I would be taking them out. Basically if I lost them, I'd promise the Department my first-born. In addition to tools, or something that could be used as a weapon, bringing in simple costume pieces was challenging because it was viewed as escape paraphernalia. I not only had to get my supervisor, the Community Resource Manager, but the whole chain of command to sign off on it. That was eight flippin' people who had to be convinced of the necessity of tree skirts and Santa hats. I stalked people for a week, walking from one building to the next, in perfect order. Following the chain of command required patience and diligence because one never asked the Captain's permission before getting the Sergeant's and Lieutenant's. That was political suicide. That would have meant that I intentionally went over their heads and believe me, I would have paid for that. "Respect the chain of command." I heard Kimsay in the back of my head.

I got some bizarre things into prison. I winked, nodded, plead my case, always promised that nothing would go wrong, and reminded them of my perfect track record. Every time the Custody Captain saw me coming, he would shudder. The Custody Captain was the big cheese cop in prison. Basically if he signs off on something that is a potential security threat (i.e. costumes in which to escape) then typically the Associate Warden, the Chief Deputy and the Warden will fall in line. A Custody Captain knows that his ass is on the line and isn't always fond of that situation. They wouldn't be disgusted, just skittish. Disgust was usually left for the officer who had to check all the shit in and out at the Pedestrian gate. That guy rolled his eyes in disbelief as he scanned the memo containing eight signatures. The officer couldn't go against anything with the Warden's John Hancock on it, but he certainly did share his disdain for my position.

Most things went as planned the night of the performance. The inmates who were performing in the show were escorted to the Visiting Room where we set up. In the summer we held concerts outside, but during the winter we had to perform inside. It was like having a concert in a cafeteria with linoleum floors and fluorescent lights. The Visiting Room accommodated about 150 inmates for the audience and every seat was filled. Guys who wanted to see the show had to sign up in their housing unit a week in advance. The shows became very popular, so there was always a waiting list if someone didn't show up or got turned away. In order for an inmate to leave the Yard and go to the Visiting Room, he was required to be dressed in state blues. They weren't allowed to attend in sweats, T-shirts, or sneakers. Blue jeans, blue shirt, standard issue leather boots and ID were required. If they weren't dressed right they were sent back to their "house." Every single inmate who attended had to be patted down for contraband, both going in and coming out. It's a huge thing to have officers pat down 150 guys, a ton of work.

On this particular night, there was one itty, bitty glitch I chose to ignore. The four black queens were absolutely gorgeous. I don't have a clue as to where they got the skin and hair care products, but these men had the most happenin' hair and flawless skin and were much prettier than I ever thought of being. They also had decided, unbeknownst to me, to wear their prison long johns under the red fake-fur tree skirts, instead of their blue jeans. They requested a room where they could drop their shirts and pants while the musicians were setting up. There wasn't any other staff around at the moment, so I directed them to a small storage room. Twenty minutes later when it seemed like they were taking an awfully long time to drop their drawers, I went to check on them. I opened the door and this bunch screamed like a pack of fourteen-year old girls caught naked by a Catholic nun. Good Lord Almighty. They were peering through a white cloud of powder. The girls were so excited about their routine that they smuggled in a little makeup for their debut. They'd gotten hold of some red pens and used the ink for rouge and lipstick. They used black ink as eyeliner. And God only knows where they got the powder. The show was about to begin. Inmates and officers were everywhere. It wasn't prison protocol, but dammit I was under a lot of pressure. I chose to shut the door. Ignore it. I couldn't get sidetracked with minutia. I let the show begin.

It was marvelous. For one moment Mr. H. was actually happy to be in prison. He looked like a happy, happy Garth Brooks. His blue eyes twinkled with delight. Inmates and staff were having a great time. Yes, Christmas was a hard time of year for inmates and staff is trained not to talk about it, but for a rare moment we were celebrating it, in all its glory.

The grand finale had come with the last Christmas song for the evening. The band started playing *Jingle Bell Rock*. The queens made a surprise entrance from the right in a line of white long johns, prison issue boots, red fake-fur skirts, Santa hats and ornaments dangling from their ears. The hair was either flat ironed or curled, the ink pen makeup very sexy, and their cleavage was looking very interesting since they had unbuttoned the long johns to the waist. They definitely had it going on dawg, as they sang,

> *Jingle bell, jingle bell, jingle bell rock*
> *Jingle bells swing and jingle bells ring*
> *Snowing and blowing up bushels of fun*
> *Now the jingle hop has begun.*

They turned their butts to the audience, gave them a little tap and Holy Moly! What thunderous applause!

> *Jingle bell, jingle bell, jingle bell rock*
> *Jingle bells chime in jingle bell time*
> *Dancing and prancing in Jingle Bell Square*
> *In the frosty air.*

The queens smiled and lifted their skirts can-can style in the front.

> *What a bright time, 'tis the right time*
> *To rock the night away.*

The girls gyrated their pelvis' and the crowd went mad. The entire audience got on it's feet and screamed "OHHHH BAAAAABY" as they thrust their hips like they were gonna' fuck these boys to kingdom come. It was insane.

*Jingle bell time is a swell time*
*To go gliding in a one-horse sleigh.*

A little touch to the back of their ass.

*Giddy-up jingle horse, pick up your feet*
*Jingle around the clock.*

They patted themselves on the bottom as they pretended to be riding a stick horse.

*Mix and a-mingle in the jingling feet*
*That's the jingle bell,*
*That's the jingle bell,*
*That's the jingle bell rock.*

The crowd went nuts. I'd done concerts many times before, but a formerly kicked-back guard suddenly spoke into his radio "I need some back up. Potential riot situation." The room was vibrating. Back up? Why do you need back up, they're not going to escape in their tree skirts!

I stood in the back of the room. I am sooooo fired. What was I thinking?

Fortunately no one had jumped up on stage and grabbed anybody. That would have been very, very bad. When the song was done, everyone sat down and laughed. Absolutely priceless! The queens were rock stars that night. I always wondered what the remainder of the evening brought for the four black beauties. I imagine it was either heaven or hell. As for me, I didn't know if I was a genius, or a knucklehead?

# Almost Perfect

We had talked about starting up a statewide playwriting competition and now were ready to do it. McMurtry was determined to get his one-act submission complete. He was one of the few inmates that ever took my advice; write what you know. He didn't want to write about the prison itself but took small talk from the CO's and concocted a fictional comedy that took place in the small desert town of where else? Blythe, California.

In his one-act play, *Blythe*, the heroine is a twenty-something waitress who sleeps around with several correctional officers from the nearby prison. While chugging down his breakfast, a local yokel at the diner has his tow truck stolen by an inmate who has just escaped from the prison.

McMurtry really captured the flavor of the officers' lingo and the dreariness of the area. It was the best inmate work I had ever read. I thought it was brilliant and decided to produce it. McMurtry had a future as a writer and I wanted to give him the experience of having an outside director come in, so I hired Nigel Sanders-Self, a short, energetic British guy who had worked at Soledad for years. He was jazzed about McMurtry's script and I was looking forward to playing Beth, the waitress. (Okay, I wasn't in my 20's, was a bit pregnant-chubby-again but hey, I was the only woman around.)

There was a fine line walked in terms of asking permission to do something or just doing it, particularly in selecting plays to be performed. In McMurtry's case, I decided to just do it. But I did provide the script to my supervisor Lucia, first. Fortunately, good-natured Lucia was humored by it as well and it was a "go." What neither one of us anticipated was that one of the Associate Wardens, a suit who didn't have much to do at the time, was standing in her office when the bold title *Blythe* caught his eye on her desk. He started thumbing through the script and was not humored. Rehearsals were scheduled to begin in a week.

I was at home in Palm Springs when the phone rang. The Warden's soft-spoken demeanor on the other end of the line was adamant that there would be no production of the play *Blythe* in his prison. It was too volatile. He believed it made fun of staff in such a way that their safety could be jeopardized and could lead to a potential riot. As much as I always respected Mr. White, that was a riot. *Who's the theater expert here? The AW? Some suit that doesn't know anything about theatre, judged an entire piece of work based on a page or two taken out of context?* Despite my pleas to Warden White to consider that I knew my business and that a riot would not be a by-product of this theatrical gem, despite all my urging, the answer was; "No. There will not be a production of *Blythe* at the prison, at this time." Mr. White was going to be on vacation the next two weeks, and that was that. He said whatever play I selected for replacement, an Associate Warden in addition to my supervisor, Lucia, would have to okay it in his absence.

I knew I lost the battle, but didn't want to lose the war and asked, "Will you approve the play for submission to the playwriting competition?"

"That's fine. I don't care what you do with the play outside."

"It's one of the best things I've ever read that was written by an inmate."

I could feel his silent laughter on the other end of the phone.

He was polite and stated, "That will be fine." I told him I'd have the paperwork on his desk when he returned from vacation. It was all very civil. I had to respect his decision, but *Shit!*

Nigel expected to keep his contract so we quickly replaced McMurtry's play with two short one-acts, *Killer's Head* and *Red Cross* by Sam Shepard. The AW who read these, quickly approved them, probably because he couldn't understand them. I think Sam Shepard was doing so many drugs back then, his early plays have moments of being incomprehensible. I did compliment the suit however, on his theater expertise.

Cowboy, my new clerk, was a tall drink of water with a long ponytail and a rugged face. Although he was a musician, he enjoyed watching the Shepard plays. But Cowboy was nervous that night. *Killer's Head* is an esoteric monologue by a man who is about to be executed. Nigel, the director, cast a black inmate in the role and Joe McGrath designed an electric chair that was painfully realistic. Cowboy nervously paced back and forth as the audience trickled out the door. He was so restless that I thought he had popped some speed or downed ten cups of coffee. The image of a black man being executed by two white guys was messing with him. Turned out that Cowboy knew something that no one else in the room did: "The verdict in the Rodney King case is out and there are riots in LA." Poor Cowboy was afraid that if the audience knew about the shocking verdicts, that watching Nigel's version of *Killer's Head* would send the inmates right over the edge and into a full-blown riot. But it didn't. Never could start a riot with a play.

\* \* \*

The Shepard plays came and went and so did McMurtry and Watts. Forty-some one-act plays were sent to me from all over the state for the competition and I made sure that a memo was sent to Warden White as a reminder that "all of the plays from CVSP were being submitted." No one was concerned, and I boxed up copies of all the plays for each judge: Oskar Eustis of the Mark Taper Forum, Robert Blacker of the La Jolla Playhouse, Ken Raskoff of Steve White Productions, Ernest Dillihay of the Los Angeles Cultural Affairs Department, television writer John Bunzel and Penny Johnson, an actor on HBO's The Larry Sander's Show."

It was amazing that we had such high caliber people in the industry agree to volunteer to read that many scripts. Each of them did so because they were connected to us somehow. Oskar Eustis from the Mark Taper was a friend of my playwriting teacher, Shem, who could coax a bear out of hibernation. Robert Blacker from La Jolla Playhouse was a former colleague of my best friend from college in Montana. Ken Raskoff was the summer theater director at Fort Peck, Ernest Dillihay used to be the Artist Facilitator at CRC and John Bunzel and Penny Johnson went to Juilliard with me.

Now that Ernest was working for the Cultural Affairs Department, his position at the California Rehabilitation Center (a.k.a. "Hotel California") was vacant. I was definitely interested. Husband had wrapped up the harrowing year at MIT and moving closer to Los Angeles was very appealing. CRC was located about fifty miles east of LA in Norco. We thought we could split the difference again and live somewhere in between. Instead of me driving 100 miles each way from Palm Springs to Blythe each day, I could cut that down to 30 miles each way and similarly for Husband. I believed I was the logical candidate: 1) I knew the place well from working there many times in the past. 2) It was the only facility that housed both men and women and it would be nice for a woman to run the program. 3) It was one of the few prisons that had quality theater space and it was close enough to LA that the Hollywood crowd, with whom I had connections, would be willing to travel there.

The other contender for the job was a Facilitator from Susanville. He was a jovial trumpet player, black, in his fifties. I always liked him but always felt like I was getting hit up on at conferences. At the interview he wasn't all that prepared. His videotape of samples wasn't cued for the panel. (A no-no in the non-profit arts world.) When I spoke to him outside, I realized he didn't seem to know much about the place. I'm a shoo-in.

I entered the room looking oh-so-professional. I had my briefcase (a holdover from appraising days) full of notes about the institution, my videotape of sample work perfectly cued and I wore a gorgeous red skirt and blouse. I walked in like I owned the place but I was taken back when the hiring panels' mouths dropped open. Boy-Child was about to pop. Unlike cleavage that can be flaunted for fun then concealed for work, there was nothing I could do to cover up this bundle of joy. They asked when I'd be ready to start. They were impressed with my tape of samples and curious how I knew so much about the place. They seemed excited about my overall plan for running the program. *Yippity Skippity I'm gettin' out of those damn sandstorms!*

It was perfect. I'd pop out Boy-Child and during my maternity leave we'd find another place to live between Norco and LA. Then I'd start my new facilitatin' job at the most kickback joint in the state. I got the call from the Assistant Director of Arts in Corrections in Sacramento, MUGsie, the Most Unhappy Gal. My male competition, had originally replaced her as an Artist Facilitator at Susanville when she opted to go corporate. MUGsie had short brown hair and sad brown eyes. When she was an Artist Facilitator in Susanville she was jovial and vivacious. In Sacramento she looked tired and defeated. "I'm sorry Leah. They decided to go with him."

"What? That makes no sense."

"I know. You did great. I think the institution was more comfortable with him. We have to go along with what they want. We can only guide them, but in the end it's their decision. I'm really sorry."

"He didn't know shit about that place. He wasn't even prepared." I paused for a long while. "You were there. Do you think this has anything to do with me being pregnant?"

I don't remember her response to that question anymore. I didn't get the job and came unglued with righteousness, but resisted the temptation to get litigious; not my style. (I liked this guy but years later heard he was fired for allegedly having an affair with a female inmate who had paroled.) *I knew it.*

I visited Dr. Rosenthal on a Wednesday and all looked well. Two days later I had lost a large percentage of my amniotic fluid. "Would you like to have this baby tonight or tomorrow morning?" I opted for the next morning. The thought of having labor induced the next morning with Pitocin was disconcerting. It threw you into hard labor quickly, which made it difficult for your body to adjust. I got up hours before to make a last ditch effort to induce labor on my own and rode my Lifecycle as hard as I could. About halfway to Upland the fruits of my labor paid off and the contractions started on their own. "Nah Nah Nah Nah Nah Nah!" I boasted upon arrival. "You don't have to touch me."

With Boy-Child I got to deliver in the water. It was strange and wonderful. The water was so soothing. I didn't need drugs or stitches of any kind. He came out swimming. Dr. Rosenthal looked at me. "Go ahead, you should be the first to hold your son." It was like trying to catch an ornery fish. It was an awesome birth.

The results were in. The three plays chosen by the panel of judges were Blythe by McMurtry, Maxine, Oh Maxine by Watts and Let's Keep Dancing by an inmate from Folsom. God I love it when I'm right.

An article appeared in the trade magazine *Drama-Logue*, written by Tom Provenzano. It began; "The newly renovated Ivar Theatre in the heart of Hollywood is the perfect staging ground for the *First Annual One-Act Playwriting Competition* sponsored by Arts in Corrections, one of the most hopeful programs of California's Department of Corrections." Info. Info. Info. "The honorary chairs of the competition include Charles Dutton, Edward Asner, Edward James Olmos and filmmaker Charles Burnett." More and more info. "Three scripts have been selected by a panel of judges for the staged readings on Monday, Nov.16 at 8p.m."

When I set up the playwriting competition my one stipulation was that I got first dibs on which of the three plays to direct for the staged reading. Naturally I chose McMurtry's. I had a great cast of professional actors who had been rehearsing and were ready for the big night.

It was Saturday the 14th of November, two days before the readings. Husband and I were frantically trying to leave to go to Shem Bitterman's wedding in LA. Shem was the playwriting program at CVSP.

The phone rang. It was Jim Carlson, good-in-a-Nordic-sweater Director of AIC. *Why is Carlson calling me at home on the weekend?* Evidently, he was called at home on the weekend, too. Some Suit(s) wanted to know if I had written permission for *Blythe* to be performed in Los Angeles, and if not he(they) wanted it pulled from the evenings' program. *What the hell?*

"Jim, I sent a memo to the Warden saying that *all* the plays from CVSP were being submitted to the competition months ago. Why would I be packing that around?"

"Leah, are you sure you had permission to perform the play?"

Now, that was a mighty big question in the world of government bureaucracy. Clearly after the debacle in the spring when the play was banned from being performed inside, I made sure that it was in writing that the play was being submitted to the competition. Granted I wrote that memo months earlier, but I was confident that it also stated the winning scripts would be performed for the public in Los Angeles. I was confident because "I planned the whole goddamn thing! I have paperwork! In fact, if I remember correctly, myself and only one other Facilitator in the state have paperwork! And by the way, Mr. White chuckled when I told him *Blythe* was one of the winning scripts. And now that I think of it, he also has a memo stating that I've been working off-grounds to rehearse with the actors in LA. How could he suddenly not know that the play is being performed in LA? As a matter of fact, I invited him personally and he just sort of smiled and shook his head like it was no big fuckin' deal."

Carlson knew I was upset, but God love the guy, he knew how to keep his cool. "Leah, do you have any paperwork with you?"

"I don't know, but I don't think so." And I didn't. I didn't normally carry around memos unless they were critical to getting something in and out of the prison; like a camera. Shit like that. *Why would I carry a four, five, who-knows-six-month-old memo with me saying the following twenty-some plays are being submitted when I just saw the Warden a few days ago and practically kissed him good-bye as I left the institution to rehearse the play? What the hell?* This was an ignoble and obviously whopping case of administrative amnesia.

But none of that answered his question. Did I have it? No. It would have been in my office, it was late Saturday afternoon, I needed to drive to Los Angeles to Shem's wedding and CVSP was one hundred miles in the opposite direction.

The whole thing was ludicrous. I ended up faxing the whole script to Sacramento. I can't even remember all the people I talked to. But phone call, after phone call, after phone call, I left Palm Springs certain that I had to cancel McMurtry's play from the program. I understood how McMurtry felt when he didn't want to get his ass kicked over a play; I didn't want to lose my job over one either.

All I ever understood about the situation was that Mr. White "got wind" of the reading (like he didn't know before) at a Wardens' meeting and was accosted by other Wardens who intimated that this play could prove to be embarrassing for the institution and that his Artist Facilitator was some sort of rogue, loose cannon, that he couldn't control. Right. I was such a loose cannon. I did scary, outrageous things like plays. I let an inmate write a play that insinuated sometimes people in the workplace get involved with local people and sometimes it's with more than one person at a time. Apparently that never happened in the Department of Corrections. I let a guy write a play where an inmate escaped from prison and tried to get away by stealing a truck. Apparently the Department of Corrections didn't want people to think that ever happened either. Good God Almighty. 1992 must have been the year when state bureaucrats started losing not only their sense of humor but their common sense as well. It was a sweet, funny thirty-five minute play being performed in a crappy part of Los Angeles for about eighty people. But they just couldn't get a grip!

Because of the crisis Husband and I missed the wedding, but went straight to the reception where the newlyweds were hoisted in the air on chairs per Jewish tradition. Patrick Hustad, one of the actors in *Blythe*, was also at the wedding with his wife. Patrick was a tall, lanky white guy with big blue eyes. He was a nice guy who was brilliant at playing disturbed people. As we sat with him and his wife, I warned him that he'd probably be getting a call from me the next day telling him that *Blythe* was yanked from the reading. Throughout the conversation Patrick's hands were either covering his mouth in dismay or waving in the air as if to say "Stop! Stop! Go back and say that part again!" Meanwhile his redheaded wife sat quietly in the corner. I barely heard her when she leaned closer to the table and said, "Have you thought about going to the press?"

"I can't do that."

"Why not?"

"I'm a state employee. I can't contact the press without permission. Besides I don't want to lose my job over this."

"What if I contact them?" Her eyes opened up wider and the freckles on her face began to dance. "This is really important, you know. How can the prison get away with this? That guy has the right to write that play and have it performed." She was kind of revving up some more. "Honestly, what if I call someone? I know some people at the LA Times."

"It's a free country. I can't stop you from going to the press."

Patrick leaned into me like a schoolteacher giving me the answer to a test question that I should have known. "My wife's the managing editor of *Buzz* magazine. " The cat really was out of the bag.

I think I had a slight hangover the next day. His voice was resonating inside my head, or maybe it was just my phone. "Leah Joki?"

"Uh huh."

"This is Don Shirley from the *LA Times*." Holy shit did I put myself together in a New York minute. I knew that I couldn't talk to the man. I could answer yes or no. "Are you Leah Joki?"

"Yes, I am." I made one statement and one statement only. I told the reporter, "The same paperwork was submitted for *Maxine, Oh Maxine* as was for *Blythe*. I don't see them pulling Watts' play out of the program." After that I referred Mr. Shirley to Jim Carlson in Sacramento and to Eric Flamer, the Public Information Officer at CVSP.

The next day I had just showed up at the theater to help get the stage ready and to go through lighting checks with the other directors, when a stagehand came up to me and said "Miss Joki, Ed Asner called. He was concerned if there was an issue with censorship?" My head ached. I didn't call Ed back. If I had I would have said, "Thanks for your concern. But my head aches Lou, I have to go now."

The evening went well. The newly anointed winning play was lyrical and thought provoking. There were raw, emotional scenes in Watts' play about a homeless woman and alcohol abuse. McMurtry's play? It was like snow on a tree that a gust of wind blew off, no one knew it had ever existed. I sat in the back of the theater and cried. McMurtry should have been there. We should have been laughing our ass off. But he couldn't be, and we weren't laughing. The actors I'd been rehearsing didn't come and Ed Asner wasn't there.

# Go Directly to Jail, Don't Collect $200, Don't Write a Play

### by
### Don Shirley

I opened up the *Los Angeles Times* the next morning and there it was at the top of the STAGE section. The greatest thing about this article was that my name was never mentioned. It told how McMurtrys' play was pulled just days before a scheduled performance. It stated that prison authorities "felt it wasn't helpful for the relationship between the institution and the community for the play to be presented at this time" said Jim Carlson. I loved the guy for knowing how to play politics.

The article went on: ...prison spokesman Eric Flamer said "the play made references and innuendoes toward the staff that were not exactly accurate" and also referred inaccurately to prison escapes. Of course, employees in the Department of Corrections don't screw around and inmates don't escape.

It went on further to say: the play as a whole is "humorous and harmless" said one of the professionals working on it. "You can't expect them not to write about their world and what they know of it. This has opened up a can of worms, where the possibility of work being screened and maybe censored could happen." I wondered which professional said that.

Oh Lordie, if only all had been left well enough alone. Talk about opening a can of worms. McMurtry's play would have come and gone like the snow on the tree: unnoticed. But no, the Department of Corrections operated with such fear and paranoia at times that mountains were created out of molehills. This was one of them. And now my job was on the line, again.

It was important enough that Jim Carlson flew in for the meeting, which was very classy of him. Carlson didn't express dismay at me for having a rubber knife made, for encouraging inmates to write about prison or for having two children within two years of working there, but then again, he himself was a "family man". We talked about the timeline of events and looked at the existing memos. He thought it was best that he spoke to the Warden alone, at first. I was fine with that. I always trusted that Jim had my best interest at heart.

He stepped into the Warden's office while I waited outside. Julian Marquez was now the Chief Deputy Warden who would one day take over at Chuckawalla as Warden. (I heard years later, but cannot verify, that Mr. White was ousted over this fiasco, however I cannot imagine that was true. That would have been as ridiculous as the situation I was in. Mr. White was a smart, decent man and a good Warden.) There I was, having to fight for my job with someone who wasn't even a player in the drama. Typical. Kim had warned me to always be nice because we never knew who was going to be holding the key to our castle in the future, and this time it was Julian Marquez.

I didn't know him well, or have a read on what action he might take. Carlson came out of the Wardens' office. That was quick. He pulled me aside. "I think you'll be fine if you agree to sign this letter to go into your personnel file."

I glanced at it. It stated something about not going through proper channels, not following through with acquiring the necessary signatures and admitting that I was at fault - but not with ill intent. Carlson must have drafted that up before he even got there. I'm telling ya', the guy was a great politician. I didn't really like the letter though. I didn't like admitting to something that I didn't do, but recognized that I needed to take some kind of slap on the hands. "Fine. That's fine. I'll sign it." I liked my job. I wanted to keep my job.

The next few months were a blur. For the first time, work was a challenge. It was the regular kind of challenge, but also an I'm-so-fucking-exhausted-I-can't-see-straight-kind of challenge.Lovely Girl-Child slept all through the night. Never woke up crying, never heard a peep from the darling creature. My lovely infant Boy-Child also slept a full eight hours happily snoozing away, needing nothing at all, but Boy-Child slept all day! There was a child awake 24/7. Sometimes at two or three in the morning when my son would cry to be held or changed or want dinner I would wake Husband up in a fearful rage and scream "Take him. I might hurt him." I wasn't depressed. I wasn't Brooke Shields thinking I didn't want him and needed medication. I was exhausted. I needed sleep. In an attempt to correct this domestic horror, the pediatrician recommended keeping him awake fifteen minutes longer each day. So instead of letting him go to slumber land at 9:00a.m. our job the first day was to keep him awake 'til 9:15a.m. That was it. Fifteen minutes longer each day. Sounds like a piece of cake, but it was months of grueling torture. We would dunk him in cold water or put ice cubes on his forehead as he screamed with his chubby cheeks turning flaming red, then miraculously fifteen minutes later each day, like a professional narcoleptic, he'd conk out.

I was going 75mph. It was 10:00p.m. It was so dark and there was no eye candy, no cars to avoid coming the opposite direction. It was like an angel descended from above and covered me with a heavy, wool blanket. She kindly took the wheel while I captured a few moments of much-needed sleep.

It was a goddamn good thing my angel was a good driver,

because otherwise I would have been dead or seriously fucked up. She somehow took my lead foot off the gas and coasted me into a sea of sagebrush. And there I rolled along in the dark at about 2mph when a truck driver coming from the opposite direction laid on his loud horn in an attempt to wake me up. And he did. He stopped and inquired if I thought I was okay to continuing driving. I assured him I was. As I finished the last leg of that one hundred mile drive I thought about how much I loved my job, how hard I worked to get it, what great things had happened with the program, how amazing it was to have health benefits and be able to take time off with my newborn children and how Jim Carlson had fought to keep me. And then, I thought about Girl-Child and Boy-Child and that it might be a good idea for me to stay alive.

"I'm quitting my job tomorrow." I announced as I walked in the door. And much to my surprise, Husband was ecstatic.

# The Big House

For months Shem had been bending Husbands' ear about the importance of being in LA if you want to have an acting career. Shem had piercing blue eyes and was losing his hair at a young age, but was remarkably handsome. He was the smartest, most articulate person I knew. As a writer he was not only prolific, he was brilliant. He could conjure up the wildest situations with laugh-out-loud dialogue, but I was concerned for his mental health. Shem didn't steer clear of dark topics; he was like a moth on the porch light to them.

Finally, Husband could get back to where he belonged: not Orange County, not Blythe, not Palm Springs. Hollywood! We abandoned our middle-class lifestyle with health benefits and paid vacations for the more bohemian one we had before. The only difference was two children. Our plan? I stay home and raise two kids; he strikes it rich in Hollywood. It was naive, but I believed in Husband. He was an extremely talented actor. We knew a lot of successful people in the business. This was his moment. It didn't take long before he snagged a manager, and out he went in search of smoky, jazzy headshots and I to buy a membership to the Los Angeles Zoo.

Husband was busy with his career. He did readings for free, starred in a play in an outdoor park and did a small role for no pay in Shem's first movie. He started teaching at the High School for the Performing Arts and continued to work as a contract artist in the prisons for Artsreach. He was ambitious, but we were going broke. Husband already was a well-respected stage actor. But it was imperative for him to make the crossover into film and television. Handsome as he was however, there was a little glitch in his physical presentation; he was wall-eyed. Never once did I call him that. "Cross-eyed" was what people said behind his back. To his face he got "What's with the eye?" One eye looked right at you and the other was focused on something three to four feet to the side. People didn't know if he was looking at them or not. My advice? "If you can't or won't fix it, then embrace it. Be like Peter Falk and make it part of your charm." He hated when I said that.

A year and change went by and it was clear that I needed a job. This time my angel steered me seventy-five miles northeast of Los Angeles to Lancaster, where the California government built a new Level III/Level IV (Medium/Maximum security) prison and needed an Artist Facilitator.

More than thirty percent of convictions in the state of California came from Los Angeles County. So much crime originated there that people bitched and moaned for years about all the prisons being built in every nook-n-cranny in the state, but never in LA. East Los Angeles had long been a focal point as a site, but always managed to escape having a state prison built in its urban backyard. Lancaster became the perfect solution. It was about as far as you could get from Los Angeles and still be in Los Angeles County.

It was a 75-mile, (albeit negative) commute each way, which was nothing after a 100-mile commute each way in the middle of nowhere with only one gas station and a convenience store in between. Another plus factor was that since it was the only prison to ever be built in Los Angeles County, it was the easiest to get to and the most kindred spirit of Hollywood, which could turn this Arts in Corrections program into a high-profile one. And besides, I missed 240 lb. hairy-chested lover. Hell, I was going broke without him.

An Arts in Corrections conference was taking place in Arrowhead, CA. With the help of Susan Hill at UCLA, Husband and I got an admission ticket. Scheduled to attend this particular conference was Lynn Harrison, the new Community Resource Manager at California State Prison-Los Angeles County (CSP-LAC). Whoever the Artist Facilitator was going to be, they would have to be approved by her. I put my game face on and headed to Arrowhead.

You would think that driving up winding roads that hugged the mountainsides with spectacular views of God's country would be a cinch for a girl who grew up in Montana, but they scared the crap out of me. I don't know why. Maybe I'd seen too many action flicks where the vehicle didn't make the hairpin curve and instead flew into the air, somersaulted down the mountain against the snowy, jagged rocks and landed engulfed in a ball of fire.

It was a white-knuckled drive getting there but worth the anxiety. Once I was there it was like putting on old, comfy slippers. It was fun taking workshops to brush up my artistic prison libido, shooting shots of tequila with the AIC poster child and former inmate, Aileen White, and watching Husband flourish in an a cappella jazz group. I missed my babies, but damn I was having fun.

It was at breakfast one day that the infamous Lynn Harrison was pointed out to me. She was intimidating. There weren't many Community Resource Managers who could put "Former Mayor" on their resume. In her early forties, she sported a mane of thick, white hair. She was a staunch Republican and had the photographs to prove it: Her, with Governor Pete Wilson and her, with former President Ford. She looked the part too; serious, conservative, wire-rimmed glasses, tasteful suits, meticulous and organized. How in the hell I thought, would this woman and I ever relate? I didn't have a clue. But I also remember thinking this about her. There was something beyond the conservative, authoritative veneer. Lynn could have been your boss, your mother, your mistress or bus-driver. She could have been the colleague that ripped you a new one, the friend upon whose shoulder you cried, or the woman in the bar who bought a round of drinks. She was like a complicated Paula Dean. Mixing all those things together, how could we not get along? Besides, that job was mine.

I had been working at CSP-LAC less than two weeks when I was handed a piece of college ruled paper folded into a small square. Before I could even open the outside door to Arts in Corrections, the inmate that handed it to me was gone. I walked through my main area past the pottery kiln and back to my small office. I'd been handed notes from inmates before. Usually they scribbled things like "Can I get on the guitar list?" or "Will you look at my novel?" or "If you need someone to work for you, I needs a job. I cans type good." Joe Schmoe, C-12345, FAC "C" Bldg 3/21L.

### Translation of C-12345, FAC "C" Bldg 3/21L

**1. "C-12345" = inmates CDC number.** They all start with a letter of the alphabet and then five digits. The significance of a guy with a "C" number is that he obviously would have been locked up for a long time. CDC started with "A", then went to "B" and "C". I don't think I ever met an A number, B's were rare and C's were your old-school convicts. The majority of guys in Lancaster at that time were D's and F's. (It's a scary thought, but they've exhausted the alphabet. They're onto double letters.)

**2. "FAC "C"" = Facility "C"** or the "C" yard or "Charlie" yard. This was the first part of his address. Most new prisons had four individual yards: Alpha (A), Beta (B) Charlie (C) and Delta (D). There could have been a riot on "C" and inmates on "A" could still be going to Chapel.

**3. Bldg 3/21L = Building #3, Cell#21, Lower bunk.** The second part of his address.

My raggedy note simply stated: "You won't be able to stay here because of a lawsuit about the library."

*Curious.* Interesting note. I wondered if there was anything to it. Turned out, there was. When they were building a bunch of these new prisons like the one in Lancaster, they made the library on each yard much smaller than in the other prisons. The problem was that the smaller library could not house all the law books that, by law, must be available to inmates. Whoops! To create more space for the law books a few institutions, including CSP-LAC, moved the library to the end of the hall to the largest classroom. But that became a problem because inmates could no longer access the library directly from the yard as mandated, by law. Instead of just walking in, they had to wait for the Education Officer to come and unlock a door and pat them down for drugs and weapons before they could proceed. Another whoops!

Note Guy was right and the inmates usually did know more about what went on than the staff. CDC wasn't going to win this one, the inmate was. The libraries were going to have to move to a larger space, accessible directly from the yard.

Hobbycraft had been in the prisons for eons. With the assistance of a full-time staff member, inmates could purchase, with their own money, a host of craft items from a pre-approved list. They bought leather, wood, beads, ink, paper, paint and they made cards, clocks, belts, jewelry and drew portraits. Most prisons had a store by the visiting area or in the administration building where inmates could sell their stuff to the public or they sold it on the yard to each other.

Hobbycraft in the new prisons was moving to an "in-cell" program only. The inmates could still buy stuff but no longer had a place to work other than their cells. CSP-LAC had four Hobbycraft buildings. Each had a main area with a large, expensive kiln, four large storage rooms, an office and a small classroom. And none of them were going to be used for what they were built for. But wait! I was there, wasn't I? Arts in Corrections needed kilns, storage, water, ventilation and an office from which to supervise. It would have been perfect for me. But no, the Hobbycraft buildings were now the new libraries.

So where was my space? Didn't I get my own building like CSVP? Turned out the "designated" Arts in Corrections' space in these cookie-cutter prisons, was built "behind the wall". "Behind the wall" was the vocational area where inmates worked in programs like Upholstery, Laundry, Mill & Cabinet. In order to get to these workshops, inmates would pass through a gate called "Work Change" where they had to strip down, do the keester squat and be checked for drugs and weapons coming and going. The problem? At CSP-LAC, most of the inmates were "close custody" or Life Without Parole (LWOP's) and were considered a bigger security or flight risk. The problem with that? Close custody inmates couldn't go through work change or behind the wall. In addition, behind the wall only operated during weekday daylight hours. Arts in Corrections was a leisure-time program that was required to offer classes during evenings and weekends, precisely when they were closed down. Brilliant!

All these fancy schmancy new buildings where my classrooms were located, where they could have had all these great vocational programs and inmate jobs and nobody in Sacramento realized they couldn't be used. The state geniuses built AIC areas that couldn't be accessed by most inmates, two vocational areas that could barely be used and remained largely empty, four Hobbycraft buildings that would never be used and four libraries that were too small. Millions and millions of dollars of taxpayer's money were gobbled up because of inadequate planning for intended purposes. Whoops again!

But hey, CCPOA made damn sure they rarely went without a pay increase.

When the space wars ended and the dust settled, I ended up with an original small library room (at least it had direct access from the yard) on both Facilities "A" and "B" - Level III (medium security) yards and classrooms I could borrow, but not occupy, on

Facilities "C" and "D" - Level IV (maximum security). The juggling Bill Cleveland who was back consulting for AIC decried "That's untenable". He thought I was getting screwed and I was, but there wasn't a damn thing to do about.

I ended up with the worst AIC space in the state. I had to run a visual arts program without a sink, storage space or proper ventilation, a band program right next to an educational classroom, a video program without studio space and a theater program with no place to perform. And despite all of those obstacles, we had one of the most prolific, active and high profile programs in the state.

Oh, and my office? It was in the Facility "B" Chapel. It was nice and cozy, a very friendly area. I just couldn't see anyone. It was difficult to supervise inmates who weren't in the same area. I don't think I've ever hired a babysitter for my kids and then told her to watch them from a house halfway down the block, or from another neighborhood altogether. Prison was comedy.

No matter what security level the prison is, minimum, medium or maximum, they all have a minimum yard. That's a requirement. Why? Because minimum-security inmates run the prison. They're the guys that clean the Administration building, serve as clerks to the Procurement officer and other administrative positions, they assist in medical, do laundry for inmates and staff, mow the lawns, paint the buildings, drive staff around in golf carts, cook and serve food in the cafeteria. Oh, and they also go out into the community and clean up the freeways and stuff. Clearly the place doesn't run without them. If you've never been to a prison before, it is an odd thing to get used to all these inmates roaming around in their prison blues in and around the Administration Building. It's kind of like hey? Isn't this a prison and shouldn't these guys be locked up?

The minimum yard is typically located just as you come onto

the prison grounds. There's a Program area with a Sergeant's Office, Hobbycraft area, Library, Chapel, Visiting Room and chow hall. There were also two dorms. Guys in minimum sleep double or triple-bunked in a massive, and very noisy, dormitory. They each have their bunk and a locker. Everything's out in the open.

There is no physical difference between medium and maximum security. The biggest difference is that medium security inmates get to come out at night, whereas maximum-security inmates have to lock up at 3:30p.m. They get to go to dinner but have to stay in the housing unit for the remainder of the evening. Basically, they can't roam around in the dark.

When my medium-security clerk, Clinton, wanted me to "write him up" for something he didn't do, I was confused at first. Clinton was tall with blond Fabio-like hair and loved to talk. He liked heroin, too. I'm not sure if he liked it or needed it, but he was pretty upfront that he did it. Heroin addicts were usually not bad people to hire. Oddly enough most of them were pretty functional, as long as they had their stuff. The agreement I had with Clinton was; "I know you're slamming, but I don't want to know when, I don't want to know where, just do not, do not do it here. Do not have my program shut down with that shit. You do the stuff in here? Bring anything connected with it here? You're done. I call the cops, you lose your job and I make sure you see more time."

I never had a problem with Clinton. He was a good, solid reliable worker. I just didn't understand at first why he was asking me to write a disciplinary report stating that he was smoking in a prohibited area, or said something foul to me or failed to report to work on time. What Clinton was looking for, I came to realize, was a way to keep his points from dropping. An inmate's security level was determined by the number of points he had. Over a period of time his points could drop if he didn't do anything to mess it up. It sounded like a good thing, but apparently that wasn't always the case. And especially not if a guy was going to be released in the near future. Maximum guys loved dropping down to medium because then they got to go out at night. But medium guys didn't always want to drop to minimum despite its' laid back atmosphere and roaming privileges. Clinton wanted to stay in his cell, not move to the dorm.

The typical cell is an eight feet wide, eight feet high, and twelve feet long concrete box. The back wall has a six-inch wide by two-foot long window. Bolted against the wall is a metal desk with a metal seat attached. Bolted to the side are two metal bunks. Each metal slab has about a three-inch thick mattress. On the other side of the room are some shelves, bolted of course and a lovely metal toilet, bolted down as well. And that's where Clinton wanted to stay, in his bolted down cell.

Walking into a housing unit was very intimidating. Unlike a Chaplain or Librarian, it wasn't something I had to do very often. If I did however, I would call ahead to an officer in the Housing Unit to let them know I was coming. Once I walked across the yard (about the size of one and a half football fields) through hundreds of male felons, I'd stand in front of the unit and press a button. Kinda' like ringing the doorbell, so to speak. *Ding! Dong!* "May I come into your big house today officer?"

"Why yes you can Mam'. But I'll need to see your ID first." The guy who just asked for the ID wasn't behind the door. He was in the control booth on the second floor. I could see him looking at me in a mirror positioned over my head. The door would open and I'd step into a long, narrow hallway. Above me I could see the control officer through the glass ceiling. I had to stand in the middle of the hallway and wait for the first door to close so that he could open the second door at the end of the hallway. In prison no two doors were ever to be opened at the same time.

Inside was a vast, open concrete area with several round metal tables with metal seats bolted to the ground, a couple TV's bolted against the wall with an officers' podium in the middle, numerous showers out in the open and a "holding tank" off to the side, which looked like a big human kennel. Along the back walls were two stories of cells.

This oppressive, behemoth structure was a preferable setting for someone like Clinton. The minimum dorms were a place to be feared, a place where all sorts of shit could go wrong. You could end up sleeping next to some guy slammin' shit all night on one side and another jerking off all night on the other. Medium guys doing a short stint on Minimum, feared being messed with just days from being released. They feared that some bozo would stash shit under their bunk to screw with their release date. The dorms were noisy and unpredictable. The cells were controlled and familiar.

I may have pushed the boundaries here and there, failed to mention something here or there, but I never put anything in writing that wasn't the truth as I knew it: even for Clinton.

But I think somebody did.




The truth about child molesters, the bottom feeders, the dung on the tread of your boot, a secret truth that most people don't know, is that child molesters are the best damn workers in the joint. Now, we know they're not the man in the trench coat flashing passersby. They are uncles, janitors, coaches and priests. Children know and trust them. They will go above and beyond to help out a parent, especially a stressed out single parent. One better then that, how about a stressed out single parent with physical, emotional, or financial problems and few resources? Pedophiles create safe, supportive and comfortable situations, which allow them continuous access to children.

But what happens when the child quotient is removed? What happens when the pedophile is in an environment where there are no children? Like prison? To be incarcerated for child molestation was a precarious position to be in. If other inmates knew what Chester (a common term for a child molester) was convicted of, he was in a heap 'o trouble. Shunned, raped or possibly "stuck"(stabbed to death). That's what he had to look forward to.

The likelihood of that happening, however, was pretty slim

because child molesters were usually carted off to a "sensitive needs" yard. (Isn't that a fun, politically correct saying?) They usually housed them there with the snitches and debriefers. (A debriefer is an inmate who disassociates from his former gang and gives staff whatever information they want about that gang; who the players are, what they are planning, where they get their money, the significance of their tattoos, whatever.) There are some inmates however, who would like to kill the inhabitants of a special needs yard; the pedophiles, snitches and debriefers. So, it' was important to protect them. Besides, no officer or investigator wants to lose a good snitch. Hell, they get information out of these guys for years. You definitely want them alive.

As for the pedophiles, most of society wouldn't mind if they mysteriously disappeared. In this day and age however, we answer to a higher power, the ACLU (American Civil Liberties Union). God forbid that a pedophile not be adequately protected. It would be a Warden's nightmare to have the ACLU up his ass. So what 's to be done? You put them all together in the same place where they all have the same problem, namely that someone wants to kill them. Then you hope the old adage "misery loves company" kicks in and they don't turn on each other.

There weren't any signs hanging up proclaiming the area "sensitive needs". Sometimes a yard would become a sensitive needs yard without the majority of staff even knowing it. Inmates would always chew the fat about a certain area becoming a sensitive needs yard. When inmates with suspicious reputations kept ending up on the same yard, one had to wonder.

Every now and then however, a pedophile was found operating on the main line. The only way he could survive there was by making sure the other inmates didn't know what he was really in for. And the only way Chester could be sure he wouldn't be exposed was to never, ever get in trouble. He could not bring any kind of negative attention to himself. For instance, if he were to steal something, be involved with drugs, have a weapon, mouth off to an officer, come on to a teacher, or even smoke where he wasn't allowed... any of these actions would demand that a report be written. The officer, for example, must write up a report but doesn't type it himself. He goes down the hall to the Clerks' Office, where there is a sea of inmate clerks all dressed in pressed blue denim, all waiting to type up what ever his heart desires. He has a clerk type the report. The inmate clerk shares the information with the other clerks. And as the other clerks leave their job at the end of the shift, they tell their cellie what they heard and so on and so forth. Then of course, that report must be filed. So the counselor requests the molester's C-file be sent from the Records Department where it has been quietly sitting, forgotten among four thousand other files for years. It is dusted off and carted in a basket to the appropriate yard, to the appropriate counselor and the little two inch report is put into the actual C-file which obviously contains his entire history. A pedophile's biggest nightmare, however, is that the inmate clerk who works for the counselor could get a glimpse of that file... and Whammo! Cat's outta' the bag!

Consequently, pedophiles rarely got in trouble. They were always punctual, polite, and went above and beyond the call of duty so their supervisor wouldn't look at their C-file and get hip to their heinous deeds.

If I had to choose between a pedophile, a psycho who raped and killed some woman, an idiot who robbed people blind, or an ignorant asshole - I always picked the perv. Pure simple logic. I wasn't fond of the idea of potentially being raped, killed, or beaten by men with "issues" about women, nor of having my shit stolen and sold on the yard for a pack of cigarettes. I had endless art supplies, musical instruments, CD's, videos, knives, cutters, art tools, clay and enough guitar strings to have the entire joint tattooed. An ignorant, asshole criminal could also jeopardize my program in a heart beat just by being rude to custody staff or not being vigilant about checking in tools and brushes after a painting class. Negative attention to the program could have shut us down. The beauty of a pedophile was that he wasn't interested in middle-aged women, he wouldn't steal from me and he wouldn't draw negative attention. In fact, he'd work his ass off to keep me out of his business. That's what I call one hassle-free worker.

Golly, I loved child molesters. The only bad part was that they were hard to find on the main line, a rare commodity indeed.

By the 1960's California prisons grew much of their own food and raised their own livestock. The prisons in Riverside and San Bernardino counties had their own dairy farm, which provided milk for every institution in the state. Most yards had their own garden. Back then being on the Sergeant's Crew was a position coveted by inmates. The pay was crap, but they could barter the fresh tomatoes and lettuce for cigarettes, candy, drugs, sexual favors, whatever. When the CCPOA came to be the behemoth powerhouse that started swinging elections in the 1980's the dairy farms were shut down, the gardens raked out and covered with concrete.

Now, the canteen was the only choice, the only deal in the joint. The prisons were no longer self-sufficient. They were becoming big business, big enough to replace the demise of the defense industry and big enough for businesses to bid for a state contract as a canteen vendor.

At canteen, the mom-and-pop store that was located on every yard, without the mom and pop, inmates did all their purchasing through a window.

"Being at canteen" was a half-day thing. Many an inmate was forgiven for missing a painting or writing class because gosh darnit they were "at canteen". Once an inmate knew his number was up for being in the line that day, he could gage when he needed to be standing there. The annoying thing about the canteen line was that if an inmate wasn't there when his number was called, he was shit-out-of-luck until the next month. If he made it, he filled out an order form for items requested, which were then placed into a plastic bag and charged to his account.

Actual money was not allowed in prison. There was currency in the form of cigarettes, cards, drugs, etc., but other than that, inmates had "accounts". A small percentage of wealthy or highly connected inmates had people on the outside who placed money in their accounts, but the majority of inmates lived on what they made at their job. Average pay for a forty-hour/ week job was $25.00 to $40.00/month. Guys who were making over $50.00 per month were the sought-after skilled plumbers, electricians, etc.

An inmate could easily spend $35.00 of his credited funds at canteen on toiletries. After the occasional splurge on soda or candy there was the all important extra-food-for-the-cell-in-the-event-of-a-lockdown. The higher the security-level, the more important extra food and toiletries became. Old school convicts knew that. They even stocked up on vitamins so they wouldn't get sick since the only toilet available in a lockdown is in the bedroom/cell. Lockdowns were hard on the "fish" (new guys) mainly because of lack of preparation. The key to handling the lockdown was preparation: having the extra food, ample supply of toiletries, books, CD's, socks and underwear.

The sunny side of lockdowns was the respect that *all* the racial groups had for that preparation. If the blacks had a beef with the whites, or vice-versa, and retaliation was in order, then word was put out to "get ready". That meant that it was each inmates' individual responsibility to be prepared to be locked down for a while and they needed to make sure that they had what was needed from the store/canteen before anything came down. An old-school convict knew that he needed lots of Top Ramen, canned shrimp, canned pork, canned tuna, canned anything-you-can-get-your-hands-on-to-make-a-real-meal while locked up in an 8' x 12' container for a couple weeks. The perpetrators of the upcoming incident would always wait for the last one to go to canteen before pulling out any weapons. That was just being respectful, before taking care of business.

That sense of respect also lent itself to pie and pizza sales. The various denominations of Chaplains and inmate activity groups were big on selling food items to the inmates to raise funds for things like a new keyboard, literature or prayer rugs. Inmates ordered their apple pie or pepperoni pizza well in advance and on a designated day, the items were delivered and distributed. Never, ever did an incident occur during a pie or pizza sale. That would have been the epitome of rudeness. No one could have respected a racial group that didn't let some poor slob get his bi-annual cheese pizza before they got busy stabbing each other.

My clerks and I looked out the window above the marine blue book-deposit drop, a remnant of the "space wars" fought early on. We watched the line of inmates picking up their apple or cherry pies and wagered bets on how long it would take to for the whole line of inmates to get their pie in a flimsy box, and get to their cells. It was benign prison gambling that didn't involve the exchange of money or favors, just verbal quips. It was curious fun. Curious, how respected pies were in the joint. Fun, to see how close you could call the timing of weapons being dug out of the ground and thrust into the ribs of an opposing group.

Surely we weren't the only ones that knew this went on, *were we?*

# Zumlarry

He was a typical, northern, urban black guy. At 6'5" tall he had a passive demeanor that belied any ambition. His eyes were fogged with sadness. Fond memories of being a "con-man" were overshadowed by years of drug addiction. Of all the inmates he talked the least and wrote the most. What jumped off of his pages was a unique, quick-witted sense of urban humor. Larry sat behind the left side of the eight-foot long table.

Past the other bodies in prison blues, at the right end of the table, was Zumpano. He had been steeped in the East LA gang life for years and by the two teardrops tattooed just under his left eye, he had served two terms in prison because of it. The guy could hardly read, let alone write. He told his story to a cellie, who "for a price" wrote it up for him. It was written in Spanglish, this East LA dialogue that glided back and forth between English and Spanish as if it were one language. It was a captivating tale of a gangbanger's life salvaged by tragedy. Zumpano's and Larry's work was so impressive, we set out to do a formal table reading of their new screenplays.

This was our first foray into screenwriting at CSP-LAC. In

fact this was the first literary class in all of the state prisons to be offered in this format; as opposed to poetry, prose or playwriting. Being the only prison located in Los Angeles County and close to Hollywood, why not teach them how to write a screenplay? A small group of inmates met with my contract artist Shem every other Saturday for six hours. I met with them for an hour and a half weekly. My job, as their beginning class instructor, was to do the "kitchen work".

"Larry and Zumpano listen up". (By now I referred to everyone by his last name. Hell, I'd been working in prison so long that I called Husband by his last name, even at home.) "Guys... listen up. Put the page number on the bottom right corner. Lookie see, here. This is dialogue. This is a stage direction. Blah blah blah." I was the nuts-and-bolts instructor who explained proper format while doling out reams of paper, pencils and pens. Shem was the program. He not only provided unexpected inspiration, but he also provided connections and had brought us all together at this table.

Shem didn't just bring in professional actors for the guys to hear what their work sounded like being performed, he brought in some Hollywood elite: Esai Morales, a well-known Hispanic film actor, and Peter Berg, who starred in the TV drama *Chicago Hope, The Fight Club* with Brad Pitt and later directed Billy Bob Thornton in the Texas high school, football movie *Friday Night Lights*. Peter's enthusiasm was contagious.

Larry was going to be at CSP-LAC for a few years, but surprisingly Zumpano was preparing to be released. With a lot of nagging and prodding from Shem and me, Susan Hill from Artsreach at UCLA got Zumpano a scholarship at UCLA Extension for screenwriting classes upon his release. Not only that, but Esai Morales was entertaining the notion of working with him on the script Zumpano had written in prison. This was phenomenal!

I didn't know what Zumpano was in for and didn't have time to find out. When he left, so did his C-file. We only knew how he seemed to be turning his life around. Per the Department of Corrections procedure I could only have contact with him about work-related issues. I only knew he was taking the class at UCLA extension in the evenings and working in Century City at an imported rug place. A few months into this experiment however, Zumpano's name on the UCLA roster attracted some unwanted attention. Unbeknownst to me, Shem, Susan Hill, or my boss at the prison, Lynn Harrison, when Zumpano was released from prison he was deported to Mexico. Apparently it didn't take him long to get back across the border because he slipped back into the U.S. just in time for his first class. It sounded scandalous, but wouldn't you? Wouldn't you come back if someone arranged a scholarship at UCLA extension for you? Zumpano probably never finished high school and had some Hollywood actor thinking about getting involved with his screenplay. Wouldn't you get your ass back into the land of opportunity? It made perfect sense to me.

What Sacramento wanted to know was what in the hell, were Susan Hill and I doing lining up a scholarship for a deported felon and citizen of Mexico who returned to the country illegally? Good question. Obviously the parole deportation process was out of our area of expertise.

I think it was more embarrassing for Susan than for me, since she was the one who answered to a board of directors at UCLA and went out on a limb for Zumpano. One thing about the fiery, strawberry-haired New England dynamo; only Susan Hill could have something backfire on her, get her hand slapped, and accept her licks with grace without one ounce of regret. She knew she messed up, but she would have done it again because she felt in every ounce of her being that she was making a difference in someone's' life, someone with undeveloped, raw genius, and it was worth the effort.

Unfortunately, to throw more salt in the wounds, it was only a few days later when Zumpano was in the back seat of a car stopped for a minor traffic violation. I'm guessing that the driver and other passenger(s) looked like him, and the chances of them all not being searched would have been zero. His little teardrops alone would have been "probable cause." That traffic stop proved to be quite fruitful for the cops. Zumpano was a two-time loser and he was packing a small amount of crystal meth. Ba-da-boom! Ba-da-bing! While in county jail he made a few desperate pleas for help to Susan and me, but there was nothing we could do. The law was the law and he screwed up. One two three; he got twenty-five to life. That was the end of the story, end of his opportunity.

Zumpano joined the early ranks of casualties of the Three Strikes law. He didn't get twenty-five to life for stealing "the controversial pizza", but he did become part of the ever-growing statistic of guys locked up under that law for a non-violent third offense. To the public it was "good riddance." But inside, staff was growing weary. We were all growing weary because it wasn't exclusively for violent offenders. Every year there were more and more offenders dumped into the system under that poorly written law. And every year, the officers worried about the growing population that had nothing to lose. If an inmate was doing life on a petty theft with a prior offense (i.e. the guy who stole the pizza) what was his incentive to behave? If he smoked "out of bounds" what were they gonna' do? Lock him up for life? He was already there. If he got into a fight with another inmate, what were they gonna' do? Lock him up for life? Still there. And what if he assaulted a staff member? He was already there, in maximum security, doing life.

Larry chose to reform. Unlike Zumpano, who was still a young man in his twenties and young enough to not recognize his last opportunity, Larry was painfully aware that his age was rapidly climbing upward and his health wasn't the greatest. He was in his early 50's, a lived-a-hard-life guy who used to serve as a lookout while his knucklehead friends would break into people's homes for drug money. At CSP-LAC he spent his last few years honing his writing skills before he paroled into the real world. His points eventually dropped and, for his last year he worked on the minimum yard as my clerk where he had the opportunity to write to his heart's content. And write the gentle giant did. His work was original and funny and I wished him luck when he left.

He left CSP-LAC completely stoked about beginning a career in screenwriting, but plagued with gout and high blood pressure. Even still, he was on a mission; to write, sell, and produce his screenplays while he was still alive. He didn't think he would have a long run of it, so he was in a bit of a hurry.

I kept in contact with Larry while he was on parole and per procedure, I made my supervisor aware that he would only contact me for suggestions for how and with whom he could peddle his work. He contacted me by phone at the prison and said he had landed in San Diego and hooked up with an ambitious group who was wheeling and dealing to the best of its' ability to get one of his films off the ground. I didn't know how he made any money, but he seemed to keep his head afloat.

When he was off parole I agreed to meet him at a restaurant in Los Angeles. I had a proposition. For a couple of years I'd had an idea of a small budget, independent feature that I thought Husband would be great in and I wanted to direct. The only problem was that between work and kids, I couldn't seem to come up with the time to write the thing. I proposed to Larry that I pay him to write a first draft and that any profit that ever came from the actual script, we'd split 50/50.

It was called *Pizza Man*, inspired by news reports in southern California where delivery guys were being held up for their pizzas. I was interested in exploring the relationship between a middle-aged black man and the younger black generation. Husband would be the Pizza Man, an honorable guy trying to make it as a musician or something, but saddled with a wife, kids and bills to pay, doing what it takes to survive including delivering pizza in the evenings. One night he is taken hostage by a gang of young black men. They think he is a middle-aged loser and he sees them as nothing but thugs. Through the course of the evening the Pizza man witnesses the complex world these kids live in and begins to sympathize with their plight. The teenagers begin to see the Pizza Man as a stand-up guy. You know, the hostage feels sympathy for his abductors kind of movie.

I figured it was Larry's cup of tea and it was fun handing him a check in a Hollywood restaurant. Larry was my success story and this was the opportunity that Husband and I had been looking for—something to jump-start his acting career. Prison had been good to the three of us.

# Visiting LWOP

The sentence of Life Without the Possibility of Parole (LWOP) had existed for a long time. It was very clear that an LWOP was never going to be released from prison ever, for any reason. It was a predetermined life sentence. A Fifteen to Life sentence however, meant that after the inmate served his minimum sentence (ideally 15 years) then he would go before the Parole Board who would determine if he was a suitable candidate. It was never shoo-in. If Aunt Sally showed up with pictures of little Suzy's naked body in the perp's basement and wailed over the loss of her only relative, how her life was cut short too soon and the rapist/murderer was enjoying strawberry ice cream and guitar classes, chances were he was going nowhere fast. That inmate could come before the Parole Board every few years, and so would Aunt Sally, and every time the verdict was likely the same. No Parole for that guy. His Fifteen to Life sentence could conceivably leave him to rot in prison for the rest of his life. But he would always have the chance to have his status revisited every few years.

It's important to understand that in the state of California a Fifteen to Life sentence meant that ideally the inmate would serve fifteen years before coming to the Parole Board, but most likely he would find himself looking at Aunt Sally in approximately eight years. It was a nifty thing called "day for day". For every day that an inmate worked he received a day off of his sentence. "Day for day" was critical to the successful operation of the prison system. How else can a facility operate at 190% capacity and not implode? For years and years "day for day" eased the burden of excessive overcrowding in the state prisons. I thought of the whole system as a tall glass of milk that no one ever drank. The glass was the prison, the inmates were the milk, the shiny metal pitcher that kept pouring infinite quantities of milk into the glass was the justice system and the milk that over-flowed out of the glass illustrated the parole system as trying to contain the inmates after they were pushed out. An eight-ounce glass can only hold eight ounces and then somebody has got to go.

Before Bill O'Reilly started to rattle his saber about passing Jessica's Law in every state in the union, there were some pretty terrible people that got popped out of prison because they had done their day for day. (Jessica's Law required a mandatory minimum sentence of 25 years and lifetime electronic monitoring for adults convicted of lewd or lascivious acts against a victim less than 12 years old.) Their minimum sentence requirement was fulfilled and they had been model prisoners during their incarceration. They didn't hit anyone on the head, didn't get busted for drug possession, didn't destroy state property and didn't smoke out of bounds. They were good little boys who didn't have an Aunt Sally crying her eyes out and they were sent on their merry way back into our world.

One such inmate was Richard Allen Davis, the guy that took Polly Klaas from a sleepover in her home and killed her. Richard Allen Davis had no business being let out of prison, but on paper he looked good to go. It was Polly's father, Marc Klaas, who led the bandwagon on the Three Strikes law that Zumpano fell victim to. Ironic that Mr. Klaas himself, in the end, lamented the adoption of the law, believing that, as written, it didn't focus on "violent offenders" but merely "three-time offenders".

When Governor Gray Davis came into Office he decided that

a Life Sentence was a "Life Sentence". There was no longer any distinction between a Fifteen to Life (with the possibility of parole) and a Twenty-Five to Life (with the possibility of parole) and a Life Without Parole sentence. Ole' Gray didn't care that a judge and a jury had used discretion in the sentencing, he was making sure he wouldn't have any "Willie Horton's" in his future political career. (Horton was the convict who ran amok while on furlough, a program supported by Massachusetts Governor Michael Dukakis and widely believed to be responsible for his loss to George H.W. Bush in the 1988 Presidential election.) Despite the fact that there was speculation for years over the legality of Governor Davis' proclamation, lifers were not being released. They were the same as LWOPS except that Lifers still went before the Parole Board every few years, but were always told "No."

It was a curious thing in the late 90's. The LWOP's still couldn't go behind the wall, the Lifers couldn't be released on parole, and the Three Strikes guys (those sentenced to twenty-five years to Life on a third conviction) well, by golly—they were Lifers now, too. Looked like nobody was going home on Level IV and everybody was staying in prison, by gum. Inside, the inmates were not happy, nor was the staff that had to contain them now triple-bunked in gymnasiums and on the housing units' common floor areas.

A juicy Hot Topic that spawned from all this life sentence crap was Family Visits. What were they? They were cool. Taking turns in rotation, an inmate got to have a sleepover with his family in the little bungalow apartments on prison grounds. His whole family could come if he wanted; the wife, kids, siblings, parents or grandparents were allowed. For twenty-four hours they could be one big happy family. The inmate could have sex with his wife in one bedroom while Gramps napped in the other. The kids could watch TV in the living room sitting on the green shag carpet and Brother and Sis' could whip up a home-cooked meal in the little kitchen. It was divine. And naturally the taxpayers didn't mind footing the bill. It was all for the public good. It was important for an inmate to maintain a relationship with his family to ensure that that family would be intact when he/she got out. I was very supportive of that.

What about the guy that didn't have a family? Not everybody had a spouse and kids who still wanted to talk to him after their money was stolen or embezzled. Some parents didn't give a rats' ass what happened to them. What about those inmates? If he didn't have a wife, or only had an ex-wife that he tried to kill, well, that wasn't a problem. He could probably get a new one before his next family-visit rotation.

There was a drop-dead gorgeous white guy with waist-length blond hair locked up in the SHU (Secure Housing Unit) in Soledad where we performed *Think Again, Jackson!* He claimed to have been married seven times, all while incarcerated in California. He didn't have trouble getting a wife. He was just unlucky in love, poor guy. Seven times the state coughed up the funds to provide a clergyman of his selected faith to administer the nuptials so he could get it right in the love department. Surely he knew all seven of them and clearly intended to keep each marriage intact until he would be released one day. Surely he wasn't just paying some hooker a chunk o' money to marry him so he could fuck her brains out in the paid-for-by-the-state family visitation apartment. Surely none of the wives/sluts ever filled up a condom with pure-cut cocaine and stuffed it up her vagina before their family visit, knowing full well that it couldn't be picked up going through the metal detector or during a pat down. Surely there was no benefit in taking a risk like that. And certainly Adonis wouldn't have thought to pull the "balloon" from her vagina, set it aside until the twenty-four hour stay was up and swallow it so that it couldn't be traced in his digestive tract but would handily show up in his feces in a day or two. I couldn't imagine that Adonis would know that the balloon gig wouldn't leave any trace of narcotics in the family visiting apartment, in his wife's blood, or in his, unless of course it burst in his system before it made it to the bowel movement phase. Adonis was way too smart to risk a massive overdose and cardiac arrest for the sake of a drug addiction or, dare I say, trafficking?

Back-in-the-day "Family Visits" used to be called "Conjugal

Visits". According to Webster's: "conjugal" is an adverb meaning "relating to marriage, belonging to marriage or the relationship between husband and wife". It must have been hard to continue to call them "conjugal" visits when the whole damn family or a string of mail-order brides showed up, so they changed the name. Ironically, the "Family Visitation" program accommodated the Pelican Bay inmate that was adopted in his late-thirties by an attorney couple in the San Francisco area. The threesome's huge exotic dog attacked and killed a lesbian in their apartment building. He obviously really needed a "family" and that wouldn't have qualified under the old definition of "conjugal".

Nope there weren't any problems with family visits, including any need to supervise or require birth control. Just because a guy couldn't physically and financially support a child conceived in the family visitation apartment didn't affect the privilege. The state could help support those children too. There was welfare, food stamps, public education and the local hospital emergency room if the child got sick with a cold. There was nothing to worry about and there was plenty of money for everything and everyone.

Under Gray Davis' regime, the only conundrum of family visits became who got to continue to have them? LWOP's never qualified because they were never getting out, so there was no protest about that. But now that Lifers and Three-Strikers were no longer going to be paroled per the Governor, there was talk that they too, might lose the privilege of family visits. Believe me, inmates weren't happy about that. Nobody cared that they no longer retained the right to vote, even when released from prison. That was meaningless. But take away family visits? Hell no!

To this day I don't believe Gray Davis had the authority to refuse parole across the board to all lifers. In addition, in my opinion, lifers who qualify should be able to retain family visits with a pre-existing spouse and their children, but not the whole damn family nor with one created by the prison chaplain with taxpayer funded children conceived in a family visitation apartment surrounded by razor wire.

Political correctness was running amuck. What would happen, theoretically, if gay marriage was given the green light in California, and not that I think it shouldn't, but what would happen in the prisons? Would the ACLU jump in and defend the inmates' right to marry the same sex? And if a male inmate could marry another man from the outside world, why couldn't he just marry another inmate and they could be permanent cellies? What about the racial thing? For safety's sake they never bunked a white guy and a black guy in the same cell, but if they were married, would they be required to? I would think that the CDC would have to come up with extra money to provide extra security for all the lovebirds.

I would also think since every incarcerated individual has a constitutionally guaranteed right to marry, including LWOPs who can never have a family visit nor officially consummate the marriage, the state will eventually have to come up with surrogate mothers or sperm donors for the incarcerated. Lyle and Erik Menendez shot their parents, reloaded and shot again. They have both been married in prison. They could still make great dads.

There was always money to afford everything and I couldn't imagine that they would ever take away any existing educational or arts programming, even when a 35% pay increase for CCPOA was approved by the Governor to ostensibly handle all the growing chaos along with supporting his re-election bid. All I knew was that there was beginning to be a lot of chatter in the joint.

# "Shakespeare Goes to Prison"

by
Steve Hayes

AMERICAN THEATRE MAGAZINE

*"Feb. 10: Joe Haj is nervous. It's the first day of rehearsal for the first full show he's ever directed." "Feb. 10 marks another first: Shakespeare performed by inmates, for inmates, inside."*

Husband established a video program as an Artist-in-Residence at CSP-LAC, like he did in Chuckawalla. When a young American actor of Palestinian descent, Joe Haj, approached me about doing Shakespeare's play *Henry V* at CSP-LAC, frankly, I was skeptical. *Why? What's the point of doing Shakespeare here? It could turn out to be humiliating for the inmates.* But it didn't take long for Joe's enthusiasm and impressive resume to win me over. I helped him write a short-term Artist-in-Residence grant. Husband was going to videotape not only the performance, but rehearsals and interviews as well because Joe wanted to make a documentary afterwards.

It was a big to-do! Joe Haj had never worked in prison before. He came in like it was a non-equity playhouse in the Hollywood Hills, clueless about the amount of coerciveness that went into getting the Warden to sign off on a project like this. He didn't understand that drumming up twelve or more inmates to perform in a Shakespeare play was no simple task. Acquiring use of the Chapel for performances was lost on him and I don't think he understood how difficult it was to get permission for the *LA Weekly* and *American Theatre* magazine to come inside multiple times to cover the story. I also acquired permission to take a state-owned five-ton truck, gas it, and drive it to Blythe and back to retrieve the nifty, portable stage set-up designed by Joe McGrath. Since the new IAF at CVSP was a visual artist it was languishing in the dust.

Haj didn't understand the cajoling and flirting I had to do with the Program Sergeant, Lieutenant and Captain to allow the inmates to bring their sack lunches and rehearse through lunchtime and how I practically had to sign over my first-born to ensure that this old guy Sal wouldn't use the play as an opportunity to escape.

Sal was an itty-bitty white guy in his sixties. He always had a big smile and an unlit cigar in his hand, but he ran every day. He was an unlikely character to be found in prison. He was of Italian descent, an old-time crooner and could bust out any tune you could think of. Before coming to prison, he owned a bar and played the piano in it in the Palm Springs area. The story I heard was that one night some teenagers practically ran him and his grandchildren off the freeway. He brought the grandkids home, jumped back onto the freeway, caught up to the car that tried to run him off and gave them a taste of their own medicine. He gave them a little nudge with his vehicle and off they went flying, resulting in the death of a teenager. I think alcohol was a factor. Prior to that fateful night, Sal had lived his life without a traffic ticket. Consequently he was considered "Close Custody," who like the LWOPs weren't allowed to be out in the evening like the other Level III inmates. Somehow I convinced the chain of command that it would all be a-o-kay for sweet Sal to come out for performances only. The significance of that however, was lost on Joe.

Joe was also miffed because he viewed my minimal presence at his weekend rehearsals as a sign of disinterest. Rather than enjoying my trust, he commented that my "training for the marathon seemed more important" than his rehearsals. And yes, quite frankly, it was. I loved my job at prison, but I also had a family and a life outside that happened to encompass training for another go in the LA marathon.

In the end however, Joe's production was quite an achievement, and it was due to his persistence and professionalism. Despite our different approach to the project, he began to see my point of view as an administrator. I also admired his determination and ability to put himself forth as a positive role model. The inmates never sang anything but the man's praises.

And Sal? In the middle of the performance series he was transferred to Facility "A". Naturally we didn't want to lose him for the last couple of shows, so I arranged for him to be brought over from Facility "A" back to Facility "B" each night. The only problem was that inmates never casually move from one facility to another and the first night that Close-Custody-Sal started to walk the hundred yards in between the two gates, the officers in Control thought he might be escaping. Poor Sal, like McMurtry and Watts who didn't want to get beat up over a play, Sal didn't want to get shot for doing Shakespeare.

I was very proud of this project. Receipt of the grant was a coup in itself, with an inexperienced-in-prison artist, a grueling trip to Blythe and back, a challenging rehearsal schedule using a huge cast of prison inmates, set-up and performances, we had, literally, pulled off the impossible.

I was quoted in *American Theatre* magazine: "The CDC experience is hurry up and wait," says AIC artist coordinator Leah Joki. "There's an elaborate approval process for everything: You can't get a key without an act of Congress." MUGsie (our Most Unhappy Gal in Sacramento) was now the director of Arts in Corrections. The Nordic-sweater guy, Jim Carlson, had hung up his political gloves, gone back to being an Artist Facilitator at Folsom and left the reins to her, his former assistant. MUGsie didn't like those comments. Or maybe some suit in Sacramento didn't like them and she was just the messenger. Somebody in Sacramento actually said I should be fired. Whatever the case, for a brief moment, my job appeared to be on the line again.

Unlike Carlson in the past, MUGsie certainly wasn't flying to my defense. It was the CSP-LAC Warden, Ernest Roe, who had my back. Mr. Roe was a very affable, portly black man who came up through the unlikely route of Education as opposed to Custody. He didn't understand why Sacramento's feathers were ruffled by prison being about "hurry up and wait". That was a military statement and we were working in a paramilitary organization. And instead of being offended with "you can't get a key without an act of Congress," he thought it was not only accurate but highlighted his staff being concerned and proactive about security. He liked the notion that we didn't just hand keys out to anyone. Those were all good things according to Mr. Roe. He'd signed off on everything we requested for the project. He liked the positive press coverage and essentially told MUGsie and her higher-ups to waste their breath on something more meaningful.

He didn't actually say that, but I wished he would have. Mr. Roe had more class than that. I, on the other hand was still a Butte girl and in the land of Evel Knievel, we enjoyed when peoples asses were righteously kicked.

# Jewish in Jail

I always thought Rabbis had the most kickback job in prison because their clientele was so sparse. The Christians and the Muslims packed the house, but not the Jews. Inmate Goldberg was fair-skinned with brown hair, blue eyes and a hoarse voice. He had spent some time at the Sierra Conservation Center (SCC) in Jamestown where he learned to paint and draw from Stacey Hay, the Artist Facilitator, and had fond memories of that well-established AIC program and it's abundant studio space, as opposed to our one classroom with minimal equipment and supplies. He was an admitted addict who used to break into peoples' homes to fuel his drug of choice, whatever that was. Although he was first and foremost a visual artist, he was in the production of *Henry V*. After that I moved him over to Facility "A" and retained him as a worker for a short stint. He had done the posters for *Henry V* and was doing them for my original play that I was directing on Facility "B", *The Big Picture*.

Goldberg' points were rapidly dropping as he got closer and closer to being released and we came up with the Big Idea. Why not let his points drop so that when he moved to the Minimum Facility, he could run our new space in the former Hobbycraft area. Goldberg could work as my clerk, set up the space and by golly, I could write him an Artist-in-Residence grant as well. Snap. I believe there had been only two other inmates in the state that had written grants as participants and gotten funded. Goldberg' idea was keen. During his eleven-month grant he would create four huge paintings of outer space as discovered by NASA's Hubble Telescope. A painting would be placed in each of the four visiting areas of the prison: Facility "A", "B" "C" and "D" respectively. The theme would embody the notion that although prisoners were the microcosm of the macrocosm, they too were a part of the larger universe as well. It was kind of a touchy, feely proposal but the practical side brought a 4' x 6' painting to each visiting room in front of which inmates had pictures with their wives and kids taken. It was a win-win deal.

As an inmate, Goldberg couldn't pocket a cool $1300/month like the normal AIR awardees, but he could get $50.00/month plus the maximum amount of supply money. For an inmate that was no chump change. We wrote it and it was funded. CSP-LAC was awarded one of the first inmate grants in the state of California in a very long time. For some reason, however, MUGsie wasn't happy about it. She thought maybe it wasn't legal, despite the fact that precedent had been set years earlier. She didn't like the attention that it brought. She didn't like attention at all. Unlike the old days when we were encouraged to get as much positive press as possible, she preferred we stayed off the public radar. MUGsie thought it was best if the public didn't know we existed.

At first MUGsie was merely malcontent in Sacramento, but then she buried my colleagues and me under a mountain of paperwork. Personally, I always liked MUGsie, but she worried me from the get-go as a Director. She didn't have the political prowess of Jim Carlson or the chutzpah of Bill Cleveland. No, MUGsie needed to know everything. MUGsie needed to ensure that every move we made was approved, that every twist and turn taken inside would be documented. Every hiccup was to be accounted for and reported to her. It would have been kinder to stuff a ten-page quarterly report in our mouths, tape them shut with clear packing tape and watch us all suffocate in the corner with our eyes bulging out of our heads. That demise would have been more humane than her chosen one; solve everything with paper. Paper. Paper. Paper. And this was just the beginning.

For a minute it looked like Goldberg' harmless space painting grant was going to fall prey to MUGsie's paranoia, but somehow it miraculously survived.

Not only did his grant survive, so did his ability to assist me in launching the first Annual Inmate Art Sale at CSP-LAC. I had always wanted to do an art sale like the Artist Facilitator at Deuel Vocational Institute (DVI) in Tracy, CA. I had toyed with the idea but unfortunately it only came to fruition by means of a tragedy. Husband was working late one night at the prison. I had given him explicit directions to call the guitar teacher, Brad Bailey, whom I had not been able to reach in weeks. Husband dutifully made the call, and got Brad's wife at home. She had just returned from his funeral. Brad had been killed in a car accident. Brad had long rock and roll hair and looked like a musician, but was aging and lived in a middle-class neighborhood with a parrot and suburban furniture. Brad was an excellent teacher, the inmates loved him, and upon his death, Goldberg and I set out to have an art sale that would benefit the Brad Bailey Foundation; established in his honor by his wife Lena. The foundation would provide professional music instruction to kids who couldn't afford lessons in the Lancaster/Palmdale area.

I visited Steve Emrick, the Artist Facilitator in Tracy, to learn firsthand how he operated his art sales. He was mild mannered, articulate and an amazing wood worker. He made beautiful, fine furniture. Steve and I discovered that we were on the same page about MUGsie: baffled.

As Goldberg painted merrily away, into our lives stumbled an unpredictable and crazy female Sergeant. From a distance she almost looked pleasant. She was short, heavy-set and wouldn't have been the first black woman to not like the likes of me. She didn't think that Goldberg should be able to work without direct supervision, despite the fact that his position had been set up to do so.

The chaplains' clerks worked that way, as they too, couldn't possibly be on five yards at the same time. In addition, Crazy Woman didn't appear to like Jews. A gorgeous, charcoal drawing of a young Jewish girl in the Holocaust wearing an armband with the star of David mysteriously had a pencil thrust through it, and things came up missing in the studio.

Goldberg wasn't her only target. Since I didn't have a key to the front gate yet, Crazy Woman would see me there and make me wait twenty to thirty minutes before she got off her fat ass and buzzed it open.

Goldberg began to tell stories of how she, without witnesses, ranted and raved about the Jews, threw things around and repeatedly threw him out of his workspace.

"Boss... I don't know if I can take it anymore." Crazy Woman had brought a grown man to tears. The guy was just months away from being released and I believed that this half-drunk nutcase was trying to make him snap before he got on the bus.

Her antics had been consistently reported to my supervisor. Numerous times Lynn came to the Minimum Yard to reiterate to Crazy Woman that Goldberg did indeed have permission to work without my direct supervision. In a meeting with the Custody Captain, an attempt to resolve our "problems", Crazy Woman pulled out all stops and announced that I, Leah Joki, was having an "inappropriate relationship" with inmate Goldberg. Of course this was said in my absence with no way to defend myself. Lynn immediately called me at home on my day off. "You're not going to believe this," and described the context of the meeting and advised me. "You need to respond to this accusation, in writing, and bring it with you tomorrow along with any documentation you have on her."

Crazy Woman didn't succeed in getting very far with accusations that normally would have resulted in me being walked off grounds and put on administrative leave without pay, pending investigation. Her allegation that I was having an affair with Goldberg was so ludicrous, that after the Warden saw the documentation both Goldberg and I had been keeping, it was readily dismissed.

She remained on the yard however, until Goldberg got on the bus. And it was not without incident. She followed him on the vehicle yelling "Jew this, Jew that" and this time there were many witnesses. It wasn't long after Goldberg was released that Crazy Woman was removed from her position on the Minimum Yard and was hidden on 1st Watch, the 11:00p.m.to 7:00a.m. shift. For weeks I always checked my rearview mirror to make sure she wasn't following me home.

Goldberg was so traumatized that when he was paroled, he contacted the Anti-Defamation League (ADL), and informed me of his complaint. Being the loyal employee that I was, I advised Warden Roe to respond quickly to anything from the ADL. I sympathized with and respected Goldberg, but I knew that the ADL wasn't the type of organization that CSP-LAC needed on its back nor did the institution need that kind of press.

That first year we made about five hundred dollars at the Inmate Art Sale with the proceeds going to the Brad Bailey Foundation. Goldberg was very disappointed with the staffs' reluctance to pay more than a few bucks for a piece of original artwork. That year I began my own collection. I bought several of Goldberg' paintings. One piece was part of a triptych: three paintings of a similar theme. Each painting featured a female standing in a ring of fire. I kept one for myself, the housewife about to launch a cake at someone, and gave the other two to my best friends. They had to agree to never give them away but they could always give them back. To my friend Ashley in New York, married for a second time with three boys, I gave the wife carrying a platter with a man's head on it. I thought she and her second husband would get a kick out of it. And to my career-oriented friend Jean who once sacrificed her underwire bra to see a prison play, I gave the woman in a suit holding a briefcase in one hand and a chainsaw in the other. I loved Goldberg' sense of humor in his artwork.

Shortly after getting out of a halfway house, Goldberg landed in the San Francisco bay area with dreams of being a professional artist. He was smart enough however, to recognize first things first. He started a small business cleaning houses. He said that it was only fair that after all the years he robbed peoples houses for drug money, that he should have to clean them for a while.

Goldberg is a success story. He stayed out and stayed clean for at least ten years. The last contact I had with him, he sent an email that read: "Hey Boss... could you use some Santas? I came across a bunch and have no use for them."

What was a Jewish guy going to do with Santas?

# Movie Stars in the Joint

Guys in prison had tattoos. They contained visual information about an inmate, information that scrolled down the back of his neck, across his heaving chest, around his bulging biceps and down his over-developed calf. If one looked across the yard on a hot day when inmates relaxing outside would take their shirts off, one would see images from Dungeons & Dragons, gang insignia, low-rider cars, inspirational jargon in a foreign language, mementos of lost loves or deceased relatives and naked women. There were naked women with large breasts, naked women with large breasts and wings, naked women with large breasts in low riders, naked women with large breasts riding giant birds and naked women with large breasts hugging other naked women with even larger breasts.

One can easily spot a prison tattoo by the absence of color. Colored ink is next to impossible to come by there. Hell, black and blue ink was hard to get. Most of the ink came from inmates who ordered stuff through Hobbycraft, Education programs or me. I intentionally kept the purchase of ink to a minimum for that reason. It was hard enough to account for the snippets of a guitar's E-string, which they snapped into a Bic pen with a battery to make the tattoo. Who wanted to worry about monitoring large quantities of ink? Who needed that headache?

Once they got all the equipment however, the question was where did they do it? Most prison tattoos were done in a corner where no one was looking, in the bathroom or out on the weight pile where no one from any distance could tell what was going on.

The newer prisons eliminated dark corners to lurk in out of their design and the weight pile eventually became a thing of the past. That was a sad day when the weight pile was taken away. The public had grown weary of the image of inmates coming out of prison all buff and strong and then attacking people. So when they took out the weight piles, the CDC made it look like a great PR campaign. Like they were keeping the public safe from super-fit, super-strong parolees. Most prison staff knew however, that the inmates who utilized the weight pile weren't the ones they typically had problems with. Not having the weight pile as an outlet wasn't worth the politically correct trade-off. But the CCPOA was down with that. That weight pile was one less activity that an inmate could keep himself occupied with. And if the inmates weren't occupied? Well, they tended to get idle, then restless and then violent. The CCPOA, in my opinion, had a financial interest in keeping the prisons violent. How else could they justify an enormous pay increase?

One inmate had a unique tattoo on the back of his shaved head. In bold, chunky black letters it stated "FUCK YOU", rude, but clever. I could imagine the inmate with his hair grown out, clean cut and no tattoo visible, working for an insurance company. When the boss required him to do something he didn't feel like doing, I imagined he'd come into work the next day with his head shaved. He'd tell the boss he was quitting for a better job, shake his hand and walk out with a swagger and "FUCK YOU" printed on the back of his head. I wanted one of those. It could come in handy in so many ways. It'd be just my luck however, to end up losing my hair in my old age and there'd I'd be in a nursing home with "FUCK YOU" tattooed on the back of my head. That wouldn't be right.

* * *

There were different kinds of movie stars in the joint. The first variety was inmates who were in a successful play at the prison. It was so mind blowing for other inmates and staff to see these guys on stage that the inmate actors were like rock stars for a week or two. My favorite tattooed guy, Alex, was one of them. He had Hollywood good looks with Edward James Olmos' bad skin. Alex had never been in a play, nor was he involved with the AIC program before. He used to steal old ladies' purses in the parking lot of the Ralph's grocery store not far from where I lived. He had a large swastika tattooed on his bicep and yet he enjoyed the comradery of the other actors, some of whom were black and Hispanic. This was the first time that he had hung around with a multi-racial group. He was my favorite tattooed guy because by the end of the rehearsal period I noticed that the swastika had been covered over with a solid, black band permanently tattooed on. Score. Good for him, for coming around.

I had written and was directing a play called *The Big Picture*, about an inmate who went to prison because of a drug problem. It began with the inmate sitting on a toilet waiting for the stash of drugs he swallowed from a visitor, to come out in his feces. The play unfolded backward in time, working its way through the main character's life before he was in prison, and ending with the first time he tried cocaine. Shorty, an inmate who had been in Joe Haj's Shakespeare play, was the star. Shorty was a natural. This guy had unbelievable comic timing, professional demeanor and embodied the spirit of a likeable fool. Alex played numerous characters, each one completely different from the other and all flawlessly executed. I had butted heads with one inmate in the play and replaced him with a professional actor, Preston Maybank. He was contracted by Artsreach and joined us with only a few days of rehearsal left. Preston brought the play to a whole new level. The command of his voice and movements were a delight to watch, but what blew the inmates away was that he was able to memorize his lines in three days. Preston was a rock star too, for a couple of days.

An Artsreach staff member, Sheila, came to visit. She was the beautiful black actress that toured with us doing *Think Again, Jackson!* Now she was working for Artsreach and was concerned. By illustrating how the inmate in the play got drugs into prison, she wondered if we were exposing them to manners of trafficking they didn't know about. I really had to laugh at that one. The inmates knew how guys brought their drugs in. They informed me, not the other way around. I considered her observation and chose not to change anything. I understood that she was just doing her job and part of that job was to seek out anything that could be problematic in the public eye. We agreed to disagree.

*The Big Picture* was one of the most gratifying experiences I had in prison. I had never seen a group of inmates work so cohesively together. Not just the actors, but also those who wrote and performed music, painted the backdrops, built props and changed the set were functioning as a unit with the same goal in mind; to do the best job they could. Driving with handsome and funny Preston, I was struck by his melodious voice and high energy level. He was flabbergasted by my 240 lb., hairy-chested lover. He couldn't believe how much I loved prison. "You're like a mayor in there, like a politician. It's amazing to watch you navigate through that place." Preston was the only "movie star" that made me feel like I wasn't a failure for working in prison, what with that Juilliard training and all.

Months after the play was over I spotted Alex walking in front of the Program building. "Hey Alex," I yelled. "Where you been? Long time, no see."

He glanced over his shoulder, then down at the ground and

quietly said "Miss Joki, can I talk to you in private?"

"Sure." I led him to my office and told him I was surprised we hadn't seen him at all.

Quickly he interjected, "Miss Joki, I can't come around here anymore. Some guys noticed that I covered my tag and threatened me if I hung around with the Arts in Corrections people."

"What?"

"Miss Joki, I've only got a couple of months left. I just want to do my time in peace and get outta' here."

"You want me to talk to someone? You want me to tell the Sergeant?"

"Noooo, please. Please. I just want to get outta' here. I don't want any problems. Miss Joki, I really need to go. I really do." He walked to the door and before he opened it he turned and said "Thanks Miss Joki. I really enjoyed doin' the play. I've never done anything like that before."

"You did good. You're a good actor. You might wanna' give it a whirl when you get out."

He smiled. "I might. Okay.... uhhh...thanks. I gotta' go."

That was the end of that person in my life. It made me cry, but it was a mini-success story. Man, I loved prison that day.

Another kind of movie star in the joint was the professional actor who usually performed in the formal reading of that year's winning screenplay. To win became a coveted achievement for an inmate; to have his full-length screenplay read and critiqued by "real" actors he might've seen on TV. Actors Brent Jennings, Deborah Van Valkenberg, up and coming star Samantha Mathis, Noah Wylie of ER fame, and screen writer Michael Goldenberg were some of those who came to CSP-LAC. For months I had a clearance for Dermot Mulroney, but alas he never made it. Boo Hoo. Chicks, even middle-aged chicks like me, swooned over Mr. Mulroney.

In order for the movie stars to obtain a "clearance" (signed confirmation that nothing in their past prohibited them from entering prison grounds based on a background check) I first had to gather their vital, personal information: Name (as it appeared on their driver's license), date of birth, driver's license number with expiration date, and Social Security number. I reveled in the fact that I had some very wealthy, very famous peoples' information at my fingertips with which I could wreak a whole bunch of havoc if they were haughty. I envisioned taking money from their overstuffed coffers and transferring it into the 401K that I didn't have. Or if they were going to be so-overly-impressed-with-themselves, I fantasized slipping their social security number to an inmate and letting him have at it.

In reality however, I went to extreme measures to protect their vital information. All of those files were kept in a locked cabinet in my office. The key to that locked file cabinet was in my desk, which was also locked. The key to my desk was on the same key ring as the key to my office door in the Chapel corridor, which was locked as well. Those keys (when not on my person) were kept locked up in the Control Room and were only allowed to be checked out by me which I did by handing over a metal chit, with my last name engraved on it, to an officer behind bullet-proof glass. And that didn't take into account the series of gates I had to pass through to get to the Control Room to get the goddamn keys. All that nifty info was locked up pretty darn tight.

The bigger and more competitive the screenwriting program became at CSP-LAC the more "stars" got cleared to come inside and play for a day. All of the Hollywood connections came through Carl. He had a knack for hitting people up at Hollywood parties and goading them into working with us. The more famous people that walked through the gate, the more credibility our program had. Name recognition was a powerful tool in the joint as well. Officers were always nicer when we traipsed onto the yard with someone they recognized from TV.

An unknown actor, however, didn't always get the kid-glove

treatment. Once I hired a Hispanic actor whose clearance didn't come through in time for the reading, so I wrote the standard memo requesting that he be allowed to come in for one day only and that he would remain under my constant supervision. Occasionally when things got backed up in the Records Department, my supervisor would ask the Warden to sign off on letting someone in without a clearance. Typically it was for someone that we could vouch for and felt confident that there wasn't something in their past that would prove problematic. Since Husband knew this guy, he was approved to come in for the day. The actor rode with me for an hour and a half to get to the institution and when we arrived at the Pedestrian Gate early that Saturday morning, his clearance paperwork had just come through. Unbeknownst to him, there was a warrant for his arrest. He'd been cited for jaywalking in downtown Los Angeles years ago and apparently had neglected to pay the ticket. He wasn't a famous actor and jaywalking was such a violent crime that threatened the public safety that the Sergeant at the Ped. Gate gave him the option to either be arrested then and there or to leave the grounds. He chose to leave. We left him at a Denny's restaurant where he sat for eight hours as the rest of us did a formal reading of inmate screenplays. Poor guy, had he been Charlie Sheen, I bet the Sergeant would have winked and let him go through with the memo signed by the Warden.

Whatever inmate won the screenwriting competition became the rock star to the movie stars. There was so much attention given to the author of the winning script it was amazing that the inmate didn't just float out of the place like a hot air balloon. One year, inmate Bly won the competition. It was a bit of an upset because Bly was on Facility "B" and the dominant writers were typically on Facility "D". That year Shem brought along this Dutch producer-guy. The script was innocuous yet full of brilliant moments. After the reading I was off for Christmas vacation.

Upon my return, I was told, the Dutch producer-guy "bought" Bly's screenplay. Misinformation #1: Dutch producer-guy "optioned" it. There's a big difference between buying a script and optioning it. He agreed to pay inmate Bly a small amount of money to retain exclusive rights to it for a designated amount of time, usually one year. Within that time frame a producer would attempt to gather enough interest in the project to acquire enough financing to go into production. By the end of the year, if nothing was happening with the script, the option would either expire or producer-guy could negotiate an extension.

MUGsie had a new boss in Sacramento, the new Director of Community Resources, who was supposed to be our savior. Miss B. was the ex-wife of a Los Angeles Councilman, Richard Alatorre. He had taken a tumble in the press, cocaine and corruption charges, but was still beloved in the Hispanic community. She was also one of the head honchos at Blue Cross/Blue Shield. She didn't know anything about an arts program, but she had very nice shoulder pads, blonde hair and red lips. *Why would she want to work as the Director of Community Resources for the Department of Corrections?*

She and MUGsie had their panties all tied up in a knot over the Bly script. It was nothing that I anticipated or approved, but Dutch producer-guy didn't do anything wrong. He simply used Bly's address on the front page of the script to contact him. It's not a crime to write to an inmate, anyone can do it. Under the "Son-of-Sam" law, however, an inmate was forbidden from profiting from his crime, so I had to make sure that Bly's screenplay was not based on his conviction(s).

Bly was an intelligent guy, impressed with his own intellectual capacity. He was a slight, white guy proud of his German heritage and a real film buff. I never knew whether Bly was wrongfully convicted or a psychopath. Reading his C-file, ironically, wasn't much help.

Bly had been living in a guesthouse in a mansion district in Los Angeles. Unbeknownst to him, the owner of the property was involved in some pretty shady financial transactions. He told Bly that he feared for his life and was leaving the country. He asked him to pick up some dry cleaning prior to his departure. None of this had anything to do with the script he wrote so I read on, something about a body in the homeowner's trunk that he either showed Bly or got him to help him dump. I couldn't understand why the police weren't called but then again, what did it matter? None of this had anything to do with the humorous script he wrote. I read on. Bly dropped him off at LAX.

Next Bly was being arrested for his murder. Someone had found a body in the mountains with no head (meaning no dental records), no hands (no fingerprints) and no feet. What the body did have was a piece of clothing with the dry cleaning tags on it, the dry cleaning that Bly was asked to pick up. It kind of looked like Bly was set-up, but who knows?

There was nothing in Bly's C-file that was even remotely connected to the script he wrote. Case closed, I thought. He owned it and had the right to sell it. And since it was "optioned" for a nominal fee, why not let it go without attracting a lot of attention?

But MUGsie and Miss B. couldn't stop there. Just the thought of an inmate potentially making a million dollars on a screenplay made Sacramento nuts. I needed to be brought to task for this. I, again, probably should be fired. Once again it was "back off" from the Warden. All Shem and I did was teach the guy how to write. We weren't optioning his script. Dutch producer-guy wasn't my contract artist. I didn't pay him to work for me. He was a guest, a volunteer who acted independently outside of my or CDC's view. Hell, it wasn't the first time that someone on the outside put money on an inmates' account in exchange for something! Fortunately, common sense had ruled.

Bly had his fifteen minutes of fame and that was that.

The worst kind of movie star in the joint was the one who had more than one shot of fifteen minutes of fame, and directly impacted my program. Enter Richard Speck. He was famous for killing a bunch of nurses in the Chicago area. He was incarcerated for years until he died in 1991. In 1996 however, this videotape surfaced. Speck was seen performing oral sex on another inmate and snorting cocaine. He proclaimed "if only they knew how much fun I was having, they'd turn me loose." On top of that Speck paraded around with female-like breasts, a by-product of smuggled hormones. They looked so much like women's breasts that most networks blurred his nipples out on the broadcast. The real kicker however was when an off-camera inmate asked "why did you kill the nurses?"

He smiled and replied, "It just wasn't their night!" Disgusting.

Knock, knock they came to my Arts in Corrections door. The custody staff was there to confiscate all of our video and editing equipment. Richard Speck's parade from the dead in the mid-west had Sacramento in a tailspin. They gathered up staff member's recording equipment so fast it was like a fire blazing through the sterile halls of prison administration buildings. No one knew what hit him. I didn't hand anything over without a Warden's signature. Husband and I had worked for years establishing a video program. We put together a top-notch editing system and had guys learning all the basics of video production. And not once, had we had a problem with inappropriate material being filmed with our equipment. It just didn't seem right that demented Richard Speck should have the final say on years of our accomplishments in that medium. *Fuck you Richard Speck. I ain't going down because of your sick ass.* And I didn't. Despite Sacramento's edict to hand all recording devices over to custody, we prevailed at CSP-LAC. But there were only a handful of us, the rest crumbled. *As if custody knew how to monitor the recording and editing of videotape. Right!*

# The "C" Files

Overcome with fatigue, I sat in the Records Department reading files of prospective inmate clerks. They all checked out, nothing I couldn't work with. *Surely there must be something more titillating than this. This is a maximum security prison for chrissakes.* I was overcome with curiosity and I handed the woman a list of names and numbers of students that I was curious about. She returned with three bulky, over-stuffed files. My eyes twinkled because, you see, in prison size mattered. *What a dandy way to work through a lockdown! What a cool job!*

**FILE #1.** I don't know if it was just beyond the edge of the woods, but it was certainly beyond the edge of comprehension. C-101 wasn't a typical inmate. He was like a west coast Kennedy. Chiseled face, six pack abs, an impressive stock portfolio and family political connections. He was the epitome of a northern California guy; resided in Marin County, attended the University of California at Berkley. What would have motivated him?

At one point C-101 was rooming with a less than desirable guy, a real troublemaker, bad news waiting to happen. In an odd twist of events, however, nice-guy 101 turned out to be more frightening than the roommate.

Mr. Roommate had some problems. He drank heavily, did drugs and tended to steal things he thought he needed, but didn't have money for. C-101 tolerated him as best he could and might have kept his distance, but clearly it wasn't far enough.

Mr. Roommate had a brilliant idea one day. He sat 101 down and laid out his extraordinary plan, the scheme of all schemes, the plot of all plots, a perfectly infallible course of action. 101 apparently had a very good friend, his best friend. At least the guy was one of his best friends at college and someone he'd known since elementary school. As it turns out, the parents of Friend were pretty well off and Roommate thought it would be grand if they pretended to kidnap Friend and get the parents to cough up some dough. In fact, in this-oh-so-grand scheme, the Friend wouldn't even know he was being kidnapped. This was to be a benign kidnapping.

I completely understand the allure of impromptu kidnappings. I remember in grade school that my friends and I snatched Laury, the smallest and weakest amongst us, against her will, rolled her up in a blanket, carried her across the street to the nun's Convent, pressed the doorbell and ran. As kids we thoroughly enjoyed our improvisational abductions. Who knows? Maybe I could have been suckered by Roommate, too. I once lured the actor Evan Handler into a room at the Juilliard School and my friend Gerald and I tied him to a chair and interrogated him as the Lobster Man. I think we kept him for about an hour. But, we were actors working on a scene from a Sam Shepherd play and having fun. We weren't extorting money from anyone.

I would have thought that 101, being the level-headed, smart guy that he was, would have detected something wrong about the scenario. But he did not. Maybe I too, would have been sickly humored by getting a friend drunk, calling the parents and asking for money, if I honestly believed it was a joke. I could see myself at college age at the other end of a phone sounding like a TelaTubby. "Pleazzzzze, Mommy and Daddy of my cute hostage, pleazzzzzzzzze. We need money for beer, we have no shoes, we have no candy on the weekend, and oh we must do our own laundry. Pleeaazzze couldn't you just send $200 to show your adoring son how much you care for him? Surely you think that he is worth at least that? We know you love your son and don't want to give him a complex, do you? Great! We'll take $300." You know some goofy phone call like that. What I can't imagine is what actually happened and what in the hell C-101 was thinking.

They picked Friend up for some college boy fraternizing with adult beverages. The trio sat by the railroad tracks downing beer after beer. They drank and drank and were shooting the breeze on a crisp northern California evening. Before long it was dark and they were drunk. Mr. Roommate nudged Friend to go for a little walk. He agreed. As Roommate and Friend walked along the tracks under a bridge, 101 cradled his head in his hands, laid back and put his feet up on a rock. He had a nice, mellow high going on. Life was just dandy and so peaceful. He chuckled to himself. They thought they could get the guy stinkin' drunk and as he lay passed out on the tracks they would call his parents to pony up some cash. 101's head was heavy. He heard a thud and looked up. Roommate's shadow was walking toward him. As he cranked his head around the dark figure, he saw his friend lying on the ground. He nodded his drunken head and gave a double-barreled wink with his bloodshot eyes. Great, he thought, *Friend's passed out. Must be time to do this thing.* In the back of his head he still thought the whole thing was a hoax and thought what a Ho-Ho for Mr. & Mrs. Friend's Parents. He'd say "we were just joshing you about your son. He's our buddy. We just wanted to see the look on your face." The look that parents get when some guy calls up and says they're holding their son hostage and pay up in a couple hours or he dies. That would be such a funny look to see, wouldn't it?

As Mr. Roommate got closer, 101 noticed a large hunting knife in his hand. It was covered in blood, his friends' blood. I don't know if the guy died immediately or was left to die. What I do know is that despite the shock that Mr. Roommate stabbed his friend, an act of violence he'd not foreseen, 101 didn't call the police or an ambulance. Instead, he made the call to the parents. The parents recognized his voice in spite of his drunken attempt to disguise it. I don't know if the parents were panicked or thinking it was a joke, but I know that his elementary school buddy was found dead under that bridge the next day and 101 was found making arrangements to get out of the country.

101 represented to me the epitome of what is missing in this day and age. He had good looks, money, nice home, nice parents, good education and lots of opportunities, and not one ounce of courage. Maybe his friend could have lived if he would have called the cops or 911. Maybe he didn't have to die. Maybe the parents didn't have to sit in horror in the courtroom as the district attorneys unfolded the cold-blooded murder that was aided and abetted by someone they drove to the baseball field, someone who slept at their house in a GI Joe sleeping bag, someone they fed Oreos and milk after school, someone who threw his graduation cap into the air, shoulder to shoulder with their only son. Someone who lured and then cowardly left their only son to die, alone and cold under a bridge, his face smashed against the metal rails of the train track. 101 lacked the courage to put his best friend's life ahead of his ass. C-101 thought only of himself. *I like C-101, have known him for years. Maybe I am judging him too harshly. Maybe when I was young and in college I might have made a similar mistake.* I moved on to the next C-file.

**FILE #2**. The wrinkles around his eyes gave away years of severe drug abuse. His long, neatly twisted, two-foot long dreadlocks embodied his former, carefree lifestyle. He was no different than the others there, serving 25 to life with no possibility of parole.

C-102 was special though. He wasn't a gangster or a psychotic murderer. He didn't torture people or rape women. He simply had hit hard times. For years he frolicked in the Caribbean waters with his Jamaican wife Melanie and their five daughters all with light brown skin, black eyes and soft curly hair. Their life was carefree, bohemian. Then they moved to Long Beach. Like many others, his downfall came with the introduction of crack into the community. It was cheap, fun and destroyed his family like a pancake being flipped and landing on the uncooked side, sizzle and burn. His wife became so debilitated from the crack and heroin, she walked into the ocean late one night, naked, babbling to herself, and scratching incessantly. She floated up in the harbor two weeks later.

C-102 was a renaissance man even back then. He stayed at home and raised the children while his wife worked as a paralegal in a local law firm. He contributed financially by being the master of budget consumerism, and by occasionally selling some of the numerous paintings that he had created over the years. When Melanie was pronounced dead on the beach that day, it finally hit him. He was indeed, in a bit of a pickle. The true breadwinner of the house was gone and there was no back-up plan. No savings. No 401K. No life insurance. No money put aside for rainy days or freakish incidents. When a woman appears in the water like a buoyant marshmallow in a cup of hot chocolate, and her body is naked and bruised, the police tend to scrutinize the husband carefully. Careful scrutiny wasn't on the list of C-102's manageable tasks at the time. He certainly was no Scott Peterson. He didn't have that lovely ability to look all teary-eyed at Diane Sawyer and then yuck it up with Amber Frey during his wife's memorial. The only thing 102 was trying to hide from the police was his persistent drug use. It wasn't exactly easy to stay high with the police breathing down his back. He barely had time to grieve as he kept care of the house and the kids. 102 knew that he was a mess, in a horrible mess.

He also knew that he did not kill his wife. He adored Melanie. He was mad at her, but he didn't kill her. In fact, the night before she wondered off to her demise, he had forgiven her for bringing the shit into their house, the shit that broke them down to barely functional. He would never know for sure, but he suspected that his act of forgiveness might have given her permission to let go, to let go of a world she once knew but in which she could no longer function. She was once a respected member of the community, a professional with an adoring, painter husband and five gorgeous children. It was over the course of just a few months that she went from being a working mother to a crack-head. That too was a full-time job and she did it with zeal. Melanie couldn't foresee a future. She just wanted the present to end.

Not knowing where to turn at first, C-102 thought that after the funeral the most compassionate thing for him to do was to leave all the children with their aunt, Melanie's sister, until he sorted things out. At first 14-year old Naomi, the eldest, was going to stay with the younger ones, but it was summer and he realized he needed her help more than anyone. He had no one. In the back of his mind, he thought that if he kept Naomi with him while he looked for work on the streets, he would be able to straighten himself out. You know how teenagers are, the way they can be so blunt, so straightforward. He figured all he needed to kick his nasty habit of crack and heroin was a good swift kick in the ass and a couple of flippant remarks from his eldest daughter. She could be the ticket to putting him back on track. He was vehemently committed to the new plan. His daughter would set him free.

As for Naomi, it was hard to predict what grief would do to a teenager who lost her mother to a drug induced lunar eclipse. Who'd have thought that she would seek the same comfort her parents did, cheap crack and heroin? Unbeknownst to 102, his daughter had been addicted for some time. He'd never been a careful junkie, but since Melanie was gone he had to remember such things as how much stuff was left and where the money was to pay for more. Gone were the days of losing himself in his painting. He hadn't picked up a brush in weeks. Hell, he didn't even know where any of his brushes were. When he discovered his shit was completely gone, he looked to Naomi. 102 snapped. He knew it was her fault, and as high as he was, he made sure she was going to pay for it. First she paid with bruises, next with a tooth. When he broke her arm and they made a necessary, but suspicious trip to the ER, he finally realized his abusive tactics weren't working. *What the hell*, he thought. *If she wants to do the shit, fine. So be it.* But from now on she was going to have to pay her fair share and earn money, cash money. They don't take credit cards for crack and heroin.

He scratched his head in unrefined dismay. 102 looked for the silver lining in this cloud. "What could a 14-year old do for money?" he asked himself. She couldn't hold a regular job that was legal. Babysitting? Mowing lawns? Recycling? 102 saw that Naomi was a beautiful girl and men would surely pay to sleep with her. Who wouldn't want to sleep with a 14-year old girl? It was a no-brainer. He was concerned that his daughter was a virgin and might not be up for the task. So like the good crack-head father he was, he fucked her first. As much as he could remember, she didn't seem to mind. Now they had something special. Now he didn't miss his Melanie so much, he had her daughter.

They became quite the team roaming from place to place. Sometimes they would spend days with men who not only paid for Naomi's services, but also paid them to leave. One can only have sex so many times before most people have to return to work or something.

It was a particularly dreary day when they lured their last john. He was the typical easy-score-guy; no wedding band, middle-aged and balding, okay car, high school education, small town. They didn't bother to ask his name, but liked the fact that he was willing to take them to his house. It never occurred to the fella' that 102 was the girl's father. He assumed that he was her pimp and protected his goods. No problem. He was an upstanding guy and wasn't gonna' do anything to hurt the girl, just have a little fun. Like any good host to a pimp, he offered 102 a sandwich when they arrived.

While the stranger took his daughter upstairs for casual sex, 102 got to eat pastrami on rye with a small bag of chips and a cold beer. It was the best food he'd had in days. Hell, it was the only food he'd had in days. After filling his bloated tummy, he leaned back for a bit of R&R. It was so quiet that all he could hear was the wind brush up against the window and the sighs of his daughter being sodomized by the nice middle-aged man upstairs.

It's hard to say if 102 went upstairs out of concern for his daughter or if the filling meal reinvigorated his own sexual desire. But join them he did. He took off his clothes, set them neatly on the chair nearby and knelt in front of his daughter. While the bald guy penetrated Naomi in the ass, he thought it would be dandy to give her some fatherly love from the front. Naomi didn't seem to mind, she was so high she wouldn't remember what happened anyway. What C-102 didn't expect however, was a comment about the size of his penis. What the john didn't expect was that the dutiful father always carried a buck knife in his pocket in the event that someone ever messed with his daughter. He suddenly thought that the guy didn't deserve her anymore, despite the fact that she was bought and paid for. In the blink of an eye, 102 pulled the knife from his picket and slit the man's throat ear to ear. Naomi didn't remember that part, but she admitted she helped drag the body downstairs. They stole the man's car, any cash they could find and, by golly 102 even had another pastrami on rye before they left.

The blood and DNA evidence were overwhelming. With a public defender at hand, 102 didn't have a chance. He was convicted for life without the possibility of parole.

I thought 102 was one of those cases where drugs had overtaken a man, temporarily robbed him of his conscience. *It had to be the drugs. Please God tell me it was the drugs. This guy is so respectful. He's so talented.* I shouldn't have looked at the legal-sized pages that were kept hidden in a military green folder. I should have left that file to languish in the back of the Records Department. It could have sat for years with no one disturbing its ugly memories. The kaleidoscope of visions of pimping, eating a sandwich, fucking his daughter and slitting a man's throat made me sick to my stomach. I thought I was going to puke on the teal blue industrial carpet.

\* \* \*

**FILE #3**. Her hair was caught in the closed door of his car. One usually envisions kidnapping, terrorizing, sodomizing and raping a 14-year old girl synonymous with a dark Buick or a Ford Pinto; either a big cruiser or a little junky piece of crap, but I imagined it was a nice kind of car, not a BMW or a Lexus, maybe a Toyota Camry kind of nice car because C-103 was that kind of guy.

C-103 was another handsome, well-educated guy who piqued my curiosity. He was an accomplished musician, an excellent guitar player. He had the skinny rock n' roller look.

*Okay, now I'm obsessed. I have a headache.* C-103 was cruising down an alley one hot, sunny day south of San Diego and saw two young girls walking home from school. He stopped his car and picked one. She was most likely the shy one, the weakest one because sexual predators have a knack for picking off the kid who has self-doubt written all over her face. He grabbed her, stuffed her in his car, slammed the door catching her hair and left the friend in the rearview mirror, standing glued to the hot pavement in blowing debris. He sodomized her repeatedly and when he was done, he was chivalrous enough to give her a ride back to the alley, dropped her off where he snatched her. What a nice rapist! Most victims who endure such cruelty usually end up dead in the trunk of an abandoned, stolen car or with their nude body dumped somewhere in the mountains or desert. This little girl was returned alive, hopefully to overcome the nightmare.

I single-handedly pushed gargantuan speakers from one end of the prison to the other. The wind was unbearable. It was like pushing them up a mountain. I did that, so C-103 who raped this young girl, could have better acoustics for the band concert. I mumbled to myself "You are such an idiot." The wind pushed against the forty-pound speaker and made it feel like 1000 lbs. My fine, white-girl hair got tangled into knots that didn't comb out easily later. This is what the Juilliard girl did with her life? This is what the next-best-thing-since-whipped-cream did with her life? She chose to schlep Peavey speakers, fit for a professional rock band, for a guy that didn't give a shit about the girl he raped.

"Miss Joki, we have to have those speakers," he said. So doing my job the way I always did, going above and beyond, I went and got them. All I could think was *loser, loser, double loser*. And that was in reference to me, not the inmate.

My head was pounding, I felt nauseous. There was no way I could go back behind the wall. There was a reason that knowing about actual crimes of the inmates in the art program didn't serve us well: It was hard to go out of my way to get guitar strings for someone that killed his best friend's grandmother in the middle of the night for drug money. It wasn't a priority to get hooker's green paint to an inmate who tortured his female co-worker because he was convinced she was in love with him, instead of the man with whom she'd lived for years. I didn't care that a guy, who shot and killed an innocent bystander in an armed robbery, wanted pens and paper.

Reading C-files was making me physically sick. It was time to stop.

# The Force

"Bah bah bah" she bleated at her shepherdess, Miss B. in the tailored suit and matching high heels. MUGsie bellowed again "Bah Bah Baaaaaahhhhhh." I heard that sound come from her mouth as she handed out stacks of paperwork regarding our "new direction". I could never quite get a pulse on who was really the ventriloquist and who was the dummy with these two.

MUGsie was a nice lady, but I felt badly for her. As Assistant Director to Arts in Corrections she was bubbly, fun and enthusiastic. With her promotion to Director she seemed to take a turn into the land of duress; it all looked so goddamn painful, so stressful. Maybe her home situation with an ornery husband and two belligerent teenage daughters was finally catching up with her.

Her prior leadership skills were completely nullified when Miss B. hit the scene. When she was in the room MUGsie was *bleating bleating bleating* like Mary's little lamb that didn't know where to go. But once Miss B. was gone, the sheep's clothing came off and there stood MUGsie, the wolf, growling. "I know this isn't right, but this is the way that Miss B. wants it and there's nothing I can do about it".

"Bah bah bah" she bleated.

The dynamic duo was on a mission: To rewrite the Request For Proposal (RFP). The RFP was the document that dictated how Arts in Corrections did business with their contractors: Artsreach at UCLA in the south and the William James Foundation in the north. Almost from its' inception Arts in Corrections had a "single source vendor" stipulation with both of the aforementioned foundations. There simply were no other groups in existence that did what they did, and they both did it incredibly well.

When so many prisons were being built in the Central Valley (what we referred to as the "Middle Kingdom") the IAF's there grumbled about not wanting super-qualified artists from LA coming to their institutions and having to pay them travel and per diem, thereby eating up their budgets more quickly. They wanted local artists and complained when Artsreach couldn't find any. It became a bit contentious, and the Middle Kingdom definitely had MUGsie's ear. MUGsie was very willing to listen as she resented a few things herself: #1 the amount of power and flexibility that Susan Hill from Artsreach had and #2 the amount of money Susan made *AND SHE DIDN'T EVEN HAVE CHILDREN!*

It didn't take long to figure out why Miss B. was so goddamn interested in being the ringleader. It was called "pet project," the implementation of a facility where incarcerated females could go to give birth and bond with their infants for a period of time. I wanted to know if I could go there too. While convicted felons would have such care, I as a state employee had to pay out-of-pocket for my children's births at such a center and I was only in the facility about twelve hours total. Then I had to go home and fix dinner.

In the background was the new mothers' facility in Norwalk while in the foreground the new RFP loomed. Artsreach and The William James Foundation were both well-oiled machines that knew their prison business and they "worked" for all these years. But the new RFP was unbelievably onerous with the most simple of tasks requiring vast amounts of paperwork. And on top of that, it now was incredibly restrictive. Planning a year of arts programming in prison had always been a goal-oriented declaration with lots of wiggle room since we were, mind you, operating in prisons, a.k.a. places guaranteed to be unpredictable.

The new RFP was pure MUGsie and like planning a dinner party at a homeless shelter eighteen months in advance down to the last detail, not knowing who was going to be there or if the place would be open. We now had to designate a location, the dates of the class, the name of the instructor, the time of the class, content and cost of the class. That was all well and good in theory and eventually had to be done at some time, but impossible to do eighteen months beforehand. Impossible to do in a prison where a classroom could become unavailable in a heartbeat or a lockdown could stifle programming for months. And how do you get an artist to commit to teaching once a week for eight weeks on a designated night one year in advance without being allowed to contact them, let alone hold them to a schedule so far in the future. It was crazy making.

It was so much so, that Artsreach at UCLA wisely pulled out of the bidding process all together. MUGsie had her dream come true: Goodbye Susan Hill. With or without Artsreach in the mix, the new RFP also required that the contract go to the lowest bidder. Drum roll, the lowest bidder for the south half of the state of California was the Imperial County Arts Council (ICAC).

ICAC was a small arts council that operated out of a post office not far from the Mexican border with no prior experience working with prisons. We went from the resources of UCLA to a post office in the middle of nowhere.

The current director of ICAC, however, had a very impressive resume. He had a Masters in Arts and he spoke well. That was a good sign. The only problem was that once ICAC got the contract, he was out of Dodge and things were left to ole Granny, the office manager.

I remember my first encounter with ICAC. Ole Granny, a doting grandma-type who never shut up, was handing out purple and gold gift bags (like they were business colors?) to her southern Artist Facilitators (as if she was soliciting our business?) This was our contractor and we had no choice but to do business with them. One of the items in each bag was a pound cake with a nail file baked into the center. I could never have imagined attending a meeting with Susan Hill passing out brownies with razor blades in the middle and laughing about how much she didn't know about prison. This was a prime example why government contracts need the "sole source vendor" line item, to prevent bullshit like this.

We had certainly stepped into the land of OZ and it didn't take long for frustrations with ICAC to set in. ICAC didn't have a list of qualified artists from which to work. When Susan Hill didn't just fork over ten years of work compiling information on artists all over the state, they were sorely disappointed. Since ICAC couldn't come up with new artists for us to work with, most of us used the ones we already had, provided they hadn't quit the program and jumped ship in support of Artsreach. That worked for a while, until they failed to get paid. Yeppers. Contract artists who, for up to ten years, were used to being paid for the work they did, were no longer getting paychecks on time. It would string out thirty days, then sixty, then they'd get righteously pissed off and I'd have to make another humiliating ninety-day phone call. Eventually Sacramento realized that ICAC wasn't properly handling, maybe mishandled, maybe embezzled state funds and eventually, the doomed-from-the-start contract was revoked.

Meanwhile, Miss B's personal project in Norwalk was going off swimmingly. It was a lovely facility. The convicted mothers were just going to be oh-so-comfortable there. Arts in Corrections had also decorated it with such beautiful, original artwork and she was very thankful.

MUGsie bleated "Bah bah bah" in the corner.

The only thing better than leaving the prison to attend a conference (which MUGsie and Miss B. pretty much put a stop to, although they'd blame it on Headquarters), was leaving the prison to attend a meeting in Sacramento. It was an opportunity to network with colleagues. This particular meeting wasn't just a run-of-the-mill get together, this one had some cachet to it: It was a "Task Force". Oooooohhhhhhhh. Task Force! That's where policy was discussed and designed. I'd never been on a task force before. I felt honored, privileged. This wasn't just for Artist Facilitators, MUGsie, Miss B., and some Community Resource Managers, by golly there was an attorney present as well.

I was happy as a clam to be on a Task Force. I loved prison, but sometimes I needed a break. Even though meetings in Sacramento took place in a "tomb", the CDC building downtown that had nary a window, it was a relief to not have to go through a series of iron gates, to not have to dress like the phone-lady and to be able to put on a skirt and wear perfume. It was fun to feel like a professional and not a packhorse hauling instruments and art supplies all over the goddamn place. And besides, we could buy lattes downstairs and take them up to the meeting with us. La-tee-da!

The small group that fit around the one, large conference table was there to discuss "Ownership of Artwork". In Arts in Corrections inmates were not supposed to profit off of work that they created with state materials. If an inmate paid for his own paint through Hobbycraft, then he had the right to sell that painting. But with AIC, the state paid for the paint. "Ownership of Artwork" was a touchy issue that was intentionally left vague for years because had it ever been put into writing, the Facilitators feared the inmates would lose the privilege to own any of their work. Most of us utilized a one-for-one system. For every two pieces of work, the inmate got to keep one to send home and donated one to the program to be used for fundraisers and beautification projects. For the most part, that arrangement worked pretty slick.

With literary material however, no one questioned the ownership of a song, play or book. It was a "product of the mind" and was legally protected as such, provided the inmate wasn't profiting from his crime (the Son of Sam law). I was there as one of the few performing/literary folks and certainly Bly's Big Win was probably what landed me in that grey-cushioned, state-purchased seat. I didn't quite understand what compelled MUGsie and Miss B. to take this on, but they certainly seemed motivated.

Jim Carlson and Skelly were, as usual, the most vocal of the visual artists and the most eloquent. The "one for one" policy that had unofficially worked so well for years seemed to be the ticket. Everyone agreed it was simply a matter of writing the procedure in a manner that protected the state and still allowed the inmate to keep some of his work.

When the literary discussion came around however, it was much more adversarial in tone. No one gave a rat's ass about poems. "Sure the inmates can own their poems, they're poems!" the attorney quipped.

Of paramount interest were plays, screenplays to be specific (even though they did throw the word "novel" around a bit). Sacramento's objective was clear; to find a means in which the inmate didn't have complete control over a large piece of work. (Basically they were scared shitless that some random inmate was going to sell a screenplay for a million dollars and that would be a public relations nightmare.) No matter what the discussion, we came back to the same point every time: Product of the mind.

Miss B. seemed to be frustrated by the "product of the mind " crap. She leaned over in her crisply pressed blouse and waxed brows and inquired "What about the paper?"

"What do you mean, what about the paper?" I asked.

"The paper. Where do they get the paper to write the script on?"

"I give it to them."

"Uh huh. That's right." she nodded in glee. "That's state paper!"

Dang this was an interesting road we were going down. "Well of course it is, but how could we verify that I gave it to them?"

"You just said that you give it to them!" Miss B. was gettin' kind of pissed.

"Yes, I did just say that... and I do. I give them paper. But, my question is how can that be verified? Inmates can buy the same paper at canteen, they can get it in an education classroom or from their job or from the Program Office. It's all the same; yellow legal pads and eight and a half by eleven typing paper. How can anyone verify that it came from me? Couldn't that be easily disputed?"

Miss B. was scratching her head now! "Okay fine. What if... what if they were only allowed to own a certain number of pages per quarter, what about that?"

Now, we had entered the Twilight Zone. If I understood correctly, Miss B. thought that CDC could control the ownership of a screenplay, a product of the mind, by parsing out its' ownership in segments of paper. Okay.

I had to scratch my own head on that one. But only one thing made sense. "If, for example," I began, "an inmate can only own twenty-five pages of his material a quarter, then fine. That's what he can own. Typically, it takes a person/inmate one year to complete an entire screenplay, which averages one hundred-ten pages. So, the first quarter I hand him the first twenty-five, the second the next twenty-five, and so on and so on and somewhere along the line I'll throw in the extra ten pages. At the end of the year he's going to have all the pages and still own the thing. How in the world do I stop that without completely censoring everything he writes?" Not particularly eloquent, but hey?

This was the first meeting in Sacramento that I didn't enjoy. The task forced upon me was making my head ache.

# The Good Doctor

It was an absolutely glorious day. There I was, perched on two water-skis. The water was like glass. I was so cool, crossing back and forth over the wake with such ease. Little drops of water came up to kiss my face. Life was good. WHACK! The tips of my skis crossed and I fell like a rag-doll. Silence. WHOOSH. I floated to the top. The boat seemed far away. I couldn't hear or feel anything. My legs and arms floated beneath me, supported only by the life vest. The boat started to draw near. *How in the hell am I going to tell them I broke my back?*

I also thought of shaking Christopher Reeve's hand once in New York and wondered if Superman had placed a curse on me long ago.

"Jesus Christ!" my younger brother with blue eyes and premature grey hair declared as he pulled up in the boat. "That was some wipeout. Are you okay?"

I couldn't speak. They pulled me up by the padded, blue shoulders of my life vest. Although I wondered if I was paralyzed, I was more perplexed by my potential girth. I wondered what the women's movement had done for me lately, because I was unable to move one muscle and all I could think about was my weight. I was wondering if I would walk again, I was lying on the thin carpet of my brother's speedboat like a fish with a hook it's mouth, flapping around, wondering if I were a *fat(?)* fish.

A couple of years after that nasty water-skiing fall, I began to have severe pains shoot down my right arm. I would be washing dishes after a home-cooked meal and BLAM, the plate would fall out of my hand and shatter. I started dropping dishes unexpectedly quite often. The gnawing pain in my right arm occasionally kept me home. Murphy's law dictated that I would go through all the motions of getting ready for work; take a shower, make lunch, floss teeth, load up car and then suddenly, Whoa Susanna!!! By golly, I could not move the gearshift on my truck. For some reason the motion required of the right arm to push the gearshift down, then back and forth with some resistance was impossible. I would stand with the phone to my ear, looking at my blue Toyota pick-up and say "I'm sorry, but I can't come into work today, for some reason I can't seem to drive my car". That must have sounded terribly lame at the time.

Chiropractors, acupuncturists and orthopedic surgeons all searched for this lightening bolt of pain. The traditional Western world found a calcium deposit in my right shoulder and promptly shot it up with cortisone and sent me on my merry way to physical therapy. When my eyes welled up with tears as the cortisone rushed into my body, creating a sensation of panic and numbness accompanied with great pain, the first doctor said "Oh stop it. It's not that bad." He tapped me on the shoulder and trudged out. His brilliant theory was to just "get on with it." I tried physical therapy and found no relief, so I sought an acupuncturist. I had tried several before, but I felt I needed something more aggressive. Like most things, it was a phone call away. My king-of-vegan-living-guitar teacher gave me the number of a guy who was supposed to be worth every cent and the long drive too.

A 4'10" Vietnamese man said in broken English, "OOOOOhh-hhhh... 'dis not wook good." He looked at my tongue, listened to my breathing, a man of few words. Prior to Dr. Little Saigon acupuncture was typically quite benign. Occasionally a needle would feel slightly uncomfortable and frequently just droop over like a flower after a cold nights' frost. But the Dr. Little Saigon experience was unique. He used more needles than I'd ever seen. It felt like they were put deeply into muscles knotted with tension. After placing them, he burned the tips with moxa, a mugwort herb that smelled suspiciously akin to marijuana. It brought about a sensation of pain unknown to my body, extraordinarily freaky. He insisted that I lay in the dark for a full 20 minutes. Tears began rolling down my cheeks. The pain was excruciating. "Dr? Dr? Hello? Anyone? I think I need help. Hello?"

He entered quietly. He only wore socks. I wasn't sure if he was there. Like a spider on the ceiling the morning of a hangover, I wondered if he'd been there the whole time. I didn't hear or see him come in, but it would be weird if he was there the entire time. "Dr. this really hurts," I sobbed. "Should it hurt so much?"

He grabbed a tissue from across the room, wiped the tears rolling off my cheeks, knelt next to me and calmly said into my right ear "You... you bery, bery strong. Dis ... dis bery good." And before I could open my eyes he was gone. *That's it? I'm strong and this is good but, I can't even fucking move.*

Some little Vietnamese guy in a relatively dumpy commercial building in Little Saigon had quietly left me crying and paralyzed in pain. It reeked of pot. No one spoke English. I had paid for this. *I am in a Quentin Tarentino film.*

Dr. Little Saigon was my hero. The next day I woke up pain free for the first time in months. I never questioned his methods again. I just went back and forth for two months to the Little Saigon district to have my pain magically disappear. I thought I was normal again.

\* \* \*

My mother is amazing. At the age of 74 she was still attractive and vibrant. Complete with pedal pushers, canvas sneakers, a sheer scarf to protect her hair from the wind and big sunglasses, we were leaving on vacation. She got on the train like she was Jackie O in her later years, going incognito.

Husband couldn't accompany us. He was shooting a TV series in Vancouver. We had come to a good place in our lives. We had two great, healthy kids who went to a great school, a beautiful old house we couldn't afford to properly furnish, good friends and neighbors. And after months of visiting Dr. Little Saigon, life was virtually pain free.

Deciding to take advantage of the good life, my mom, kids and I hopped on the Starlight Express. It was one of life's delights with the dining car and its fresh white linen and endless stream of comfort foods beckoning you to scrap your diet. It was dandy as the train giggled down the tracks along the western coastline. There was wine tasting at three o'clock. My mom sipped on Pinot Noir made in Oregon while the children happily watched a movie in the theater car.

The only down side to the Star Light Express was the coach section at night. People were tired and it wasn't easy to sleep sitting up all night. There were infants and toddlers who were too annoyed to sleep and some teenagers- gone-amuck that drove us nuts by roaming from car to car. The lesson I learned from this? Get a sleeping car on the way back.

We traipsed through the streets of Seattle, drank coffee, listened to music and went through the butterfly exhibit at the Pacific Science Center more times than should ever be allowed. We made a trek to Vancouver to visit Husband and watched him play a CIA agent with a couple of lines in a sci-fi series. We missed each other.

We did get that sleeping car on the way back. It was glorious. We could shower and there were chocolates on our pillows. I slept tucked in, with my children nestled above, as the train swayed back and forth, like a lullaby. I realized that the acupuncture treatments that gave me relief were only a mask for something else. I came back to Los Angeles in excruciating pain. Something was very, very wrong.

Sandra, my benevolent chiropractor who had nursed me through marathons, car accidents, and the last waterskiing fall, could no longer help me. Her usual bag of tricks came up empty with the exception of a good recommendation. What took me off guard about this Good Doctor wasn't that she was "young, gifted and black" but that she seemed to take an interest in my health. Most doctors shuffle you in and out like cattle on a dairy farm. She looked at me with those brown eyes and then seemed to stare as if somewhere "out there" was the answer. She may not have won any beauty contests, but her charm was in her athletic stance and tomboy presence. I could tell that she really dug athletes and had a passion for helping people get back to their former active life style. As unconventional as she was, she still wanted to treat me cautiously and recommended starting with another injection of cortisone. No one but her could have got me to sign up for that bull ride again. I warned her that cortisone and I were not good friends. It entered my body like an enemy trying to choke me from within. But cautious she was. In honor of my extreme distaste and mistrust for the handy drug, she allowed me to rest for a full thirty minutes afterwards. Most doctors would have tossed my ass out the door as soon as the needle left my supple skin.

It was a restful thirty. Euphoric. I even had a stupid smirk on my face as I was writing the check for my co-payment. I adored signing my name and I was beginning the most beautiful, languid "L" when the pen didn't stop at the end of the paper. Everything went black and I thought I was doing one of the trust exercises they teach in theater where someone stands behind you and you fall back knowing they will catch you. I trusted the black, marble floor. I smiled as I greeted it with the back of my skull. OUCH. I *told you I didn't like cortisone.*

I awoke on the same table, but this time with an ice pack on the back of my head, dazed and confused. The Good Doctor knew a thing or two about litigation: She had every ounce of my head, neck and back X-rayed before releasing me and she never billed me for those X-rays. She walked me to my car herself.

The Good Doctor had a good therapist, Mindy. She was a petite, whiter-than-white-blond chick with extremely fine hair gracing an angelic face with blue eyes. For a therapist that was maybe 100 pounds dripping wet, this gal could do some serious damage, strong as an ox. But unfortunately the therapy didn't lead to improvement.

MRI was inconclusive so the Good Doctor scheduled surgery. The calcium deposit was finally coming out.

I was excited. I thought I'd take two, three weeks off, max. You'd think I was off to Disneyland rather than an operating room. I left the program in the hands of my Lead Clerk. Inmate Chesney had been with me for some time, hands down my favorite. He got into screenwriting and good golly that guy could write. He'd won the screenplay contest the year of the largest competition in terms of submissions. The inspiration for his comic screenplay was a buddy of his in prison, Cal. Cal was the sweet, Italian crooner who almost got shot when he went from Facility "A" to Facility "B" to do the Shakespeare play. Chesney wrote about an old guy who is so driven to perform in this dinner theater in the Catskills for the rest of his life that he sells his soul to the devil. It was a very clever piece of writing.

I never would have told Chesney this, but I must say I did have a soft spot for the old boy. He was in his mid- 50's and one of those guys that I wondered *what in the hell did he do to land here?* He was fairly well educated, finished high school, attended college and went to X-ray technician school at one point. He was bright and affable and one of the few inmates who admitted to belonging in prison. That's a rare bird. I can't forgive Chesney for what he did, but I can understand it.

His wife had left him to raise their daughter on his own. That wasn't exactly a good start. Being a single parent is surely one of the most challenging undertakings. I guess having at least two jobs was in order for him to make ends meet. As time went on, he met a girl who moved in with him. But as more time went on she coughed up the fact that she'd been having an affair, but had put it behind her. Chesney now needed not two jobs, but three in order to make ends meet. He found that third job where he picked up money for a convenience store and deposited it for them. Apparently he needed to carry a gun for this afterthought of a job. He kept it in his glove box. Combine a new gun in the glove box of his car, with the speed that he was taking so he could stay awake for all of his jobs, with the suspicion that his girlfriend wasn't on the up and up; it was a recipe for disaster. He followed her one afternoon right into the arms of her lover. On the stoop of a building they hugged and kissed and before Chesney knew it he had grabbed the gun from the glove box and started to fire. It was a completely avoidable tragedy. Chesney acknowledged that he had committed the ultimate sin and probably didn't deserve to ever be free. It was that candor that appealed to me, that was a rare thing in prison.

There I was saying goodbye to Chesney as if I was sailing to the Caribbean and would be returning with a tan. Life was good. Husband had just completed a pilot for a new TV series, money was in the bank and I was going to be pain free in just a few weeks. Yippy skippy.

The surgery was scheduled for 7:00am. I left in a cab at five o'clock in the morning while Husband stayed with the kids. As I stepped into the cab in the dark I envisioned being driven to a dark alley and raped. What a nut cake I'd become!

I filled out paper work and told the anesthesiologist that I had a low tolerance for drugs. As soon as they started that drip into my system I was out like a light. It was lonely waking up in a corner of the recovery room with no one there. The green walls didn't seem particularly inviting or talkative. I was relieved when a nurse came by and patted me on the head like a sick puppy. "Everything was fine." She said. "They'll move you to a room soon."

Husband hadn't arrived yet. I was sure he was busy getting the kids off to school or trying to sneak some work in before picking me up. My entire right arm felt like some asshole had beat the shit out it, and then wrapped it up in bubble wrap and taped it to my side. The Good Doctor entered with her usual enthusiasm. "Excellent" she declared, "you look excellent." She pulled up a chair and took my hand in hers. "We called your husband and he should be here soon. Go home. Rest. Take your pain medication and I want to see you in three days."

Three days later I was back in her office. She walked in with her usual I-just-got-off-the-handball-court-and-could-probably-kick your-ass-but-I-won't-because-I-like-you demeanor. She pulled up a stool about two inches from my face. "It went great," she said. "I expect a full recovery." Then there was the pause.

Since the MRI was inconclusive going into surgery, she didn't really know if there was any damage to my rotator cuff. She suspected that there might be a small tear or something, but nothing prepared her for what she found once she cut into my arm. All the while that I was having my shoulder shot up with cortisone and then moved around by physical therapists for six months under other doctor's care; all during that time, the golf ball-sized calcium deposit inside my shoulder, shredded my rotator cuff apart. Not torn. Not damaged. Shredded. She removed approximately 35% of my rotator cuff. This was not a good thing. You only get one rotator cuff per arm and one of mine was like a rubber band that was cut shorter and stretched around the shoulder joint.

"We need to make sure this is completely healed before we start moving your arm. Because if it tears again, you could need a shoulder replacement." *Does she mean plastic shoulder?* "I need you to stay home and allow that shoulder to recover, without using your right arm at all, for eight weeks. Don't do anything. Don't use your right hand. Don't even use your right index finger. Don't even look right!" *Some fucking trip to the Caribbean that was!*

# Manipulation

I was on a mission to rest as much as possible and catch up on movies. I thought I'd died and went to heaven. Husband and my neighbor Ed, a 6'4" black man with a big smile and the deepest voice this side of the Mississippi, moved my bed to the other end of the room, so that I could look directly at the TV. I had *Up in Smoke, Mephisto* and some other independent movies that I'd always wanted to see but just didn't have time with work and children. I pumped that baby into the machine. This was cool: staying home, taking narcotics and watching movies. Within twenty minutes I was sound asleep. I tried three days in a row to watch one of those suckers and every day, like the one before, I fell asleep. How pathetic. I felt like a big loser for not taking advantage of this time to watch movies or read a couple of books but all I could do was sleep.

The upside of spending hours sleeping during the day while the kids were in school was that when they returned home, I had some energy. I realized how much I missed being able to be with them each day, helping with homework and having dinner together. For years, three days out of the week I missed that part. I was at prison working like a good soldier; organizing classes, fundraisers and performances, while Husband picked them up and got them dinner. Now, I felt closer than ever to them. I loved being in their presence on a daily basis.

Husband was the real trooper. I couldn't cook much because my left hand wasn't particularly adept at being dominant, so he did. He also did all of the cleaning, and every ounce of driving. I was basically homebound and incapable of much more than some medication-driven repartee at the end of the day. Husband proved to be a true gentleman and didn't complain about how much he had to do. Instead, he was grateful for the fact that he wasn't working much and was able to take care of us. He was also grateful for the work he had done prior because now we had a nest egg stashed away to draw on if needed. The weeks rolled by and before I knew it Christmas was upon us.

Another reality however, was that the artists at prison were beginning to grumble. They would call me at home. "Leah, what do I do about this? Leah how do I order this paint? Leah why can't I pull the inmates out during a lockdown? Leah? Leah? Leah?" I attempted to answer their questions as best as possible, but I was so loopy from pain medication, that 50% of the time I didn't even remember talking to them. They thought they were getting the usual me, but I was high as a kite.

Just as Christmas was approaching, I had begun to see Mindy, the angelic, strong-as-an-ox physical therapist. I had started moving my arm with her help. The muscles had atrophied so badly that the scapula of my right shoulder basically hung underneath my armpit, a lovely sight. At the Christmas party I boasted about how I could move my arm six to eight inches from my side and implied that I didn't know if I would go back to work. Husband was doing great and this could be our opportunity for me to quit the job at the prison and take a year off to write. Ever since Grandma and the Imperial County Arts Council came to town, my love affair with the big, hairy-chested guy was waning.

\* \* \*

It was late afternoon on Christmas Eve when the phone rang. Husband's black face turned grey. The producer of the James Elroy pilot—that Husband had a good role in—had called to tell him that they were dropping him and another actor if it went on to series. Husband had turned down an audition for a sizeable role in a Schwarzenegger film to do this pilot. Just weeks before his manager was jabbering about him creating his own website and buying Husband.com, before he got famous. Welcome to Hollywood.

The Good Doctor sat six inches from me, her eyes locked into mine. I was in trouble. My shoulder joint was frozen with scar tissue. Since I had no prior surgical history, no one could have known that my body built up scar tissue at an alarming rate. Now I needed a second manipulation surgery to pull the scar tissue off of the joint or that six to eight inch radius was going to be it. Forever! No lifting my right arm straight out in front of me, not over my head, behind me, or scratching my own back; just those six to eight inches slightly forward and off to the side. Crap! Bad Crap!

Next complication: My first surgery was covered by Husband's Screen Actor's Guild insurance and was far superior than my primary HMO stuff. As of January 1, 2000, however, SAG would no longer cover spouses using their secondary insurance to cover procedures that should be covered by their own primary insurance. I had to go back to my primary HMO insurance to see if they would do the surgery and pay for it. The problem? I only had two weeks to have it done. The Good Doctor believed that waiting any longer would make the scar tissue unmalleable, and the success rate of the procedure drop dramatically. She sent me on a mission; talk to my primary HMO doctor and see if they could have someone do this ASAP.

My HMO surprisingly sent me to the most prominent shoulder surgeon in Los Angeles. His practice was located on an upper floor of a high-rise in Century City. He was obviously successful and important. He quickly evaluated my shoulder and stated, "In my opinion, the surgeon should never have left you immobile for so long. That's why there is this build up of scar tissue around the shoulder joint. A second manipulation surgery is risky and unwarranted. The possibility of sustaining permanent nerve damage is high. I wouldn't consider performing such a surgery. I don't know what you do for a living, but I suggest you collect disability and get on with your life. You are not going to get the use of your right arm back. I don't mean to be blunt, but it's important to know the truth." *I'm disabled?*

I needed to broaden my census so I set out to consult additional doctors. Another HMO doctor agreed with the famous surgeon; "You're screwed." But when the famous surgeons who do all of the Dodger's rotator cuff surgeries refused to see me, I took their recommendation and saw a well-known surgeon in the San Fernando Valley.

Dr. Next-Best-Thing-to-a-Dodger studied the pre and post op MRI's. He asked questions, peered over his wire-rimmed glasses and studied me, then he smiled. " Do it. I recommend you do it. You are young enough and strong enough to handle a surgery like this. If it were you, I would take the risk. You have a career and small children that need your attention and you need the use of your right arm. I also recommend that you have your original surgeon do it, because she was the one who was in there the first time and knows what she's dealing with, the delicate nature of it. No one could have predicted that you would build up this much scar tissue. So don't think that any of us could have done any better. It was a judgment call. I might have left you immobile for a long time too, I don't know. But, do it." Dr. Next-Best-Thing-to-a-Dodger made up my mind and I was headed back to the Good Doctor. My primary HMO insurance had ruled that it was "medically unnecessary", medically unnecessary for me to use my dominant right arm at the age of 43. So I paid for it myself.

The night before my manipulation surgery Husband and I

went to a Hollywood dinner party on Los Felix Blvd. Once again, Husband made me so proud. The young, trophy wife of a producer threw out "Why do men cheat on their wives?" Husband looked baffled and said, "I don't know why someone would do that. But, I don't think it has anything to do with looks. But what do I know?" *What a keeper Husband was!*

Manipulation surgeries aren't done very often and they're not exactly based on new technology; they're barbaric. My physical therapist Mindy, asked to witness this unique procedure. Ultimately, they knock you out, put a scope with a camera into your arm and then start to lift your arm away from your body. The problem is that when they lift the arm it begins to tear the scar tissue away from the bone. When that process begins, there is massive bleeding inside the arm, and the blood rushes into the camera not allowing the surgeon to see anything. From that point on, maybe ten seconds, it is one big leap of faith. Mindy almost threw up. What was astounding to her is that the surgeon was pushing my arm up trying to get to it closer to the side of my head, raising it above me. As she did so, Mindy said that you could hear the scar tissue ripping away and then see the blood flowing into my arm. The only thing they had left to guide them was sound. They listened carefully as the tissue separated from the bone. They didn't know if they were breaking my arm or tearing the rotator cuff again. Evidently the Good Doctor looked at Mindy and asked just how limber I was, because the point to which she pushed my arm would be the point of my furthest range of motion for the rest of my life. Mindy went out on a limb, "Go for it. She's strong."

The Good Doctor pulled a stool right up in front of me, looked me squarely in the eyes. "Leah... it went great. Now let's look at that arm." She proceeded to lift my arm with extreme caution above my head. That was now the standard for my new range of motion. "This is not going to be easy. The next four to six weeks are crucial. You need intensive physical therapy. Your HMO insurance will only cover physical therapy twice a week at Cedars-Sinai. You need therapy daily. Mindy has agreed to treat you Monday through Friday at no cost. The therapy in collaboration with the pain medication is the key to making this work." Wow! I was high as a kite, but I understood what she was telling me. I was to start therapy the next day. What I didn't know was, where in the heck was Husband?

It was a schedule. At 7:00am I got the kids out of bed and out the door to school by 8:00am. Then, I rode my Life Cycle for an hour to get rid of all the drugs in my system, so I could put them back in again. Twenty minutes before I saw Mindy, the physical therapist, I took two Percocet. That was the miracle narcotic that allowed her to work on me. The goal of each session was to get my arm from my side to up over my head. I couldn't lift my arm. It took Mindy thirty minutes to get my arm to its' final destination; above my head. She would start out just a little at a time, pushing the arm slightly and bringing it back. Mindy was careful because if she forced anything, she could have torn my rotator cuff again. Even with painkillers it was excruciating; when she got to the place where my arm was just about flush with my ear, I was in tears. Afterwards I spent time in their gym doing exercises designed to regain strength and then spent an hour in their 98-degree pool. At first the only thing I could do in the water was put my right arm on a styrofoam noodle and push it back and forth. In addition to that, twice a week I ventured to Cedars-Sinai for more physical therapy with Bob. I took more drugs to do that. After dinner, Husband worked on my arm for thirty minutes, I took more drugs to do that. I hooked myself up to a pulley in my breakfast room every day. I took drugs to do that. At night I needed drugs to sleep. It was a full-time job that required lots of drugs.

The Good Doctor warned me that the most difficult aspect of the first six weeks was managing the large amount of pain medication. She'd had other patients who three weeks into it, felt that they could no longer take such high doses of pain meds and started backing off and ended up losing a substantial amount of their range of motion. My plan of attack to handle massive amounts of narcotics: exercise, bagels and cheese. I didn't exactly lose weight with this regimen, but the bagels and cheese somehow made all of the medication tolerable to my stomach. I wasn't thinking about body sculpting, I was focused on regaining the use of my right arm.

It was twelve days after the surgery and right smack in the middle of when it was becoming difficult to carry on. The kids were asleep. I had brushed my teeth, taken my pain medication and was ready to slumber. Husband was, as always, in the office on the computer. He worked constantly. "Leah, come here. I want to show you something." I came to the door and there he sat facing me, sitting at the computer. His desk was, as always, covered with books and paper, and what not. As I poked my weary head in and looked, he hit the keyboard quickly. From the corner of my eye I thought I saw a woman's naked breast on the screen. He gave the keyboard another quick stroke and the screen went blank. "What was that?" I asked.

"Nothing."

"No, what was that?"

"Nothing." I glared at him with the quizzical look that always drove him nuts. "Fine." He said. "It was just a little bit of pornography."

"A little bit? What does that mean? Do you look at that often?"

"Look Leah. It's nothing. Okay? I called you in here." He looked tired. I felt bad because he had been carrying the lion's share of work at home for months. "Leah, I had two affairs, ten years ago."

# Crap

They were the original windows. The wood trim encased the wavy glass. The walls were painted a dusty rose, than rag-rolled with white. On one section of the top border there was a patch of antique stenciling exposed. The breakfast room was referred to as the "owner's room" and historic pictures of the original owners hung there. We lived in the historic Estudillo house, built in 1908. Mr. Estudillo owned another home in the Old Town district of San Diego. Once a wealthy landowner from Mexico, his full-length portrait exuded confidence. There he stood at the end of a chaise lounge sporting a husky mustache and a floor length coat. To his right was a portrait of either his mother or his wife. No one knew for sure. On the opposite wall were several pictures of his daughter standing on the porch wearing a typical 1950's dress and apron. She lived in the house alone for over fifty years. There was a photograph of her husband who looked like a 1930's playwright, sad and gloomy. He had died at a young age and they had no children.

Husband and I had bought this house less than two years ago. As his acting career started to take off, so did a lucrative job as a dialect coach. For his first gig he went to Hong Kong for ten weeks to help Jean-Claude Van Damme tame his French accent. I held down the fort solo, and he came back with enough money for a down payment. In ninety years we were only the third owner of the Estudillo house. We'd bought it from Leland, a middle-aged white guy with a fetish for old houses. Leland had renovated houses all over the neighborhood and rarely made much of a profit. He'd sat on this gem for years, thinking it was the one he'd retire to. Then, he met us. We bought it over a handshake and Ethiopian food in the Fairfax district. His only requirements: 1) Respect the historic integrity of the house and not paint over woodwork or pull out original light fixtures, etc. 2) Be involved in the neighborhood.

I didn't have a picture of Leland for the breakfast room, but figured that since we were the owners now, our picture should grace the wall as well. I put up our family favorite; an 8" x 10" black and white portrait in which everyone is in motion. Husband and I were literally caught in mid-air as our children were seen landing as they spun around. We'd coined it "The Happy Family Picture".

Right behind his head as Husband spoke I could see the space between the floor and his feet in the air in "The Happy Family Picture". My legs shook. The drugs had kicked in, I felt wavy like the glass. *Yeah, so what? So you had two affairs ten years ago. Who gives a rat's ass now? That was then, before kids, this is now. You had your fun. Nobody has AIDS. Let's just go to bed and call it a wrap!*

Husband stared at me with a this-is-bad-but-you-can-do-it-look. "I met someone. I did a reading with her at LATC (Los Angeles Theater Center)." *What the hell? I thought I brought my wobbly, highly-medicated ass down here to hear about some past affairs?*

"What do you mean you met someone?" I blurted. Apparently he found himself attracted to this black actress. I remembered seeing her at that reading. I also remembered that at the reception afterwards I wasn't introduced to her like I was to the other actors, but she was there. She was fourteen years younger than I. Evidently she made it clear she didn't date married men, but he confided in her about those prior affairs. She suggested that he have that conversation with his wife. *That would be me.*

My eyeballs hurt as he trudged through the details of his lurid past. I wondered if I had eyeball cancer. I was really high. The first affair was with the white chick Louise that he did the prison play with while he was in Kansas City, the white chick that wasn't at all interested in talking with me. Wasn't I a fool? He was so much in love with his Miss Kansas, that when he moved on to Texas for the next six months, he replaced her with Candy, his Miss Dallas. I talked to her on the phone when I called him about getting the Facilitator job. They were making pottery together. She yammered about what a great guy my husband was, and I thought they were just having a grand time throwing pots together. What a flippin' idiot I was!

I mumbled a few words. "I thought you were my soul mate. Soul mates don't fuck each other over." Then, I left.

Upstairs, I lied on my bed sobbing into the morning. The kids woke up, heard me crying and came in with wide eyes, welling with tears of sympathy for their mom. I was hanging over the side of the bed so my tears could fall on the floor. There were so many. "Mommy, mommy what's wrong?"

Husband turned to them and callously replied. "Mommy's shoulder is hurting. She'll be fine." *He's a good actor.*

It was Saturday. The kids were staying at friends' homes. We were in the breakfast/negotiation room. He had a prominent forehead that sat over his large brown eyes. His lips couldn't stop forming three syllables; "I love her." He felt a passion for her that he had never experienced with me, but he didn't know why. "It's like the tree in the backyard that blocks the sun from the breakfast room. That's what it's like." *What? There's a tree blocking passion between us? What was that? Am I the fucking tree? Am I the sun? What the hell? Is it him or the drugs I'm on because I'm not getting it!*

What I understood about his relationship with TOWie (The Other Woman) was that it was something ours was not. But I was confused how he could feel so passionate about someone he barely even kissed. His chest inflated. "Jesus Leah. That's the problem. You don't understand. You don't listen. You roll your eyes and constantly interrupt me. You don't understand."

"Then explain it to me." I pled.

"Look, I didn't get involved with her because I chose not to go down that path again. She did nothing wrong. The problem is you and I can't talk."

"Whatever. But you cannot see her again."

"You don't control me. You can't dictate to me. Besides, I have to see her."

"Why?"

"She's hosting a reading of a script that she wrote and I'm going."

"You should not be going to a reading at her house."

"Well, I am. I'm going.

"Why? " I yelled.

At the top of his lungs, "BECAUSE SHE WROTE A PART FOR ME."

"FUCK YOU." I screamed. "I THOUGHT YOU WERE EXCEPTIONAL, BUT YOU'RE NOT. YOU'RE COMMON." I downed a couple glasses of wine on top of the pain medication, packed a bag and left.

I drove through Hollywood into the Valley, to a condo in Lakeview Terrace and arrived at my friend Jean's door at 10:00pm. I stumbled past the Mexican pavers in the entry onto the carpet in living room, fell to my knees and wept and wept and wept. "Leah, what in the hell happened? Did someone die? Leah? Leah? Leah? You have to talk to me here." I wanted to talk, but the words were held captive in a throat that had shut down. I couldn't breathe. I gasped for air as my hands clawed into the carpet. When I finally blurted everything out, I had a whole-body shattering of my heart.

Jean made scrambled eggs with wheat toast in the morning and insisted that I eat all the while saying "I am so sorry, Leah. I am so sorry."

I kept thinking that I needed a guy to talk to Husband. I couldn't reach his brother so I called Walker, the husband of my dear friend, Penny. Penny was my classmate at Juilliard, a gorgeous black actress. We'd known them for 20 years. They were religious, in Hollywood! Penny had a successful career, but put family first. I went to their beautiful home near Baldwin Hills. After I bellowed out my tale of woe, Walker felt compelled to act. They went to my house, he to speak with Husband and Penny to retrieve the children.

Penny relayed how she told Husband that she was taking our kids so he and Walker could talk. "Leah" she said. "I've never seen him like that. His eyes, the look... it was vacant." She was troubled by his dismissal of her.

It was February 13th and I had completely forgotten about Valentines Day. It was late on a Sunday and while we were at Pick-n Save, Penny and I had a brilliant idea. We bought a hundred toothbrushes. We convinced the children that it would be the most popular Valentine of all, a toothbrush to brush-away all that sugar from the candy they were about to receive. We thought the parents would think it was the coolest of cool. We tied ribbons around them and attached a Valentine to each one. The kids were a bit dubious but went along with the hair-brained scheme. (Unfortunately they were embarrassed the next day when their classmates asked, "Why did you give me a toothbrush?")

As we were putting the ribbons together, Walker returned. He took me by the hand and sat me down in their family room. Walker was an accomplished musician. He sang at our wedding. He took me by the shoulders, cocked his head to one side as if to get a better view, then he looked right at me. "You go home to your husband, Leah." He waved his hand in front of my face, asking if I could feel the slight breeze that it produced. "Do you know where that comes from?" I nodded my head. "That's God, Leah. No one can explain the air. You trust in God, and go home to your husband. That woman means nothing to him. But you need to listen to him and let him guide you to find what is missing in your relationship. Look at me." He held my face in his hands so gracefully. "She means nothing. You are everything. You are his wife and the mother of his children. You go home." He held my hands and quietly prayed. I trusted Walker. I did as he said.

It was the first time I had seen a physical therapist since news of my so-called life emerged. I struggled to take my shirt off. Combing my hair, hooking my bra, zipping up my pants; these were a major challenge when I had no use of my right arm. The chatty, happily-married-with-whacky-stories Leah of the past, didn't show up. As Mindy rubbed her hands across my shoulders and neck, the release of tension brought me to tears. They fell onto the carpet in slow motion. With every touch of her hands, the diameter of my windpipe shrank. "Leah, what happened? Are you okay?" Nothing came out. "Leah, it's okay. Let's stop for today. It's okay. Take your time. And I'll see you tomorrow."

Bill, the physical therapist at Cedars-Sinai was aggressive in a different way than Mindy. When he started rubbing my shoulders and neck I crumbled. His manner was gentle, but very matter of fact. "Okay, let's have you get dressed and I'll be back in a minute." *I'm such a good little Catholic girl. I always do as I'm told.*

He came back and sat next to me. "Leah, I don't know what happened to you. Do you want to talk to me about it?" Two sentences and the tears welled up in my already-puffy eyes. "Leah, do you want me to get someone for you to talk to? There are plenty of counselors and therapists in this building?" I shook my head no. I couldn't speak. He took a deep breath. "Here's the deal. And I want you to listen and listen hard. I don't know what happened to you. It's fine if you don't want to talk about it. But what I do know is this. You've taken a heavy dose of Percocet and are still shaking inside. Your muscles are contracting in there and I can't work on you like this. I need to be able to feel what I'm doing and how far I can push you, but I can't do it when you are tense like this. I could tear your rotator cuff again and you would end up needing a shoulder replacement. The amount of pain medication you are already taking is astronomical and you simply cannot take more. Which by the way, you are handling great. But, every day for the next three weeks, every day that I cannot work on you, you lose about 3% of your range of motion. And that 3% lost each day is 3% for the rest of your life. You will never get that back. I don't know what to tell you. But whatever you need to do to get your act together, you need to do it now. You cannot fall apart now. Not if you want full use of your right arm back."

Now, crying in therapy had ceased to be an option. I couldn't even throw Husband out even if I wanted to. I needed him to drive me to therapy, drive the kids to and from school and activities, and I needed him to move my arm through the full range of motion twice a day.

We had come to the place where we had hit the darkest moment before the light. Husband sought therapy. I thought his therapist was a bit harsh. He came home shaking his head and muttering, "He says I am totally self-absorbed. I let no one in. I think only of myself." *Wow! Harsh indeed. But I'm digging this remorse thing.* He expressed how sorry he was for hurting me, and we prayed for us to heal and stay together.

We also started seeing a counselor together, Leslie, Counselor in Training. She was cheaper than a licensed therapist. We were doing well, and since we'd already spent so much money on my arm and I was out on disability, we had to be frugal. After numerous sessions of venting, she looked at us in her I'm-such-a-good-mom-and-wife manner and said, "There seems to be a lot of love in this relationship, but you certainly have your problems. I don't know whether to blow the candle out, or to fan the flame to keep it alive. You tell me." I know that she was cheap, but I thought we paid her to do that. Leslie was concerned with feelings. My feelings. His feelings. Her feelings. (She failed to mention the kid's feelings.) *We're in a play with no ending. Next?*

There was a well-known family therapist at UCLA. His fee

was $150/hour. Husband wouldn't go for that. But he liked the option where we could see a couple of his graduate students for $25/hour. We committed to four sessions of exploration, so the students were guaranteed credit. We walked into the room to meet the male and female counselors, and burst into uncontrollable laughter. They looked like my niece and nephew. The thought of sitting down to talk about infidelity, pornography, custody of children and emotional damage to children with these two green kids who'd never been married was hilarious. We completed the obligatory four sessions and called it quits. Husband stopped seeing his individual therapist due to work conflicts.

I made it through the crucial weeks of rehab on my arm and somehow we stumbled along. There were moments of bliss. We were more connected sexually than ever before. Certainly it was more frequent. One evening, we were dancing to Irish rock music with the kids. We each did our version of Irish step dancing. I became easily fatigued. I was still taking medication and flopped on the couch and watched the kids dance with their dad. He picked our daughter up, held her in the air and twirled her like a princess. Our son went flying between his dad's legs and was flipped upside down. Then, they all flopped on the couch. I leaned over and whispered into his ear, "I'm so glad you didn't throw this all away." We were "The Happy Family," again.

He couldn't find anything. He was frustrated. He didn't have work. Our house was his cage. He roamed from one room to the other, then would walk outside and plop himself on one of the white wicker chairs on the porch. There, out of his kennel, he could vent.

"I never wanted this middle class life style."

"The Joki girls are all alike. You all have to have the big house and private schools."

"I never really wanted children."

"I never really liked you."

"You never understood me as a black man."

"I never felt any passion for you."

"I resented having to take care of you."

"You want to know my dirty little secret? I think about her all the time."

But one evening when the kids were gone, we were making out on the grey couch. The fire crackled. Husband had always been an unlikely candidate for such random intimacy. He was an at-the-end-of-the-night-before-we-go-to-sleep kind of guy. He was my children's father. I relished his large tongue in my mouth, but he pulled it out. He stood up holding his head like nerves were firing off. "All right. Fine." he pronounced. "We did everything but penetration. Are you happy now?"

Paying bills is a pain in the ass, but I was enjoying it because it had been months since I could write with my right hand. Money was tight again. I was about to write out the check for the full amount when I opted instead, to peruse his cell phone bill. There was one number dialed repeatedly. It didn't take a brain surgeon to figure that out. It was TOWie's. My eyes fixated on a certain date and my heart stopped. There, in black and white, it had been documented; a lengthy phone-call the morning of January 31, 2000. At the very time that I was in the recovery room, alone, wondering if I had permanent nerve damage after the manipulation surgery, husband was chatting up TOWie. The nurses had been trying to reach him. He was late picking me up. Tears rolled down my cheek with the phone bill in hand. Husband strolled through the breakfast room and saw me. He took one look at me and quipped, "Now, what's wrong?"

"You were talking to her while I was in the hospital, in recovery, alone. You asshole. And I'm supposed to believe that you never slept with her?"

He trudged around confused and caged, then burst back into the room. He growled with anger, "Fine. You win. The reason I didn't sleep with her is, because... well... because... she's a virgin."

Later, at bedtime, he microwaved wet towels and placed them on my back, like some foreign mating-ritual he learned while gone. Then, he rubbed my back with massage oil. He was engaging with me again. Just as I was about to go down on him, he gently took my face into his hands and looked into my eyes. Finally, it's over. She's gone. She's been purged from him. The corner of one side of his lip turned up and he whispered "Leah, I've lost my attraction to you. But, go ahead."

# On Trial

"Shem called. He'll pick you up at 6:00am. Later." He closed the front door behind him. I didn't know where Husband was going, but Shem and I were going to San Diego the next morning. We were scheduled to speak at a sentencing. My success story, Larry, had been convicted of multiple charges and was looking at a minimum of nine years. Just before I had left work to have my first shoulder surgery, he had called the office seeking advice. He had been charged with petty theft, assault, and making a terrorist threat. He had been released on bail and wondered what I thought about him taking a plea bargain. The District Attorney's office offered him two years and he'd be out.

Larry had been actively working on his screenwriting career since he was released several years ago. He had contacted several actors about his script and gotten them to verbally sign on. If you are trying to make an independent film, getting anyone with a name to commit to the film is a good way to interest people with money. He needed to meet them in Los Angeles to sign a letter of intent, a legally binding document committing them for a certain length of time in the event the film finds financial backing. Larry made the appointments with the actors, but he didn't have a car, a friend who could lend him one, nor did he have a credit card. So he went to a Rent-a-Wreck and gave them a $600.00 cash deposit for a beater to drive from San Diego to LA. It broke down mid-way. He didn't have a cell phone. He was an ex-convict who'd just missed his appointments. The car was towed back to San Diego and he along with it. When he reached the Rent-a-Wreck place, not only did they not apologize for the malfunction of their car, they refused to give him his $600.00 deposit back, stating that he was at fault, not they. He was righteously angry and argued vehemently, but he realized he was getting nowhere, walked outside, picked up a pay phone and called the police. He walked back into the rental place and a small elderly, Korean woman started ranting and raving. He ranted and raved back. Back and forth they went. Then came the defining moment. As the little woman was talking to another customer, she popped open the cash register and Larry made the fatal mistake of putting his large, gout-ridden knuckles into the tray and grabbed a $20.00 bill. She "karate chopped" his arm, he said. And he in return, shoved her to the wall. Then what happened? Murphy's Law. At that very moment, the police that he had called witnessed a 6'5" black man with his hand in the register pushing a 4'10" elderly, Korean woman against the wall. *WHOOPS!*

"First of all, I am so sorry that that happened to you. But I must say... you should have never, ever put your hand into the cash register. That was completely fucking stupid. And ... you should accept the plea. I know you don't want to hear this but you're a black man with prior convictions, you've done time and unless you have one helluva' lawyer, you're going down. Two years is nothing compared to what could happen." I declared.

Larry didn't take my advice. Instead, he took the case to trial. He was appointed a public defender, but chose to get his own attorney to whom he paid $6,000.00. God knows where he came up with that.

Larry was out on bail. He missed his first court appearance because he thought he was having a heart attack, and went instead to the emergency room. Larry had insanely high blood pressure and I'm sure the whole fiasco had thrown his body into utter shock. Although he paid the attorney handsomely for a small case, he wasn't able to convince the judge that his client was in the hospital with a valid medical concern. So off they sent the police to the emergency room and when they were done checking Larry out, they carted him off to jail where he remained until his trial. He had been labeled a "flight risk."

Shem and I went to San Diego bright and early that day. I don't know how, but I kept my composure. Courthouses are so antiseptic. Even though many of them are historic and examples of beautiful architecture, they always feel cold and unwelcoming, a gloomy place to have one's future determined. As Shem and I walked up to the courtroom I saw Larry's former girlfriend, Aimee. I knew they weren't together anymore, but I was impressed that she cared enough to be supportive. She was a very attractive, middle-aged white woman, slightly matronly, but very voluptuous with a beautiful mane of long brown hair. We walked into the courtroom and quietly sat in the back. The bailiff was meandering around, the court stenographer was at her desk and suits were chatting each other up. And then Larry came in. He was brought in handcuffs and led to a table at our left. We were not able to have any contact with him, but the moment his eyes hit mine, I just wanted to bawl. The tears were welling up as I looked through the fog and saw a man so broken down it was as if he had aged ten years. His skin looked absolutely gray. He had lost a fair amount of weight and his hair had radically thinned. But it was his labored gait that was jarring. Despite dealing with chronic pain for numerous years, he had always exuded energy from his chest. He was a large presence, and had a twinkle in his eyes that was remarkable. But his eyes were full of humiliation. In a glance he conveyed, "I'm so sorry that I screwed up Miss Joki, but thank you for coming." His eyes filled with tears and he looked away in shame.

In came the Judge, typical white man in his 50's with gray hair, black robe and glasses. We sat in silence. There was murmuring around the judge's bench. I looked to Aimee, wondering what was going on. Apparently we were waiting for Larry's attorney for twenty minutes, in silence. Finally the door at the back of the courtroom burst open and in came a pudgy black man with black glasses and a briefcase. His watch looked expensive and his skin glowed like he just had a facial. "I'm sorry, your Honor. I apologize."

"This behavior is not acceptable in my courtroom." He gave the attorney a verbal bashing that was quite delectable. When the judge asked what made him so late, the attorney replied that he had forgotten his son's lunch and had to return home to get it, which put him about 20 minutes behind. That didn't fly well with the judge who reprimanded him with a "Give the kid three bucks next time and be on your way, but do not ever be late in my courtroom again."

This wasn't like the movies where you know exactly when things begin and when they end. It all seemed a jumble to me. Apparently there was some sort of paperwork missing that prohibited the judge from going forth with the sentencing and before we knew it the judge hit his gavel and said "See you in three weeks." *What the heck!*

I raised my hand, stood, and said, "Your Honor, we came from Los Angeles to speak on Mr. Larry's behalf and are not able to return in three weeks."

The judge muttered, looked at papers through his reading glasses, glanced at the attorneys and looked up. "Fine. Your testimony will be recorded and considered in the final sentencing which will take place in three weeks."

Shem stood up, stated his name and went on to tell how he knew Larry, how he had worked with him for years in prison and how he followed his progress after he got out. The judge was curious and asked if signing a letter of intent was a valid way of doing business in Hollywood. Shem told the Judge that what Larry attempted to do that day was completely legitimate and that he himself had played a hand in orchestrating it. "Interesting," the judge muttered.

I placed my hands on the rail that divided us, the public, from the lawyers and clerks. I took a deep breath and began. "Your Honor, thank you for allowing me to speak in your courtroom today. My name is Leah Joki, and I am the Artist Facilitator for the Arts in Corrections program at California State Prison - Los Angeles County located in Lancaster, California. I have been an employee of the Department of Corrections since 1990. As an Artist Facilitator I hire artists from all mediums, painters, potters, writers, musicians, etc. I train them to work with inmates. In addition to being a participant in my program, Mr. Larry also worked as a clerk for me on the Minimum Security Facility prior to his release. As a clerk and inmate worker, he was extremely proficient and professional. After his release I maintained minimal contact with him through my office, per CDC guidelines. Your Honor, please allow me to share with you my observations about this morning and the incident that brought Mr. Larry here today. No disrespect to you sir," referring to Larry's attorney "but… I was appalled that you couldn't find a way to be on time for a sentencing that will determine the rest of a man's life. I understand the challenge of being a parent. I am one as well. But it goes further than that. Not only did you show up late but you failed to file the appropriate paperwork. And in addition to that, I spoke with your office months ago and agreed to appear as a character witness and I wasn't even contacted or interviewed. Your Honor, I truly mean no disrespect but I seriously question the quality of Mr. Larry's representation. What Mr. Larry did in the Rent-a-Wreck that day was undeniably stupid. Putting his hand in the cash register is a mistake that he should absolutely pay for. It was unequivocally wrong. But if I had done that, I wouldn't have even been arrested let alone be looking at a minimum of a nine-year sentence. You must admit, that the sight of a very large black man, looming over a short, elderly Korean woman played a part in their initial reaction. No doubt she felt threatened. But I wonder if Mr. Larry's lawyer ever questioned that woman about her business ethics. Rent-a-Wreck's are notorious for ripping people off. They prey upon people like Mr. Larry, who live a hand to mouth existence and don't have a good credit history. The fact that they blamed him for the car's malfunction is absurd. And why is it not a big deal that this woman refused to give him his money back? He had already lost face with the actors he was supposed to meet. All he wanted was his deposit back. I mean, what criminal calls the police before he robs the store? Mr. Larry called the police. Doesn't that count for something? Your Honor, I understand that Mr. Larry did not behave well that day, but I seriously question the wisdom of a courtroom that would send this man to prison for nine years. I am well aware of Mr. Larry's past. I know that for many years he was a horrible drug addict and did a lot of bad things to fuel that habit. I am aware of that. But Mr. Larry has been clean and sober for many years. He has paid his debt to society and has successfully stayed out of trouble and carved a life for himself. He's not a threat to society. I would trust him with my own children. Is it really necessary to spend $27,000 a year of taxpayer's money to incarcerate Mr. Larry to protect me, the public, from him? Take a good look at him. He suffers from severe gout and is not a healthy man. If you send him to prison, he most likely will die there. That's a fact. And the truth is, I won't feel one bit safer when I lay my head down at night. Thank you, your Honor, for giving me the opportunity to speak." The court stenographer was crying and Larry was gasping for air.

On the return trip Shem commented, "You were like fuckin' Portia, man. I didn't know you could speak like that? Have you ever thought about running for office? Seriously Leah. You should. I know people who can help with financing a campaign. For real. Maybe you should run for Nate Holden's seat." *Shem, are you high?*

We had heard that the judge would consider reducing his sentence to seven years, but when Larry made his final appearance in the courtroom he was released. Unbefuckinglievable! The judge must have accepted the amount of time served as adequate for the conviction. Never, ever, had I heard of such a thing. Shem and I did something extraordinary that day in San Diego. It was rumored that after we spoke, even the prosecutors felt badly for pursuing him so vehemently. Husband had flowers sent to me. He did it for Larry.

# Returned

It was my 44th birthday. I put on my Jones of New York dress, because it always looked good no matter how much I weighed. Husband, the kids and I piled into our 1986 boat-of-a-Mercedes and headed to El Cholo, the Spanish cafe on Western Ave. south of Pico Blvd. It had been my favorite restaurant for 15 years. No one made better margaritas and the kids swooned over cheesy quesadillas and Shirley Temples with mucho marachino cherries.

Afterwards, I focused on getting my unsuspecting children to bed. Our marriage was crumbling, but they had no inkling, whatsoever. There were no fights in their presence. In public, we were still "The Happy Family." It was behind closed doors that his disdain was expressed in muted tones, it was there that he could be dismissive and no one suspected. Now, I understood the irony of my frequent quip, "Oh Honey, if I want to have a good time with you I need to invite someone over. Ha, Ha Ha." After all, we had lived most of our life with an audience and were always together; from stage performances and teaching in prison, to meetings, writing grants, shooting videos, at parties and fundraisers, together at the kid's games, together at kid birthday parties, at holidays with family and friends. The two of us were rarely alone. Alone he was tired, disinterested and unaccounted for.

After the kids went to sleep we sat on the porch. It was my birthday. Against the brick wall of the porch, there were jade plants in large clay pots that were dying. They had been there since we moved in. Everyone in the neighborhood had at least a dozen. I wanted them to die. I enjoyed being a spectator of their demise. One was covered in spider webs, yet still was surviving on air.

I drank wine and smoked several cigarettes as husband ranted. He felt disdain for prison. He felt that I had let my Juilliard training go to waste. He looked at me and saw prison, kids, bills, and responsibilities. "I don't want to be the guy who does the play in Los Angeles, but doesn't get taken to Broadway. I am not gonna' be that guy!" *Well, that's nice honey. But how many plays go from LA to Broadway? One, every couple of years. At most? And how many parts do you think there are for a middle-aged black man in one of those every-couple-of-year-at-best, plays? This a big concern? Why?*

We heard someone approaching on the sidewalk. There was a halfway house in the neighborhood just blocks away and I assumed it was a parolee coming our way. Even at home I couldn't get escape my ability to pick out a convict. I could tell by the way they dragged their feet that they hadn't been out of prison long. Guys who do a lot of time forget to pick up their feet over the years from walking around in a circle with nowhere to go. The gentleman passed by slowly.

Husband rambled on. "I need to focus on my career."

"I didn't want this life style."

"I need to spend some time alone, thinking."

"I want. I need. I think. I want more. I need more. I, I, I and I!" Twenty minutes passed with him talking non-stop.

It was my 44th birthday. It had been a hard year. Husband just wore me the fuck out. I felt like the jade plant being suffocated by spider webs. I was living on air. I looked at that plant, with its' burst of green just hanging in there somehow. *I will not survive on air alone.*

There was a splotch of red wine on my Jones of New York

dress. I hated jade plants and declared, "You need to leave this house. Find a place. I need to go to bed." Pause. "And by the way, I'm going back to work. Thanks."

It had been more than eight months, almost the length of a pregnancy. When you watch your body morph into a pumpkin shape, you're hyper aware that your life is being completely transformed. But staying home for eight and a half months to recover from shoulder surgery and to rehab my arm didn't initially seem to be that life altering. As I drove through the canyon, I could only think of my secrets. I was no longer happy Leah. Happy-Gemini-spaghetti-loving-good-soccer-mom-married-to-the-funny-black-guy Leah. The Leah who still bites her nails, I lost that Leah. It was the oddest thing. I think I lost her the day after I found out about the original affairs. I took her into my physical therapist's room, laid her down on the therapy table and squished her into the brown leather. She's probably still stuck in the foam. I tried to suffocate the old Leah. I wrestled with her to get her down into the milky, colored foam of the therapy table and shut up. She was so weak that it wasn't that hard to overpower her. Once I had her in the foam, I sewed up the leather seam with darting glances of my eyes. Like the needle of a sewing machine moving over a heavy fabric and piercing through it, I could hear each stitch. "Chick. Chick. Chick." I did leave one tiny hole on the corner open however, so I could peek at her periodically. Each day I laid on that table, I felt her sadness. She breathed long and hard, with a whimper.

Today was the first day that the new so-angry-I-can-take-your-head-off Leah, or the so-sad-I-will-burst-into-tears-if-you-look-at-me-wrong Leah was brought out in public. Nobody knew her. No one had met her yet. Personally, I didn't care for her much and wasn't sure what in the world I was going to do with her. If I'd known then how difficult it was going to be to return to my old job as a different person, I might have thrown in the towel right then and there. Gauged by my level of anxiety, I knew this wasn't going to be a picnic. When your head is filled with secrets, your thoughts are consumed with protecting them. You cannot let anyone know what those secrets are, nor let anyone in. There is no wincing, no breaking down or crying. You're in prison.

I used to be superwoman in prison. I was asked to speak at a Warden's Conference about women working in a men's prison and how they could be safe. The crowd of one hundred and fifty people was made up of wardens, community resource managers, teachers and artists. I told them, "Don't go behind the wall if you're not emotionally stable. Turn around and go home." They laughed as I explained the importance of double knotting your shoes. "The last position a woman wants to find herself in, in a men's prison, is bent over to tie her shoes." "Never be alone with an inmate no matter how long you've known him." I instructed them how to position themselves with their back to the wall at all times and how to get close to inmates to demonstrate a painting technique without startling them or making them uncomfortable.

I taught them my number's theory. One guy alone with you, that's a problem. One black guy and one white guy with you, that's okay. A black guy could never support the idiotic attack of a female staff member from a white guy. He's really required to take him down and vice versa. But two white guys alone with you? That's a problem. I had it all going on back then. I was the queen of prison. My Hollywood friends referred to me as "The Prison Lady."

But on the day of returning, the queen got into her car and cried for seventy-five miles. How in the hell was I going to face my boss without falling apart? How in the hell would I handle inmate Kelley? I could picture the smile on his face as I would walk onto the yard, ear to ear, his shaved head and black glasses with blue eyes beaming out. But I knew that he would pick up in a heartbeat that something was wrong. I was no longer present. I had joined their club: I had offed somebody.

For the first time ever, I was nervous about seeing the

inmates. Hell, I was nervous about the doors, the big steel doors on the outside of the buildings. They had had their pull handles moved away from the edge of the door because, when the prison was activated, two officers had fingers amputated by those doors. A strong gust of wind whipped it away from them, slammed the door ferociously and chopped off their fingers. Now the handles were awkwardly placed in the center. The wind could still pull the door out of your hand, but at least you wouldn't lose your fingers. Just the thought of having my arm yanked by the wind, made me shudder. The potential for tearing my rotator cuff made me very apprehensive.

I pulled up to the entrance gate. The officer smiled as he checked my ID. His was a happy face and we had a benign exchange of chit-chat. He didn't know who I was. He didn't know that I went home from work one evening late in October 1999 and was returning for the first time in July 2000. It was weird to come back to work after so long and realize that most people didn't know I'd even been gone.

Nothing had changed in the prison parking lot in Lancaster. There were ravens everywhere. As I put my car into park, one jumped onto the hood of the car taunting me as if it wanted to restart Hitchcock's *The Birds*. I burst into tears. I hated ravens, the desert scavengers who prey, yet mate for life. The raven looked at me as if it had some God-given right to scratch the hood of my car. I started my car up again, so it would get off the hood, but it stood its ground. I felt like I was looking at Husband. I tried to jump-start him too but just like the raven, he glared at me with disdain. He stood his ground. Husband was as bound and determined to leave, as the raven was to stay on the hood of my car. Two black, selfish creatures, giving me grief!

Eventually I got up the nerve to get out of the car. The raven looked at me as if I had been a nuisance, and hopped over to join his brethren eating garbage in the parking lot.

I felt like everyone stared at me, but hardly anyone noticed me. Most people just walked right by me as if I'd never left. The anxiousness subsided. I made my way down the hallway to my sanctuary, the Warden's office. There was so much catching up to do. It was great to see Lynn Harrison. She was her usual, gracious self. She made it very clear, that although Husband did what he could to keep things together in my absence, I had been sorely missed. Everyone had struggled without my assistance.

I listened to hours and hours of what went on while I was gone. I did not want to be there. For so many years, prison was my place to create, the place I belonged. But now, it felt like prison.

# The Runaway
# Kaleidoscope

I pulled up to the curb in my recently acquired 1998 Toyota 4-Runner, now covered with autumn leaves. I'd just driven 85mph from Lancaster to get to my kids' school by 5:50p.m. Boy Child walked out of the building first. Mr. Gonzalez, the yard attendant, opened the back door for him to get in. He climbed up onto the seat and put his seat belt on. The attendant's dark eyes peered into the car with him asking, "One more, right?"

"Yes, please." I responded. While the attendant left to call my daughter's name on the blaring playground P.A., Boy Child sat motionless. I glanced at his round cheeks. Girl Child came toddling off the playground shouldering her enormous backpack.

As soon as her seatbelt was buckled I heard Boy Child's deep man-voice declare, "I hate you." Naturally I thought he was referring to his sister, but as I looked into the rearview mirror I saw his dark brown eyes glaring at me like two chocolate chips set onto a small round cookie. "I'm running away."

"Okay... honey." I floundered as I pulled away from the curb. "What's going on?"

"Nothing. I hate you. I'm running away."

He was a boy of few words. His sister darted a goofy what-in-the-hell-is-his-problem look to me in the rearview mirror. She and I silently concurred that neither of us had a clue. We drove on.

I pulled into the driveway, put the gear into park and again heard "I hate you."

I didn't crumble but wondered instead how a father could leave when his son's teeth were missing. I sat in the breakfast room as Boy Child packed his Lego Land backpack and stared at "The Happy Family" picture. Those people didn't exist anymore. We rarely saw that funny black guy in the picture. That woman rarely smiled anymore let alone jumped for joy in the air. That little girl with the dark skirt, white top, and long black hair twirling in mid-air didn't dance with glee anymore. Now she made up sullen plays with her friends about couples getting divorced. And that little boy landing on his feet in style—he was upstairs angrily packing to leave home.

Boy Child made a lame attempt to run away that day, just days after his father moved out. After walking a half a block away in a couple of directions, he realized he didn't know how to navigate his way through LA any further than that. He didn't hate me; he hated the situation we were in. The notion of an eight-year old boy wanting to leave his loving and nurturing home should have been disturbing—but it wasn't. It was now commonplace. When Husband went to find himself in an apartment in a sketchy area of Los Angeles, we initially shared custody of our children. But it only lasted two weeks. Twice in fourteen days my children weren't at their father's apartment, they were two blocks from my house with neighbors. His Hollywood schedule just wasn't conducive to caring for minors.

He was understudying the lead role in a new August Wilson play at the Mark Taper Forum, and was in rehearsal until eleven o'clock most nights. I'd become something of a Doormat Debbie and offered to baby-sit our children at his apartment until he was done with rehearsal. I was exhausted from the commute. It was already dark and my head was congested from the abrupt altitude change in the mountainous canyons between Los Angeles and Lancaster. I needed permission to access the older Spanish building where my children would spend half their time. Husband quickly buzzed me in. I walked into the apartment that was knee-deep in clutter and saw my children on a cheap vinyl sofa crying. Boy Child looked up with big tears. "I thought Daddy was supposed to take responsibility for his children but he doesn't."

Joint custody was over in an instant. I shuffled the kids to my car as I yelled profanities to their father. I barely attracted attention in the narrow street that never had a parking spot after 5:00pm because my verbal rant was in English, not Spanish.

It was decided. The children would stay with me. He would take them every other weekend, so long as his schedule permitted. Husband liked the arrangement. I was exhausted.

It was determined. He would take some time to think about things. I would remain in a holding pattern so long as he had no communication with TOWie. If he did, then I would file for divorce.

Husband and I walked around my neighborhood littered with newly renovated Craftsman homes, seedy apartment buildings and unkept houses with cars parked on the front lawn. It had taken weeks to get this appointment. I utilized my five blocks of talking time to convince him that it would be in our children's best interest to remain an intact family—the situation in which they had the best chance to flourish and thrive. He considered it.

It was near the end of October, barely two months into the separation. He wanted TOWie in his life. I contacted an attorney who would file the papers so long as we could come to a settlement. It all seemed so easy. One phone call and a twenty-year relationship could officially be ended and we would be legal strangers. The holidays were just around the corner though, and we thought it best to wait to tell the children. My family from Montana came to visit for Thanksgiving. Husband graciously took my mother to lunch at her favorite Mexican restaurant. My family knew that we were separated and we had requested time to sort things out without any interference. My seventy-five-year-old mother returned from lunch with a big smile and a sparkle in her milky blue eyes.

"Oh honey," she consoled. "It's all going to be fine. He just needs time to focus on his career. He said that he loves you and that you guys are definitely not going to get divorced. He just needs some time." Upon hearing this lie, I dissolved into a class IV whitewater rapid; I was gushing and churning away.

My antique oven couldn't accommodate a twenty-five pound turkey so my neighbor down the street offered to let me use her oven in their absence. Husband and I walked back and forth checking the status of the turkey. On one of these trips my eldest sister followed him into a neighbor's home. There, she reportedly threatened, "If you don't take care of my sister and those kids I swear I'll do something about it. I know people in the Butte mafia."

Husband and I sat at different ends of the table. It was a sit-down meal for at least twenty-five people. He was restless. My eldest sister peered over her glasses and glared at him. His siblings were boisterous and cheerful. My mom merrily drank her wine. I quietly cried on my corn-on-the-cob.

The sounds of late-night laughter and reading were replaced with wistful, saddened commentary: "I don't like this divorce thing." "Daddy makes better chicken." "I understand that Daddy doesn't want to live with you but why doesn't he want to live with me?" The smell of rosemary chicken and brown rice was replaced with the waft of pizza: Pepperoni pizza from Pizza Hut, cheese pizza from Domino's and sausage pizza from the frozen section. "Hey kids... how about Pizza again?"

"That's sounds yummy. I love you mommy!"

Months later I looked at them in the rearview mirror and my slender daughter had a muffin-top and her brother now wore husky pants. I had warned Husband on our appointed walk that day, "Don't leave the kids under the care of someone with food issues." I guess he considered it.

\* \* \*

My thin lips opened slightly to accommodate the brush with too much toothpaste. Before I began however, I leaned on my 1908 bathroom sink with separate faucets for hot and cold water and gazed at the curious, gray rings on my mysteriously, shortened teeth. A few days later, I opened my mouth for the hygienist and she gasped. Then, I opened my mouth for my dentist of fifteen years who exclaimed "Oh my goodness! That's a problem!" Although I'd never had an issue with grinding, serious enough to warrant a mouth-guard in the past, I had ground down most of my lower teeth to the nerve. Clenching my jaw so frequently with anger and rage was what had done me in. It was a $20,000 problem.

The phone was ringing as I struggled to disengage the home alarm system. Before I could even say hello his gruff manner exploded, "Leah. He's very difficult and uncooperative. I thought you had an agreement." It was the inexpensive lawyer I never met, but retained to handle our divorce. " I can't keep going on like this. The fee I quoted you was based on having an agreement and this guy doesn't seem to be agreeing to anything. I've had it! I'll give you forty-eight hours to come up with a settlement or you need to find another attorney."

Later, I opened my mouth for Husband. "Please. I beg of you. There is nothing to fight over. Please don't have me lose the retainer fee to this guy and give money to lawyers that we don't have. I have a $20,000 dental problem. Most of my lower teeth need to be rebuilt. Please... no more." He considered it. We settled. I was exhausted.

I found a kaleidoscope in the attic collecting dust behind the TV. I remember holding the cardboard tube up to my eye and peering in. Twist. Twist. There were pink and purple loose bits of colored glass in symmetrical patterns. Twist. Twist again. There were blue and yellow bits of colored glass in a different symmetrical pattern. What could have possibly come next? Sparkles here, sparkles there. Lame, unreal sparkles changing shape everywhere.

I envisioned my life in that cardboard tube. Twist. Twist. There I was, a baby with a loaded diaper crawling on the wood floors of my parents' first home. Twist. Twist. I was plagiarizing a book in the third grade. Big double-barreled twist and I was getting divorced. What color were *those* bits of glass?

I should have hit the kaleidoscope against the wall and shook up some of those loose bits of colored glass and then I could have tossed some of the characters in my life into other sections of it. Maybe EX (formerly known as Husband) would get jostled over into the section where I was crawling around on the wood floor - with a loaded diaper. Maybe he was in the truck outside working for Tidy Didy and picking up my shitty diapers, instead of giving me grief in the present. Maybe TOWie was the nun who caught me plagiarizing a book instead of the reason for my divorce. Maybe my dentist could have been pulling EX's wisdom teeth when he was a teenager *without* anesthesia, instead of replacing cracked crowns and doing numerous root canals on me. Maybe instead of EX and I continuing to share my job in prison, we could have just shared a bus ride in Butte one day in the 60's. That would have been less bizarre than our current reality.

The phone rang. I tossed the kaleidoscope in the garbage and went downstairs. It was EX's sister, the sister to whom I was closest. Evidently she had talked with him and felt the need to speak with me. Her message was clear. "Leah, you need to let go of your anger. Your anger is interfering with your and my brother's ability to raise your children."

*Wow.* It was me that was screwing the kids up? Gee, I hadn't thought of it that way. I always thought that his disengagement, his going from living with them thirty days a month to three or four days a month was the problem. I thought that his departure from the household in which he used to help cook, clean, mow the lawn, do home repairs and read bedtime stories was the issue. But according to his Sister, it was my anger.

After the call I realized it was true; I was failing as a mother. Anger had consumed me. Suddenly, there wasn't much point in me being around doing such a piss-poor job as a parent. Visions of unused Percocet, Darvocet and Vicodin in my medicine cabinet danced in my head. The idea that the children would be better off without "angry-Leah-mom" took hold of me. My head ached. The lure of a simple narcotic escape from the pain of it all, with everything in the house to make it happen began to be very appealing. But Catholic-guilt quickly kicked in and the thought of going to hell or even spending eternity in limbo with the un-baptized babies made me more nuts. I needed help.

I called Baby Sister in Seattle, my only family confidante throughout the whole debacle, but she wasn't home. I tried my best friend Jean at work, but she wasn't available. I called my shrink, but didn't want to leave a message. Then, in a most desperate attempt to not do something foolish, I called my older sister in Orange County, The Warden.

It didn't take long for her to surmise through all of my blubbering that EX had left not to attend to his career, but to another woman.

"WHAT?" she yelled. "You mean to tell me that that asshole is screwing around and his sister is doing the dirty work for him by calling you and telling you the problem is that you're angry. How dare you think of hurting yourself over that fucking asshole! What a fucker! I knew it! I knew there was something wrong with him. Get your ass out of bed. Stop feeling sorry for yourself. You're the only one taking care of the kids! What would happen to them if you weren't here? Do you think that he and the girlfriend would raise them? Hell no! Get up and get more pissed!" It was like being thrown into a freezing cold lake. The Warden had such a way with words.

# Thanks for Stabbing my Secretary

The energy crisis was in full swing. There were rolling blackouts, 115 degree days, and talk of a gubernatorial recall. I drove onto the parking lot and saw a helicopter land right next to an SUV. That was a first for me. I'd seen them circle overhead during an incident or assault, but I'd never seen one land in the parking lot. It was also the first time I was prohibited from entering the yard. Before this people had been stabbed, assaulted, incidents were in mid-progress with officers jogging as their equipment clunked behind them and I was always let in.

This time it was different, because about three hundred inmates had organized when the guards told them to lock up. They sat down and said no thank you. The riot occurred because the inmates were fed up with the deal that the prison authorities made with the state government during California's energy crisis to defray energy costs. Prisons throughout the state had agreed to turn off the air-conditioning when the temperature reached a certain degree. To implement this inmates were "locked down", they had to remain in their cells, in some cases for many days. Lock downs in general were hard on inmates. But these "energy lockdowns" were even worse because they also didn't have air-conditioning or electricity of any kind. Two inmates had the fabulous privilege of sharing an 8' x 12' container with a toilet for several days in the dark and blazing heat where they couldn't watch TV, listen to music, use an electric typewriter, turn on a light to read or even shower. After days of being locked down with only emergency lights flickering, the inmates came out pissed off and gnarly. Who could blame them? They had enough. Lucky me, I went home.

The day after the riot, the sun was beating down, the air crackling. I walked onto the Yard and there was an inmate in shorts jogging, another group doing pull-ups and officers hanging outside the Program Office smoking cigarettes and telling jokes as if nothing had happened. I opened the door to my office my and my two inmate clerks came in behind me. I asked what the upshot of the riot was and heard that a negotiation team finally got the inmates to lock up and some of the issues were going to be addressed by the administration. Much to my surprise my clerk Douglass stated that he inadvertently ended up being on that negotiation team. Apparently as they were evacuating the Education wing where our arts studio and his desk were located, custody staff singled him out. He was well read, literate, in his mid-50's, and had already been in prison more than a decade. Douglass was one of the older convicts who lamented the wave of the future where inmates didn't know how to do their time like men. He believed there was massive corruption in the Department of Corrections and that the world government would be taking over and black helicopters were just around the corner.

Being part of the negotiation team meant that he was the white guy, along with a black and an Hispanic, who went out to the inmates who were refusing to lock up, inquired about their complaints and reported it back to staff. The hope was that this would appease them and get the inmates to return to their cells. The negotiating team was successful because they had convinced the inmates their grievances would be investigated.

Since Douglass was the most literate on the negotiation team, staff asked him to write the memo detailing the inmates' complaints. He pulled out a copy. It looked neat, well written and had no spelling errors. Unfortunately, it was also reflective of his personal views. After years of writing memos in the CDC I was painfully aware of the importance of stating the time in military fashion, the date, the purpose for writing, the facts and only the facts, along with a disclaimer in case anything blew up in my face. Douglass' memo immediately went into listing the inmates' grievances; the unbearable conditions which accompanied lockdowns for energy savings, the loss of conjugal visits for lifers, the lack of inmate jobs available in the institution, the inability to attend church services during lockdowns, the lack of fruits and vegetables in their diet and the inability to exercise properly since they took away weight-lifting equipment. Then the memo culminated by stating "that inmates were planning to attack staff if some changes weren't made immediately."

I had no doubt that threat was vocalized during the riot. It was common knowledge that inmates in the state of California had just about enough and the water cooler talk among them was frequently about when were things going to start rocking and rolling like in the good 'ole days of George Jackson, the Soledad Brother. Everybody knew it, including non-custody staff (teachers, cooks, plumbers and secretaries) administrative staff and custody staff. Unfortunately Douglass didn't know that it was dangerous to actually document and report this reality with his name on it. "Oh my God, Douglass. This is so not good." I told him.

"The writing isn't good?"

"The writing is fine, but Douglass, man. You can't say these things."

"I didn't say them. I just said what the guys told me and you know damn well it's the truth." His veins were popping in his forehead.

"Yes. I know it's the truth. Staff knows it's the truth. But you can't put it in writing. You can't threaten the staff in writing. No one will back you up. You've got to write something different."

I recommended that he write another memo to the staff

Sergeant and Lieutenant saying that he in no way meant to imply there were immediate or direct threats to staff, that he was only relaying comments given by inmates in the sit-down and could not verify their validity, and the memo in no way reflected his personal opinions whatsoever. That was my advice.

I was laughing and joking around the next day. When Douglass was late for work, I popped my head into the hallway and yelled, "Where's Douglass?" A Chapel clerk came to my door. He knocked on the glass, making sure he had permission to come in. I waved him in just as I picked up the phone and was preparing to call Richard's housing unit to see where he was. Before I could dial the number the Chapel clerk blurted out "Miss Joki, They took Douglass out of here this morning. Didn't you hear? He was stabbed on his way to breakfast."

"Oh my god I knew it, I just knew it. I knew he was asking for trouble. Crap! Did they kill him?"

"No Miss Joki, he got hit and they took him out of here for medical attention".

"What in the hell happened?" I thought for a moment. "It wasn't an accident was it?" After begging and pleading with them, after reassuring them time and again that I wouldn't tell anyone, that I wouldn't go to staff about it, the Chapel clerks finally relented. And I knew when I asked for the truth that I could never tell staff what I was about to hear.

As it turned out, my instincts were right about the memo. It wasn't staff that got upset. It was the inmates. Any formal memo that goes to a staff person almost always passes through the hands of an inmate clerk. Inmate program clerks can usually verify what is real and what is not. Evidently inmates on the Yard got wind of Douglass's memo stating they threatened to assault staff if changes weren't made in the near future. Despite the honesty of the remark, no one wanted to be associated with it, especially the blacks and Hispanics who didn't have one of their own write the memo.

If custody suspects that inmates are planning assaults on them, a lockdown is called and investigations begin. This is not only annoying to inmates, but could turn up actual evidence resulting in charges. The blacks and Hispanics wanted to remove themselves as far away from the threat as possible. It wasn't so much that they needed to silence Douglass, as they needed to make a statement: a white guy does not have the authority to speak for anybody other than whites.

The Chapel clerks told me that the black inmates went to the white shot-callers and gave them twenty-four hours to deal with Douglass. In prison that usually means "if you don't deal with the guy, we'll kill him." The white shot-callers didn't feel that Douglass needed to die, but just injured enough so he would be removed from the Yard and put into protective custody. The message would still be sent. The whites decided to do the right thing. They found a young white fish that needed to score some points. (If a fish/newbie wanted some protection in the future, he had to do something to earn it and carrying out a hit like this definitely scored some points.)

As Douglass complacently walked to get his breakfast that morning, the youngster came to him from behind and reaching, stabbed him in the back of the neck. The fish wounded Douglass enough to make him "go away". The generosity of the white shot-callers kept Douglass from being left to the mercy of other prison factions who would have killed him. I believe their punishment was generous for two reasons: first, Douglass really wasn't much of a threat to anyone, he just talked too much and second, he was my worker. Without tooting my horn too much, I believe that I was liked and respected in the joint. If I wasn't I could never have gotten the clerks to tell me the truth. I know the clerks themselves had nothing to do with the hit, but I believe it was on their recommendation that Richard's life was spared. My eyes swelled with tears, "Thank you, I guess, for stabbing my secretary."

"You're welcome Miss Joki."

# Down Hill

The phone in my office rang. "Arts in Corrections. This is Leah."

"This is Lynn. Can you come by my office? I just got something from Sacramento that you need to take a look at."

"What is it?"

"Mina. Mina sent a letter of complaint to Sacramento."

"About what?"

"About you." She half laughed. "You gotta' see this."

I sat in Lynn's office reading Mina's scathing letter. I knew that there was some tension between Mina and me since I returned to work, but this? MUGsie, our Sacramento boss, was on the speakerphone. "These are some pretty serious allegations." According to Mina, I didn't do my job nor did I help order the supplies she needed. Of course there was no mention that I was off work for eight and a half months. No mention of the numerous calls I took from her when I was in excruciating pain, trying to help her as best I could, from my home. Apparently when EX was still Husband at the prison, he wasn't giving her much assistance either. (That part probably had some truth to it.) But the big kahuna of Mina's rant was that I allowed my Facility "A" inmate worker Kelley to run the program and that he made anti-Semitic remarks.

Mina was working as a contract artist when I encouraged her to apply for an Artist-in-Residence grant at CSP-LAC. My track record as an Artist Facilitator for getting grants was perfect; nine out of nine applications were funded. Mina and I worked at my home with numerous copies of her grant sprawled out on my ten-foot knotty pine dining room table and while putting it together at the last minute we laughed and fretted but still got it to the post office in the knick of time. Grooming contract artists for residency grants was one of my best attributes as a Facilitator and every grant submitted for CSP-LAC was personally ushered along, including hers.

Mina had an awesome resume that included numerous exhibitions. She was a gentle soul and a skilled painter in her fifties with grown children. Her husband, a hemophiliac, had died years ago. Her hair was darkly colored at home, her skin was like porcelain, she had bodacious breasts and a big smile. Her work was bold, intricate and mystical. Almost all of her paintings had lizards, skeleton-like Day of the Dead characters, and yellow fish. I didn't pretend to understand the significance of them in everything, but her work was striking.

I knew that Mina was high maintenance but her biggest problem was how to handle Kelley. Kelley definitely needed handling. Kelley was the antithesis of political correctness. He looked like Mr. Clean; big, muscular white guy with piercing blue eyes and a sparkling smile. This Mr. Clean, however, not only had black wrap-around glasses but a tucan tattooed on his chest along with an entire body full of inked art. That's how he taught himself to draw. He was locked up over a bar fight gone bad when he was eighteen years old. Kelley was almost forty years old now. He grew up in prison, was an old-school convict and totally institutionalized. He had pride in his work and didn't tolerate bullshit. But he did have a mouth, and out of it came very bold declarations.

In my opinion, his ranting was worth the trade-off. While he worked for me there were never any tools missing, instruments stolen, there was no drug trafficking in our work area, paints and canvas were not sold out on the yard, the room was always clean and the output of work was off the charts. There were whites, blacks, Hispanics and "others" all working together. And there was a ton of work created and donated to the community for the art sale. Kelley actually did take care of the program. Did he strong-arm a few guys he didn't like out on the yard against participating in the program? Not to my knowledge, but if I were a bettin' man, I'd guess *probably*, but I never knew for sure.

It's hard to say what Mina thought would come of her vicious memo. Even though it rattled MUGies' cage for a moment, it was handily dismissed. It wasn't long after that her project was done and she was out of there. We never spoke again. Mina felt that I had let her down while I was sick and gave Kelley too much power in my absence. Whereas I felt she had thrown me under the bus to distract from her own inadequacy and frustration in working with maximum inmates, one of whom jerked off in front of her. I felt badly for Mina. She didn't have an easy life as an artist and single mother and working in a maximum-security prison was stressful. She had spent many hours painting alone because the inmates were on lockdown and struggled to comprehend the onerous procedures for ordering supplies during my absence and the absence of EX's involvement. In the end, under all of this I think she just "snapped". Last I heard she followed the Dalai Lama somewhere and if she did, there are surely lizards and fish painted nearby.

As for Kelley, Mina's attack made him pissed off more than he usually was. He sensed however, that I was under duress upon returning, so he did something completely uncharacteristic; he shut up, backed off and went to work painting with a vengeance. Yes, Kelley had a long leash.

Gray Davis, still Governor of California, was in a tailspin. The California Arts Council was reduced from a $26.5 million budget to a

$1.5 million budget. The entire Artist-in-Residence grant program was cancelled. The only thing remaining at the CAC was a small staff and maybe a porch light on.

It was Christmas of 2002 and all of the contract artists had wrapped up their sessions for the quarter. Then the call came from MUGsie. "The entire program has been cancelled." That's all I remember her saying. I hated the path MUGsie took us down more than I hated my life, because other than my children, that was the only thing left of my life.

It broke my heart to tell my contract artists that they no longer had a teaching job in the New Year. Many of them had been with me for years. Many of them attended my annual Christmas party. They were my teachers and they had become my friends.

The early months of 2003 were weird. I was still an Artist Facilitator, but the only thing left to facilitate was myself. According to Webster's I was supposed to be "making things easier, less difficult"- for myself? Showing up to work was strange. There were no phone calls to make, no contracts to write, no grants to submit, no money to order equipment and supplies, and no teachers to train or with whom to schedule classes. It was flat-out bizarre.

But then, we got *the memo*. The memo from Sacramento Headquarters stated that by the end of June in 2003 we could anticipate no longer having a position as an Artist Facilitator. MUGsie had fired her last salvo. The program that she passionately advocated for; she assisted in destroying through ineptitude and spineless mismanagement.

*Which disaster is more inevitable? The one at work or the one at home?* Standing in the kitchen with her brow furled, my daughter looked at me point blank. "Mommy, why are you so angry?

"I'm not angry sweetie" I replied.

"Yes, you are."

I was always astonished at her beauty, the beautiful brown skin, curly black hair and the blackest of black eyes. She could have been in her own collection of porcelain dolls. I was a deer in headlights. She looked directly at me with the composure of an adult and announced. "I think the reason that you're angry is because you hate your life."

*Busted by my daughter.* I had sat on an aluminum folding-chair outside the back door in the corner of my new, wood deck rocking myself back and forth, back and forth, thinking *I hate my life.* How could she have known that?

The love that I had for my children wasn't enough to conceal the disappointment of my personal and professional life. I was no longer in a suicidal kaleidoscope, just disillusioned. When I returned to work Dr. Xena, always my Princess Warrior, insisted that I only work twenty hours per week, which meant EX picked up the other half. We were divorced now, but shared my job. It took about six months to realize that absent-in-personal-life-EX was also doing so little work at the prison that my program was suffering greatly. I had no idea what he did and didn't do anymore. I knew he picked up a paycheck and that there were numerous complaints. On Facility "A" my new inmate clerk, Jensen, a devilishly-handsome-guy-to-end-up-in-prison was always calm. But... Kelley? Kelley never heard of calm.

"Miss Joki, HE didn't pick up the supplies from the Warehouse."

"Miss Joki, HE didn't show up last week."

"Miss Joki, we haven't seen HIM in weeks!" screamed Kelley.

While the inmates moaned and groaned about the lack of his presence, I prayed that the inmates didn't realize that HE was my EX. It was apparent that prison held little interest to him anymore. Without straying too far from the doctor's orders, I suggested he work ten hours each week, and I would work thirty.

Surely it was driven by years of prison paranoia, but I always fretted about the notion of someone knowing what had transpired between EX and me. Kelley was a convict, he'd done hard-time all of his adult life and he had prison-bred ethics and I don't think that he would have been happy with EX if he'd known what I'd been put through. I imagined a scenario in which Kelley whispered to some guy in a quiet, concrete corner. The gate would pop open for EX and he would walk onto the yard. Seemingly out of nowhere, some random inmate would jump EX and beat the ever-living-daylights out of him, at least 'til he was pulled off by a couple of CO's. I secretly wanted it to happen, but knew that if it ever did, I'd end up in prison myself because how could I defend my fantasy against something that could have been actually orchestrated from within?

EX and I went from being the poster-child for nepotism working in special circumstances to the poster-child for it going horribly awry and the very reason why it should never be done. The phone in my office rang. "Arts in Corrections."

"This is Lynn. Can you stop by my office?"

"Sure."

"I need to leave precisely at 5:00p.m. Make sure you get here before that."

"No problem."

She handed me a phone bill about fourteen pages long, to the tune of approximately $450.00. It wasn't the first time I had to explain a large phone bill or lengthy calls. It was common knowledge that after twenty minutes on the phone in prison, a call was automatically flagged, sometimes listened in on or even recorded. We all knew that long phone calls for *any* reason other than business were a no-no.

I took the bill back to my office and studied it. Obviously my minimum yard guitar teacher liked checking his voicemail frequently with one-minute calls from the phone in my office. The real perpetrator of the inflated phone bill, however, was making forty to sixty minute calls to TOWie. (I had a knack for remembering numbers. I'd never forgotten hers since the day I realized Husband was talking with her while I was at the hospital.) After our divorce was final however, I thought those two had parted company. But I was wrong. They were back together. EX explained she was directing an American Film Institute (AFI) short film and he was getting a producer credit. Well, he always got something from anyone he slept with. From me he got entree to teaching in prison, a starring role in a play for which I won Best Director, years of prison Artist-in-Residence grants where he purchased and utilized expensive video and editing equipment, a joint grant from the Los Angeles Contemporary Exhibitions, lots of positive press coverage, health benefits, invitations to all the fun conferences, as well as family members who helped buy our first home and, of course kids. All of which were no longer available to, or of interest to him.

EX claimed he was on the phone so much because he was helping to plan her film shoot. No wonder Kelley and Jensen only saw him occasionally. He wasn't *working* working. He was busy talking on a work phone about another job he was doing for free.

I wrote a report citing that the person my colleague (EX) was calling was "an individual not affiliated with the program, nor on my list of approved contract artists." TOWie had inserted herself into my life and into the lives of my children. (She gave them Christmas presents that year – Harry Potter note cards and address books. Who gives a nine-year old boy an address book?) She also sullied the waters of the one place I'd loved the most; prison. Lynn and the Warden followed up on the report. EX was written up and reprimanded. I was never allowed to know to what level or what extent. I just knew it was embarrassing, for everybody.

# The Final Bridge
# to Art

I wore a slinky, black dress to a prison event. That was a first, and Lynn was spending two nights at my home in Los Angeles on the "sleeping porch", the coziest place in the house. This was our last "Annual Inmate Art Sale" so we decided to move it from the In-Service Training classroom in the Administration Building of the prison, where we had held it for years, to the Big Time and to hold it on a weekend. I contacted art galleries all over the metro LA area, and even called the new Catholic cathedral in downtown LA. I thought with the amount of money pumped into that thing along with all the priests' past molestations popping up, the Archdiocese would be game for some good PR, but I couldn't get my calls returned. All I was looking for was a proper space. In the end, the best I could do was the multi-purpose room of my children's elementary school. It didn't sound like much but it was actually a huge room that allowed us to display the artwork nicely, it was accessible from the street and conveniently located in Mid-Wilshire. In addition, the biggest coup for the sale was we had press coverage in the *Los Angeles Times*. Not big coverage, but coverage.

Instead of our traditional silent auction we opted to do one "live" for the major pieces. Violette, my friend and theater teacher at CSP-LAC, agreed to take the auctioneer role. Saturday evening, before we got rolling, I addressed the crowd as an Artist Facilitator. I spoke about the unfortunate demise of the Arts in Corrections program, how privileged I'd felt to be part of something so special and just as I was about to mention some of our success stories, in walked Larry. *Gosh he's a big guy!* The last time I saw him was in a courtroom and he looked gaunt and deflated, even ashen. Now he looked like a stallion. He stood tall and strong and looked very classy in a suit and tie. Just the image of him looking so healthy and put-together, standing amongst all this artwork and not being in prison blues, made me cry. It was people like him for whom the program was designed. And it was all just such a damn shame to lose it.

We raised ten thousand dollars that weekend. Ten thousand dollars was collected for inmate paintings and pottery to help abused children. That was incredible with the prior "record" being only a fraction of that. Lynn winked at me as she whispered, "We did good."

The irony of the art sales' success was that every step of the way MUGsie tried to shut us down. "Arts sales are illegal." "You can't sell inmate's work." "The prison can't sell or profit from their work." "Bah bah bah" she bleated.

#1. Artist Facilitator Steve Emrick had done art sales for years at Duel Vocational Institution, a Level IV state prison.

#2. Yes, I understood that the inmates owned their artwork, but from the time I became a Facilitator the *unofficial* policy was: the inmate got to keep one, send it home if he liked, and he donated one to the program. It had worked for years. We provided all of the supplies and instruction and fifty percent they kept and the other half went to institutional beautification or was donated to the community. Never once did an inmate complain. For chrissakes, they got to pick which pieces went home, and could even keep all the good stuff and give me the crap!

#3. The prison wasn't selling the artwork. All of the artwork was donated from the inmates to The Children's Center of the Antelope Valley, a non-profit organization, and that organization provided staff to handle the money. It was a benefit for them. We merely assisted in setting up and taking down the event.

Good Lord Almighty, MUGsie had become a whacked out version of the ACLU, and she couldn't stop herself. She even tried to prevent Larry, a free man, long ago paroled—from showing up. That woman made my eyeballs ache.

So did the videographer. EX wasn't available to videotape the art sale and since it was bigger than ever before, I didn't want to do it myself. I asked an education instructor from the prison who was familiar with the equipment and had actually done some filming for us before to make the trip. He was a sweet guy with a gray beard, a Greenpeace guy. His heart was in the right place and he was always looking out for the inmates. All went well, in spite of Mugsie's protestations.

I had asked Greenpeace to let me view the footage before he allowed the inmates to see it, and I hadn't given it much thought until I came back to prison after the sale. The inmates had already seen the videotape of the live auction and extemporaneous footage, but he must have forgotten that part. Kelley accosted me with "How much did my painting sell for?" I didn't want to say because I knew that one large painting of desert cactus in bloom, that was sold in the live auction, went for much less than its' worth. In fact, I bought it and felt like I stole it. I only paid $150 because few were bidding against me.

I heard an inmate inquire, "Who were those kids running around?"

Then I was pissed. "Those kids" were my children. Greenpeace didn't think twice about putting a camera on my children. He had no idea to what lengths I went to keep my private life, private. And he certainly had no idea that we were one of the few Arts in Corrections programs that didn't have our video equipment confiscated over the Richard Speck debacle. Green Peace just didn't get it. Fortunately, I confiscated the videotape before Greenpeace aired it on the institutional channel.

Several days after the LA art sale and auction, a phone-call came in my office. "Arts in Corrections."

"Is this Leah Joki?"

"Yes, it is."

"Steve Kaufman."

Okie Dokie. Had never heard of the guy. He said he saw the blurb in the Times about the art sale and was unable to make it, but he thought he could help us out. Turned out Steve Kaufman was quite a successful artist and protégé to Andy Warhol. He had a studio not far from Melrose Avenue (in the funky part, not the trendy part) and offered to let me come by and load up my vehicle with donated art supplies for the program.

Steve Kaufman was somewhat of an enigma. He was like a gentle, Jewish giant. He must have been 6'5" with shoulder-length, curly black hair and talked like a New Yorker. His studio was very unassuming from the outside but highly operative and impressive inside. He liked to give young kids out of juvie a break, so there were several guys with tattoos and baggy pants stretching canvas and moving artwork around.

When I was getting ready to leave, Steve was leaning against my car talking about being a widower and how crazy it was that all these young women wanted to get involved with him and how one of them had a cocaine problem and another needed financial help and how money wasn't everything. He said he just wanted a simple life. I put out some friendly, sympathetic vibes but I wasn't exactly a young woman.

For months Kaufman provided us with a generous amount of paint and canvas. He was like a Jewish Santa Claus for some time. He was very generous to us and that made the guys in the joint happy. Personally, I would have preferred a date with him. I knew the program was on its last legs, but I wasn't... yet.

MUGsie had a slight problem. It turned out that the memo that stated the Artist Facilitator position would be terminated June 30, 2003 was illegal. MUGsie, Miss B. and the Sacramento bureaucrats forgot that we, our puny little group of Artist Facilitators, actually belonged to a union and they weren't supposed to be terminating anyone without first notifying and negotiating with that union. We didn't have a program, but we still had our jobs. (The irony was that the only way Sacramento was able to save our positions, was by screwing up.)

From that faux pas, "Bridging" was conceived. What was "Bridging"? None of us knew, but by golly we were gonna' find out.

The California Department of Corrections (CDC) was in quite a pickle. Their deficit was staggering. So the bureaucrats of the CDC worked with the state bureaucrats and elected legislature of the state government to figure out what excessive fat could be trimmed. Gone was Arts in Corrections, the California Arts Council had its entire torso lobbed off, vocational education programs were eliminated, the weight pile had been gone for years, and by golly the Community Resource Managers were looking like the three-centimeter slice of fat that was weighing the whole steak down.

Yep, all the promises made to the communities who allowed prisons to be built in their backyards weren't important anymore. Why keep somebody on the payroll to nurture community relations with a prison, to provide PR or advocate for the Department? Sacramento figured that since the prisons were all built, if a community had a problem or a question they could just contact the Warden. I mean letting the community have a say, and to have staff assigned to listen, was just too damn much fat on the steak. So, the Community Resource Managers would be eliminated in the upcoming months as well. There was however, one really good thing to come from all this. The CCPOA, the prison guards union, negotiated a substantial pay raise. (None of the meager, three percent cost-of-living-crap.) They got a 34% pay increase in 2002 when the state was in the middle of a fiscal crisis and a potential recall of the Governor. That made for more union dues, more contributions to state election campaigns and support for Grey Davis. Now that the weights were gone, the arts programming was gone, half the education programs were gone the inmates were gettin' kind of idle, kind of violent. Of course they needed more officers and training to keep a lid on these violent institutions. As long as they were handling the violence, that over-inflated pay was all steak and no fat. CCPOA loved Grey Davis!

Since the Community Resource Managers were no longer going to exist, the Facilitators would be under the Supervisors of Education but we wouldn't be "facilitating" for them, we'd be "bridging" for them.

It had been a very long time since the entire group of Artist Facilitators was together in one room. The days of conferences and training sessions had long been gone. There must have been seventy-five people in the room that day at headquarters in Sacramento. We Facilitators were accompanied by our new supervisors from Education. The group was too large for the room. We were so cozy I could have practically sat in my supervisor's lap. My new supervisor was Bob Garcia. Fellows didn't come much nicer than Bob Garcia and he was professional.

MUGsie seemed all excited about the new "Bridging" program. Her enthusiasm was coupled with this you-should-be-goddamn-grateful-for-this-bridging-crap-because-at-least-you-have-a-job-and-I-probably-don't attitude. There were a fair number of Artist Facilitators in the room who were a couple years from retirement and they readily agreed, whatever "bridging" meant, "bridging" they would do, because yes, they were goddamn happy to have a job. I understood their predicament, but at the same time they looked like a pack of homeless dogs fighting over a rotting bone.

Up to now, most Facilitators had two to six inmate workers assigned to them. My clerks and artist workers like Goldberg and Kelley were all assigned to me, but all worked on different yards. Inmates who have a job or go to classes need to be tracked during the day, so to comply the majority of my workers had their time cards kept by nearby officers since it was impossible for me to be on five yards at the same time. Chaplains have a similar challenge.

Bridging, however, was a new, exciting and nifty concept, we were told. The Artist Facilitator, now "Bridger" would have 50 inmates assigned to them. We would have our own "gang" of guys. But unlike the normal teacher in the Education Department who had a classroom for their inmates to gather, our "bridging" inmates were in their cells and we were going to them!

If a new guy was assigned to me, I went to his cell to get the "bridging" going. *Mmmmm, I could have a list of fifty guys and need to go to fifty cells for starters. Mmmmm. I wonder if I'll have time to read fifty C-files before I go to visit my homies in their cell. I never go to an inmate's cell without knowing something about his background. Now I have to visit 50 of them in their maximum-security cells not knowing if they're violent offenders, on psychotropic meds, or what!*

I raised my hand. "Excuse me. Are you aware that the Artist Facilitator classification does not have safety retirement? If I get hurt on the job I'm not covered like the officers or teachers. As a female who works in a Level IV institution, I don't think that going to inmate's cells without familiarity of their background is safe. Is that legal? Wouldn't we be working out of class?"

Now there was a buzz phrase: out of class meant working outside of one's job classification. Unions frown on that. A group of Facilitators, long spear-headed by Graham Moody, had worked tirelessly without success for years to get our classification changed and safety retirement added to it. We checked tools and cutters and sharp stuff out to inmates, but evidently we weren't in any *real* danger. The officer sitting with his feet up on desk, in a classroom with only desks and chalkboards at the end of the hall, watching TV, must have been in danger because he had safety retirement.

It was gettin' hot in that room, literally. The real beauty of the bridging program was "the packet". When an inmate was assigned, we would track him down, find out which discipline of the fine arts he would like to explore; visual arts, music, literary, etc., then we'd give him a packet for that discipline. For instance, if a guy wanted literary arts, I could give him some poems to read and some paper and a couple pencils. He could write a few poems and check in with me in a week to verify his assignment was complete. If a guy wanted visual arts, I could give him some handouts on beginning drawing techniques, some drawing paper and pencils. He could then make two or three attempts to draw maybe his tennis shoes in the corner of his cell.

MUGsie thought it was all pretty darn exciting. We could be creative! We could come up with all sorts of interesting packets! We could basically do whatever in the hell we wanted! It was awesome! Of course, I wasn't quite sure how long it would take for me to run out of paper and pencils and packet materials since we had no budget. Clearly I was being a bit pessimistic because MUGsie assured us while we were bridging we could also continue to operate our studios and teach whatever classes we wanted, just like in the past. Although we didn't have a budget, there was nothing to keep us from writing grants for supplies and equipment. Naturally, the California Arts Council wouldn't be accepting them with only a porch light left on, but the possibilities were endless. Personally, I thought MUGsie should have been submitted for the Genius Grant with the MacArthur Foundation.

I just *had* to raise my hand. "Yes, Leah. You have a question?"

(Mind you "day for day" allows an inmate half-time credit on their sentence by earning it either by working or going to classes. For every day spent in an "assignment", their sentence is reduced one day.)

"I'm just curious, I guess. We've been told the last few years to keep a low profile, that the farther off the radar screen the arts program was from the public the better. Now we're going to give inmates day-for-day for drawing their shoes once or twice in their cell throughout an entire week? My guys get a day's credit for doing a full day's work. I have an inmate (Kelley) who cranked out over eighty paintings in a year and we just raised $10,000 for a community non-profit. Don't you think that the public would be upset if they found out felons were getting out early for drawing their shoes?"

I swear they were smoking something in Sacramento those last few years. MUGsie looked pissed. I guess my gratitude just wasn't coming through.

The icing on the cake of our bridging training day in Sacramento however, was still to come. The new Director of the CDC was coming to talk to us! Wow! That actually was something. By this time, Grey Davis had been recalled and Schwarzenegger had fired the last Director. The last time a Director addressed our crowd was at a conference in the early 90's. I remember Director Jim Rollins speaking eloquently and his forewarning us that the CDC was going to become a "lock and feed" system. That's where he predicted the political tides were headed and he was a Director that believed in education and rehabilitation. It had taken more than ten years, but he was absolutely correct.

It was odd that the new Director was going to speak to us now. It was kind of like somebody finally visiting the deathbed, a little late. Mr. Terhune seemed like a smart guy but he'd been handed a huge mess and there wasn't much he could do about it. He talked about how unfortunate it was that we lost our program, the seriousness of the deficit and the numerous other cuts that had to be made. Then he let us know how excited he was about the bridging program.

I had a question for him. "The cost of the Arts in Corrections program averaged about $25,000 per institution. At my institution there are over a dozen rank and file officers that make more than the Warden. It's common knowledge that excessive overtime is paid out to officers who manipulate their schedules by calling in sick, having a buddy cover for them at time and a half and then he does the same in return. Also at my institution there were two Sergeants who were rumored to be paid $50,000 each in over-time to set up an employees' gym in the administration building. They had the inmates clear out the room, had the inmates paint it and then purchased a couple treadmills and some weights. Why doesn't the CDC look at stuff like that instead of canceling our program which is a spit in the bucket by comparison and more beneficial?"

Damn the room was quiet and very, very hot.

My Supervisor Bob Garcia was very courteous on the plane ride back to Burbank from our Sacramento "bridging" briefing. He was willing to work with me, provide whatever I needed, but I now loathed my 240 lb. hairy-chested lover. Like EX, he too had become an unrecognizable disappointment.

"Bridging" was just a mere shell of "facilitatin". It was like getting a job as an attorney and then finding out you will clean the toilets instead, but at least the work is in the same building. Although I liked Bob Garcia, I didn't like "bridging".

# To Live and Die in LA?

When I returned to the institution the following Monday, I found out that Kelley had already been transferred to another prison. I didn't get to say a proper goodbye and thank you. The guy raised thousands and thousands of dollars for the community and worked his ass off. I never got to shake his large hand, with incredibly thick fingers always covered in paint, and say "Thank you Kelley. Thank you for having my back and for your very large contribution". Tears were welling up as I stood behind the education building loading Kaufman's supplies off the truck. Kelley was supposed to be here a few more days. He was going to help with this. The other inmates could sense my despair. My weeping ass had no business being behind the wall, on the mainline, in that condition. *Fucking prison, fucking here today, gone tomorrow prison.*

As I walked into her office, Lynn had a smirk on her face and obviously couldn't wait to tell me something. I sat down on the familiar rose-colored, upholstered chair facing her desk. With a devilish pat she closed her door on the busybody secretaries and the foot traffic to the Warden's office next door. "You're not going to believe it!"

Lynn had survived Stage 4 breast cancer, a mastectomy, a

stem-cell trans-plant and one bitter divorce from a wealthy aerospace executive who always had trouble finding money for his two boys' medical bills. After all that, she had a whole new lease on life. Nothing brought her more delight than an unethical being brought to justice or fools being exposed. I knew it had to be good.

"What's going on?" It seemed like there are a lot a people running around the Warden's office. "What's up?"

"You're not going to believe it, but remember when I told you about the two sergeants who were getting paid to put together a staff gym? Remember? Well..." she smiled. "Sacramento sent down an investigation team today. Shit is going to hit the fan—heads are going to roll. I love it."

This was indeed good and just news. But... *oh shit!* "Oh my God Lynn. Last Friday in Sacramento at the bridging meeting Terhune actually showed up to talk to us."

"Terhune the Director did?"

"Yes, and I asked him why we were losing our program when these sergeants were being paid to put together this lame staff gym and some of the other crap we talked about. Oh my god!"

"Oh Jesus, Leah. I promise I won't tell a soul that you made that comment to the Director. Oh man... this is good."

As we salivated over the notion that some custody idiots were in some well-deserved trouble, I stopped our conversation with more pressing news. "Lynn, I'm done. I can't do the bridging thing. I'm giving my two week notice."

Yep, there I went. Like a woman in menopause, trying to control her hot flashes, I was trying to control the onslaught of tears that accompanied almost anything I said anymore. Whaaa whaaa whaaa. What a blubbering fool I'd become, almost incapable of working in the environment in which I'd once been smitten.

In typical Lynn fashion, she handed me a box of Kleenex and rolled off a litany of accomplishments we'd racked up over the years. No one was a bigger advocate and better cheerleader for my arts program than Lynn. She was an incredible boss and over time had become one of my best friends and confidantes. As she gave me her big bear hug she whispered, "It's probably good that you're choosing to leave at this time. This investigation could get ugly. I'd watch my back when you drive off the grounds the next two weeks."

She opened her door and even though both our eyes were red and puffy, we returned to the foot traffic to the Warden's office and the nosy secretaries with smiles on our faces.

Over the next two weeks I said my goodbyes on the "A" yard and was primarily focused on packing up my office on Minimum. I needed more boxes. Every day I was carting out box after box of documentation. I knew slides of artwork and videos of plays and concerts would end up in the garbage. Files containing personal information of artists and Hollywood guest stars could become fodder for inmates and staff alike. My mission was to salvage any documentation I had to boxes that would probably gather dust in my home. Spott, my new worker on Minimum, was a big help. He was one of those people who unfortunately tried meth and suddenly had an addiction that was the biggest of all monkeys on his back. Spott was a damn good guy, a hard worker. He was one of the few who understood the error of his ways and would probably never come back to prison.

On my final day at CSP-LAC I called EX from my office to tell him that I was done packing and leaving for the last time. But I couldn't even complete a sentence. I was overwrought with grief. The two things I had loved the most, prison and my marriage, were forever gone. The two institutions where I excelled, no longer wanted me. I no longer recognized my former husband, nor my 240lb. hairy-chested lover.

Spott and I packed the last boxes into my vehicle. I couldn't shake his dry, rough hand without crying. The thought of hugging him was appealing but I'd been in prison so long I instinctively knew that was wrong. I just held onto his grasp for a few moments longer as the goddamn tears welled up in my eyes again. I felt badly for him and Jensen and the other workers, because I could not predict what would happen to them after I left. I said goodbye to Lynn in her office, who reiterated, "We did good." She and I both knew, with the end of our careers along with the few hundred others like us, the march to "lock and feed" in the nation's largest, most expensive prison system, would barely miss a step.

Then I drove out of the parking lot for the last time. I didn't get a cake, or a lunchtime celebration. There were too many of us now for such sentiment. The Warden wasn't there when I left. The officer at the gate didn't recognize me. I did check my rearview mirror however, to make sure no one was following me.

My objective was twofold: find a new job and write something about prison. Over the course of four months however, neither one of them came to fruition. Hell... Susan Hill couldn't find a new job! Artists of every discipline were fleeing the state of California because the non-profit world had imploded. There were no jobs in the arts! And the part about writing something about prison? Well... I tried. My former writing teacher, Shem, agreed to be my partner on a prison project. It was a nifty deal. I would write the synopsis, he would pitch it to Hollywood execs then, I would write the screenplay and we would split the fee 50/50. Sounded awesome. But the reality was, that every idea I presented to Shem – well, quite frankly – it sucked. I couldn't wrap my head around what about prison to write about. Whose lurid tale should I tell? What horrific act should I expose? Could I make it a comedy? Nothing was dark enough for Shem, nothing was thought out well enough for Shem. I couldn't understand why I couldn't come up with a storyline, when no one was better placed to talk about prison than me. One idea after another tanked like a heavy rock attempting to skip across the surface of the water. Not!

I was eating up the equity in my house while I was trying to figure out what to do. I spent weeks rocking back and forth on that metal chair on my deck, gazing at the razor wire that surrounded my back yard. Someone had recently gone into my garage in the back and stolen $1800.00 of food from a freezer. The policeman who came to my house to file a report with the insurance company remembered my yard well. A few weeks before, a guy had shot someone in a Seven Eleven parking lot at the end of my block. The police had him cornered in my backyard for a while until he jumped over the fence and disappeared in a run-down apartment building. I remembered not being able to get to my house that day. Helicopters were hovering above and the entire block was wrapped in yellow tape. I loved my craftsman house, and my new deck but frankly, it felt like I was in prison.

I made a quick jaunt to Food 4 Less. Empty shopping carts in the parking lot were scattered everywhere. It was like driving through an obstacle course. As I entered the store I was accosted by a mental case looking for a hand out. I declined. When I got into the store there was stock strewn on the floors that I had to maneuver around. The lines were ten-people deep. At least 50% of the shoppers had food stamps.

I thought of the crack addict at the Post Office banging on the bulletproof glass for her "check" one day. I thought of the night when a crack-head knocked on my door looking for my husband. He claimed he'd done some lawn work for him and needed his money right now. I was terrified because I knew many a crack-head and what they would do for twenty dollars. I thought of the sleepless nights when mice would scamper across the wood floor of my bedroom and in the walls of my closet. I thought of the long lines at the Post Office, the grocery store, at movie theaters, everywhere. The sheer numbers of people that had descended upon the city made it insane. The streets were crumbling, the traffic was snarled 24/7, crime was off the charts, and people just decided to stop putting their shopping carts away. It had all become unruly and unbearable. And then I thought... I'm broke.

Desperate times called for desperate measures. I had two healthy children. This was good. I had $136.00 in my savings account. This was bad. I had tons of friends in Los Angeles, as did my kids. This was very good. I had EX whose career as a dialect coach had taken off, but worked out of the country six months out of the year. This was not so good. But I also had a house that was worth more than twice what I had paid for it just five years ago and this was excellent!

Bam! I made an *appointment* with EX. (My best friend and lover of twenty years, my husband and father of my children... now I had to make appointments with him.) "I want to take the kids and move back to Montana. You're gone half the year anyway. I'm going broke here. I cannot find a job that gives me the kind of flexibility and income that I had in prison. I can sell this house, move to Montana and we could live on what you pay us now. I could stay home with the kids and for once in my life I would have the time to write. My family could help me out. They would get a good education there. You're always working in Vancouver. They'd be able to see you from Montana easier than from LA. You could come visit any time. You could buy a small house and spend your breaks up there. I could rent it out for you during the legislative sessions. I'd take care of it for you."

"Absolutely not" he barked.

Days later EX came back. "I've changed my mind. I'll let you go. You deserve some happiness." For the first time in a long time I cried because I was happy and this gnarly chapter of my life was finally over. I was Steve McQueen in *The Great Escape*. Like the "Cooler King" I knew a thing or two about being held in prison and agreed it was my "sworn duty to try to escape." I'd been on the motorcycle ditching Nazis right and left too and had come to my own barbed wire – literally. When I looked out my window there was a roll of it running on top of the backyard fence. While Steve McQueen got entangled trying to reach freedom and a luscious green meadow, I put that puppy into gear, hit the gas and flew over that fence and never looked back.

# Epilogue

It was the oddest thing. The only place I could afford and liked in Montana was a split-level house built in 1974 that curiously looked like the one my father built and I grew up in. My family was giddy with the news of our return. My house in Los Angeles sold in hours with just one phone call to a broker without ever listing it.

As the kids and I went through all of our belongings THE PLAN was unearthed from a blue, antique trunk. This trunk was a gift from my mother. It had accompanied me full circle from Missoula, to New York, to Los Angeles, to Fullerton, to Palm Springs, back to Los Angeles and back to Montana. THE PLAN was in the form of an adolescent letter I'd written to myself. THE PLAN said that when "I grow up I want to have at least seven children. I will always cook dinner for my children and husband. I will always look nice when my husband comes home. I will always wear a dress or a pant suit."

In addition to her booming laughter, my daughter asked, "What is a pantsuit?" When I told her, she laughed even more.

"Well I guess that didn't work out, did it?" She quipped.

The blue trunk proved to be a treasure chest of things that didn't work out: black and white headshots of their dad and me, the silver hairbrush he gave me on our wedding night but never brushed my hair with a hundred strokes for good luck, the engraved pocket watch I gave him that night that he no longer wanted and... yes, The Happy Family Picture.

Over my left shoulder if I look in the fishbowl with no water, there is a mound of hot pink rocks along with a small statue of Patrick from Spongebob Squarepants. When I purchased it, at the persistent urging of my daughter, I thought it would add some harmony to our life. You know, fish harmony. She was really excited we were purchasing healthy gold fish from an actual pet store and not winning them in a ring toss only to die two days later. Unfortunately, the first fish died in less than a week. But Marcus, the second fish lived for almost a month.

His death was a slow and painful demise, which we watched with rather perverted fascination. He apparently lost one of his flippers and only the left one remained. Without one flipper he would sort of barrel down into the pink rocks and get stuck behind Patrick's mossy armpit. I definitely didn't know what to do with a stuck goldfish. My strategy was to get him unstuck by shaking the bowl violently and then feed him. He was stuck so often that we didn't notice he'd been dead for several days. At that point, his body was starting to decompose with his bright orange bullet shaped carcass turning white. I refused to dispose of him. He was my daughter's fish. I finally insisted that action be taken when I realized that Marcus' eyes had fallen out of his head. *Enough was enough!* When eyes fell out of sockets, boy, I was Johnny-on-the-spot with stern parental follow-up. So much for harmony.

Looking at that empty bowl I am reminded of how pathetic it was that I waited so long to take action concerning our lives. Eyes had to fall out of the skull before I said to myself, You know, you may want to make some changes. You may want to take some action - *NOW!!! RIGHT NOW LITTLE MISSY BECAUSE EYES ARE FALLING OUT OF FISHS' SOCKETS.*

Right behind the empty bowl is a window that looks at a large ponderosa pine tree. I can see my yard with two feet of snow, my neighbors' house with smoke gliding out of the chimney, and the mountains. I can walk from room to room and see nothing but trees, snow and mountains. Lovely. I can hear myself think here.

My home in Montana is a showcase for inmate artwork: Jensen's first oil painting, an acrylic painting by a descendant of Puerto Rican drug dealers which depicts immigrant workers gently enclosed in a chain link fence, a still life painted by a sixty-year old heroin addict and Goldberg' mixed-media piece of an old man's face with a woman on a gurney in the background. It depicts the author William S. Burroughs, who accidentally shot his young wife in target practice while he was perhaps, drunk.

I have the large Kelley piece of the desert cactus in bloom from the last art sale, the posters that Goldberg drew for Joe Haj's *Henry V* and my original play *The Big Picture*, and a painting of a crazy housewife standing in a ring of fire and holding her husband's head on a platter. (My constant source of amusement.) Overlooking them all is a large painting called *See No, Hear No, Speak No Evil*. Numerous hands cover the eyes, ears and mouth of a Picasso-like figure. In the iris of one eye is the reflection of a man behind bars. An inmate painted that in response to the prison guards who were investigated in Corcoran for orchestrating and even betting on fights between inmates of rival gangs.

I even have the painting of outer space that was a prototype for inmate Goldberg' grant, as well as some of Spott's first pieces. I purchased all of them at the annual art sale. If the painting was in the silent auction or live auction I paid top dollar for it. If not, I paid the amount asked. I tried to insure that I purchased a piece of artwork from every inmate that meant something to me, although a few escaped me. Each piece has a story. Each inmate has a place in my heart and memory.

My two favorite pieces of artwork are a 6" x 8" miniature model of a prison cell and another Goldberg painting. Inmate Alameda gave me this Arts-in-Corrections-specific cell because I was consistently outbid every year for them. The first year he sold a couple of cell models for $25/each. The last year he sold a *DUI Santa* cell and a *Welcome Bill Clinton* cell for $250/each. In my AIC cell the head of the inmate on the top bunk is carved from soap. The posters on the wall are miniature copies of actual AIC performances. There is a guitar on the lower bunk, and sitting in the typewriter is a screenplay titled *The Accused*. The detail is spectacular.

My favorite piece of Goldberg' is still tucked behind a dresser. It's disturbing. The background is black and there's a skeleton-like man hanging onto a curtain by one green hand. It feels like his nails are scratching a chalkboard and he is hanging on by a mere thread. More than any other piece of artwork I have, it reminds me of prison, of my 240 lb. hairy-chested lover. There was a time when I loved prison, a time that I longed to be on the mainline. I loved the sense of danger and that feeling is evoked in Goldberg' painting

Life is more serene here, but I have not completely escaped my past and the awareness and fear of pure evil. Even in Montana I always sit with my back to the wall at a restaurant, I flinch when I hear a loud sound, lay awake thinking that an intruder is working his way into my house and worst of all I have night terrors in which I wake up sweating thinking that some convict who didn't like me is there to kill me in a grisly manner. A hint of the smell of ether makes me suspect that somebody's cooking up meth. I am convinced that child molesters are everywhere. I study kids' tattoos and I never, ever leave my doors unlocked.

Once in a while I yearn for that heart-pounding flutter that comes with stepping on a prison yard, but I know I cannot go back. I'm not ashamed I spent most of my adult life and career in prison. It was a blast. That's where I belonged then, and this is where I belong now. I came to Montana to live deliberately. That damn blue trunk of failures is in my basement collecting dust, but my life doesn't end that way. I came to find the woman who got lost in prison, the phony Hollywood culture and a less-than-nourishing marriage. I returned to raise my children surrounded with the loving support of family. And I came here to tell the story—my story – of how I escaped the two things I loved the most: prison and my husband.

I am aware my children will not come out of this unscathed. My daughter shed many salty tears in her bed when we moved. She missed her dad. She missed her friends who were white, black, Hispanic, Asian and Other. For months my son glared at me with disdain when I dropped him off for school. I got the you-can-burn-in-hell and the why-did-I-have-to miss-my-last-and-most-fun-year-at–Saint-James looks on a daily basis.

It's been a few years and just days ago my daughter shared she doesn't like having her bedroom be the first door on the right. She's convinced she will be the first one picked-off by some axe murderer. She would prefer to sleep in my room at the end of the hall where she would have more time to get a bat and get ready to swing for her life. When my son dead-lifted 400 lbs. during a football workout, some bozo made the comment: "It's because you're colored." "No" I tell him, "it's because you're strong." These are my *Children Hear Them Roar!* Smiles have returned to their faces, they are safe and thriving. Even though I must soak up the gooey mess of adolescence by myself, they are the prizes at the end of the race.

As for me, well... the whole thing with inmates contacting me on Facebook is a bit disturbing. I won't give up my source, but allegedly the prison guards flagrantly sell droids and iphones to the inmates to make up for a recent pay-cut. I am convinced that happy-spaghetti–eating-Gemini Leah is still here roaming amongst the Ponderosa pine trees. I'm certain she will find another funny man one day; one who genuinely cares for her. And I don't believe her acting days are over either. In some people's eyes, she was the loser that ended up in prison, but au contraire; she was the winner. She survived the unexpected and got the last laugh.

*Oh Lucky Girl!* She laughs through her thin lips, her breath trickling over her lower teeth now covered with expensive, porcelain veneers. It's a good laugh. It's the laugh of a mature woman with a deep voice treasuring the memory of her 240lb. hairy-chested lover.

**LEAH JOKI** is an actor, writer and director. She is a graduate of the University of Montana and the Juilliard School's Drama Program. Before she was smitten by prison- theater she worked as an actor in New York and Los Angeles. Under the auspices of Arts in Corrections she taught and/or performed in almost every state prison in California. Her career in prison spanned over eighteen years. She was the Institutional Artist Facilitator at Chuckawalla Valley State Prison in Blythe and at the California State Prison – Los Angeles County in Lancaster. She was the first female Artist Facilitator in a men's maximum-security prison. Her arts program was profiled in *The Los Angeles Times, American Theatre Magazine* and *The LA Weekly*. In addition to *JUILLIARD TO JAIL* she has also written the one-woman show *HAIRBALL (The demystification of how one's life turns to crap!)*, the plays *Geezer's Cabin, The Big Picture* and *The Year of Baldwin*. She has had articles published in *SOUTHSOUND LIFESTYLES* and is currently working on her second novel, *The Avon Café*. She is a native of Montana.

# Acronyms
## (In alphabetical order)

| | |
|---|---|
| **AdSeg** | Administrative Segregation Unit |
| **ACLU** | American Civil Liberties Union |
| **AIC** | Arts in Corrections |
| **AIR** | Artist in Residence |
| **AMA** | American Medical Association |
| **AW** | Associate Warden |
| **CAC** | California Arts Council |
| **CCPOA** | California Correctional Peace Officer's Association |
| **CDC** | California Department of Corrections |
| **CIM** | California Institution for Men |
| **CIW** | California Institution for Women |
| **CO** | Correctional Officer |
| **CRC** | California Rehabilitation Center |
| **CRM** | Community Resource Manager |
| **CSP-LAC** | California State Prison-Los Angeles County |
| **CVSP** | Chuckawalla Valley State Prison |
| **CYA** | California Youth Authority |
| **ESL** | English as a Second Language |
| **IAF** | Institutional Artist Facilitator |
| **ICAC** | Imperial County Arts Council |
| **ID** | Identification Card |
| **IST** | In Service Training |
| **LATC** | Los Angeles Theater Center |
| **LVN** | Licensed Vocational Nurse |
| **LWOP** | Life Without Parole |
| **MIT** | Massachusetts Institute of Technology |
| **MTA** | Medical Technician Assistant |
| **NEA** | National Endowment for the Arts |
| **PA** | Program Administrator |
| **PC** | Protective Custody |
| **RFP** | Request For Proposal |
| **SHU** | Secured Housing Unit |
| **UCLA** | University of California Los Angeles |

# Lingo
## (In alphabetical order)

| | |
|---|---|
| **BTS** | Bi-racial Triangle Stare |
| **Canteen** | Prison store where inmates buy toiletries, extra food, stamps, etc… |
| **Chester** | Child Molester |
| **Clearance** | Signed confirmation that nothing prohibits an individual from entering the prison grounds; based on background check |
| **Close Custody** | Designated potential flight risk, must remain in housing unit after dark |
| **Day-for-day** | For one day worked, one day is taken off of the time of the sentence |
| **Debriefer** | An inmate who disassociates from his gang and gives staff information about them |
| **Fish** | Individual incarcerated for the first time |
| **Fishing** | The act of trolling for cigarettes with string, paper clips etc… in Administrative Segregation |
| **Juvie** | Prison for juvenile offenders |
| **Lifers** | Inmates serving a life sentence |
| **Mainline** | Living amongst the general population of that security level, not in protective custody |
| **MUGsie** | Most Unhappy Gal |
| **Newbie** | New Artist Facilitator |
| **"N" number** | Inmate serving time on narcotics-related charges |
| **Ped. Gate** | Pedestrian Gate (Main Entrance for Staff and Visitors) |
| **OBBF** | Original Black Boy Friend |
| **Queens** | Male/gay inmates who look like women |
| **Special needs** | Area of prison designated for child molesters and snitches |
| **Shanked** | Stabbed |
| **Stuck** | Stabbed |
| **Tag** | Tattoo that identifies gang affiliation |
| **TOWie** | The Other Woman |

## Acknowledgements

I would like to thank the Arts in Corrections program for offering thousands of inmates in the state of California, an opportunity to become better people. I must thank Susan Hill for her years of leadership at UCLA Artsreach. Susan was a beacon of light and hope for those of us trying to bring beauty and truth into the dark world of prison. I also thank all of my contract artists for their dedication and commitment to the program, and every inmate who dared to step into "our world," especially those who were hired as workers. Thank you for working tirelessly for the betterment of others.

Lynn Harrison, my former boss and Community Resource Manager at California State Prison – Los Angeles County, I cannot thank you enough. Without you there would be no memoir. Your unflagging enthusiasm, attention to detail and keen memory were essential. You are a great friend and inspiration as a cancer survivor, a politician, single-mother and flat out the best boss I ever had.

Thanks to Rebecca Stanfel, my teacher, mentor and friend in Montana. In the face of battling a chronic illness she remained my biggest cheerleader. From her classes emerged the Gold Rush Writer's Group. Scott Hibbard, Kate Cholewa, Mark Putman, Rebecca Stanfel and Niki Whearty provided an environment of creativity, critique, professionalism and ownership. They are my heroes. Our monthly Monday meetings around my dining room table were the life-blood of this book. They fueled me when the tank was running on empty. Thank you. Thank you. Thank you.

I would also like to thank the memoir guru, Joni Rodgers, for her inspiration and guidance. Hearing her tell her story at a conference and speaking with her was the inspiration I needed to keep moving forward, one page at a time.

I acknowledge the tireless work that Dennis Foley does for the Authors of the Flathead. For many Montana writers, this conference provides much needed direction, education and a venue to share our work.

My deepest gratitude goes to Shem Bitterman, Hugh Bickley, Lindsay Brown, Marvin Bukema, Jean Crupper, George Davis, Meg and Craig Eddy, Kate Joki, Joe McGrath, Roland Rosenkranz, Cathy Scott, Dillinger Steel and Josh Wagner. Because of your friendship, kindness, input and hard work my story is finally seeing the light of day.

Made in the USA
Charleston, SC
06 March 2013